Other books by Michael Dorris

Working Men
  (stories)

Rooms in the House of Stone

The Broken Cord

Morning Girl
  (young adult)

A Yellow Raft in Blue Water

The Crown of Columbus
  (with Louise Erdrich)

Native Americans: Five Hundred Years After
  (with photographs by Joseph Farber)

A Guide to Research on North American Indians
  (with Mary Lou Byler and Arlene Hirschfelder)

PAPER TRAIL

ESSAYS

Michael Dorris

HarperPerennial

A Division of HarperCollins*Publishers*

Grateful acknowledgment is made for use of the following:

The Last of the Just by Andre Schwartz-Bart. Copyright © 1960 by Atheneum Publishers. Reprinted by permission of Atheneum Publishers, an imprint of Macmillan Publishing Company.

Little House in the Big Woods. Copyright © 1932 by Laura Ingalls Wilder, renewed 1960 by Roger L. MacBride. Reprinted by permission of HarperCollins Publishers, Inc. "Little House" is a registered trademark of HarperCollins Publishers, Inc.

Little House on the Prairie. Copyright © 1935 by Laura Ingalls Wilder, renewed 1963 by Roger L. MacBride. Reprinted by permission of HarperCollins Publishers, Inc. "Little House" is a registered trademark of HarperCollins Publishers, Inc.

The Long Winter. Copyright © 1940 by Laura Ingalls Wilder, renewed 1968 by Roger L. MacBride. Reprinted by permission of HarperCollins Publishers.

A hardcover edition of this book was published in 1994 by HarperCollins Publishers.

HarperCollins books may be purchased for educational, business, or sales promotional use. For information please write: Special Markets Department, HarperCollins Publishers, Inc., 10 East 53rd Street, New York, NY 10022.

First HarperPerennial edition published 1995.

Designed by C. Linda Dingler

The Library of Congress has catalogued the hardcover edition as follows:

Dorris, Michael.
    Paper trail : essays / Michael Dorris. — 1st ed.
        p.   cm.
    Includes bibliographical references.
    ISBN 0-06-016971-0
    I. Title.
PS3554.O695P37 1994
814'.54—dc20   93-41420

ISBN 0-06-092593-0 (pbk.)
95 96 97 98 99 ❖/RRD 10 9 8 7 6 5 4 3 2 1

For Louise:

> *Absent by name*
> *from most of these pages*
> *only because*
> *you are so everywhere*
> *within them*

In addition to those men and women who contributed to this collection by inspiring the essays in which they appear, my special thanks and gratitude go to this book's editors, Nancy Nicholas and Susan Moldow, and to the editors of the various periodicals and books in which these pieces were originally published. As ever, I am also indebted to the keen eye of Charles Rembar and to the extraordinary intelligence and oversight of Louise Erdrich.

CONTENTS

Packing Up   1

FAMILY OCCASIONS   7
Sundays   8
The Contest   9
Father's Day   16
The New York Hat   20
The Train Cake   27
A Second Adoption   33
Growing Up   38
Mice   43

RITES OF PASSAGE   53
On the Road   54
The Quest for Pie   55
The Sentry   68

EVERYBODY'S CHILDREN   73
Thankfulness   74
Fetal Alcohol Syndrome: A National Perspective   77
Fetal Alcohol Syndrome: A Parent's Perspective   82
Crossing the Line   103
Crazy Horse Malt Liquor   107
The Power of Love   111

CONTENTS

INDIANS   119

"I" Isn't for "Indian"   120

Indians on the Shelf   122

Rewriting History   133

Discoveries   145

The Grass Still Grows, the Rivers Still Flow:
Contemporary Native Americans   163

The Hundred Year War for White Earth   207

LEARNING FROM MISTAKES   227

For Indians, No Thanksgiving   228

Native American Literature in an Ethnohistorical
Context   232

Mr. Reagan and the Indians   255

Dances with Indians   260

OPENED DOORS   265

Beating the System   266

Trusting the Words   268

Summer Reading   282

Word From the Front   301

House of Stone   303

Little Fears   316

GOING PLACES   319

Americans All   320

Martyrs   322

Pen Pals   327

CONTENTS

The Forgotten Algebra Test Nightmare   332

Life Stories   337

HOME   347

The Cherry Tree   348

Three Yards   349

Real and True Estate   353

Maintaining a Home   357

Cutting Grass   370

PACKING UP

What do we take? What do we leave? What do we stack in the front yard and invite strangers to disparage? We never meant to hoard possessions, never intended to sully our nest with unnecessary stuff, but somehow over the years it silently stockpiled, filling corners, drawers, attics, garages. Impulse items. Terrible gifts kept for sentimental reasons. Outgrown clothes, which we expect to fit into again after the diet. *National Geographics* from which we may someday cull the perfect isle to visit, *Consumer Reports* issues that we'll surely need the next time we have to replace our toaster or decide to get serious about choosing the most economical brand of dishwasher soap. Letters from those we've loved. Stationery and matchbooks from disparate motels: the Wrangler (Mobridge, South Dakota), the Top of the World (Barrow, Alaska), the Sequoia (Fredericton, New Brunswick), the Ramada Inn of Montvale, New Jersey. Dinner plates with a chip along the circumference. Good boots our children have outgrown. Pages torn from newspapers because one of the articles (which one?) seemed particularly cogent and worth remembering. Books we promise ourselves we'll read. Wedding presents still in their boxes.

Within that last category, we received an invention called a Shish-ke-bobber. It probably cost a lot of money, and who knows—whoever bought this gizmo for us might show up and rightfully expect skewered hors d'oeuvres. Several times I've thought of actually assembling and trying out the device, but when I read the instructions on the side of the carton, I realize how hard the thing would be to wash once it's dirty and so I lose my appetite for seared mushroom caps.

The Shish-ke-bobber, still full of potential, confronted me from its perch in the laundry room as we packed up to move this August. If I were a pharaoh, I expect I'd be buried with it, just in case I wanted to go to the trouble to concoct tiny little snacks in the afterlife. But will it fit into the already crowded trunk of the Subaru?

Relocation necessarily brings such dilemmas, for it is an experience prescient of death. It forces you to confront what you've forgotten, to attend to the fact that the passage of time alters the relative value and usefulness of objects and keepsakes that once seemed so important. It's a formalized sort of leave-taking, an erupting volcano of decisions that you have previously avoided. Somewhere between the two extreme reactions (take everything and pretend continuity, take nothing and make a fresh start) there's a murky gray area of insecure transition. Before you can completely look forward, you must review, sometimes let go.

Of course that process happens constantly in life, but usually not all at once. Most change is incremental, imperceptible. In the normal scheme of things, once you've established the basic contours, priorities are grooved as gently as rocks carved by a year-round stream or as a face resolving into its natural seams and lines. You're lulled with the intimation of permanence.

"Dream on," says a hatchback trunk with limited space. Already it contains cartons hastily sealed and banded with masking tape labels: Kentucky, Montana, FAS research, Dartmouth, Girls' Clothes. Now I stand with a box of children's school projects and souvenirs from the 1970s—Christmas tree garlands (some cut from poster paper and others concocted of pine cones sprinkled with glitter), handwritten essays stapled to Manila folders, report cards, letters from camp, apologies. Even the box itself is a relic carefully transported from a trip my older children and I took halfway around the world: *Fresh Rarotonga Paw Paws from the Cook Islands for Turners and Growers Ltd.*, reads the bright orange-and-blue lettering. Memories encased in memories.

Time collapses and warps, folding over and over itself into a condensed bundle. The collected evidence of my first sons' and daughter's childhoods—and, by extension, of my youth—demands to be relevant still, to warrant a place in the future, if only as articles of record.

I contemplate the box, and I wonder: will any item endure beyond the backward cast of my wife's memory or mine? Distillation is forever in process. It takes many maples' worth of running sap and a blazing fire to make a pint of syrup, and only a few stacks of pancakes to use that up. What was once much is by evaporation reduced to a little, and then, by consumption, to a single drop—before disappearing altogether from the earth's recall.

The box is loaded with the chaos of experience, the culled highlights. Praise and recrimination, worry and relief, intimations—ultimately proven true or false, or both—of what was in store for all of us. Promising starts that led nowhere. Early warnings unheeded. Viewed in the bright light of retrospect, the assemblage makes only one kind of sense, reveals only a single, inevitable set of interlinked events, but during the course of its accumulation, who knew that? Who could pin down, amid all the seeming digressions of talent or interest or shortcoming, the central path each son and daughter would follow? Who knows the story, even now, as we wait in worry for their next letter or telephone call?

My illusion in saving things has been that the past is redemptive, that its monument constructed of kindnesses and accomplishment can, when needed, balance, infuse optimism into a current period of sorrow or doubt. Our older children's lives have not developed as we and they had expected. They struggle with problems not of their own making, with the consequences of years of poor judgments, with a world that does not remember them sweetly as we do. The artifacts of their innocence, herewith exhibits A to Z, are inadmissible because we are the only witnesses, and our testimony is suspect.

I designate the Shish-ke-bobber as a housewarming gift for the next tenant. I donate the *National Geographics* to the town library, throw away the newspapers, and sell the dinner plates for a nickel apiece.

But I take the box along. I make room for it in the trunk, in the new house's closet of necessary gear. Airtight and secure, it waits like a time capsule to be discovered. Memory forgotten eventually becomes surprise. The past exists in its own continuum, valuable, if not to its creators, at least to its appreciative audience—distinct from its sequela. I keep the box because its contents mattered, and therefore matter. I keep it for perspective and because, when it doesn't make me sad, it makes me smile. I keep it because I can't leave it behind.

Hungry Mind Review
November 1991

FAMILY
OCCASIONS

SUNDAYS

After church, my Aunt Marion, who would tell you she never cooked, scrambled eggs while I read the funny papers. My grandmother pondered the serious question of midafternoon dinner, and in summer my mother, her hair protected by a cotton scarf, used the garden hose to wash the car. Aunt Ginny telephoned from her apartment in New York at exactly noon, and we each took our turn in speaking to her, not to exceed three minutes total. Later on, the four of us dressed again in our church clothes to come to the table, and we always had an iced bakery cake for dessert. In the evenings my mother and her friends Rita, Ruth Ann, Lou, and Frankie met for canasta, each Sunday in a revolving cycle at a different hostess's house. My grandmother watched Ed Sullivan on Channel 11. Aunt Marion and I played Monopoly, neither of us asking for nor expecting any mercy. Before bed, we met again in the kitchen—the Stork Club, we called it at that hour—for a second generous piece of cake. We kissed each other good-night and said our prayers and went to sleep. Every week of every year, for years and years, without fail.

Family Circle
October 1992

THE CONTEST

My mother and two of her older sisters were all quite ill during their late teens and early twenties, and as a result my mother married relatively late. She and my father, a young army lieutenant, met on a blind date while he was stationed at Fort Knox. In almost every respect—ethnicity, religion, background—he was romantically, complicatedly different from other men she knew, and characteristically my mother had high hopes, as she traveled alone to California for her wedding and then lived on army bases in Texas and Washington State during their first year together.

In 1947, my father was killed in a jeep accident near Passau, Germany, and my mother returned to live with my grandmother and Aunt Marion in Louisville. I was two, and my mother was in her thirties, more than ten years younger than my current age. A widow after less than five years— one long war—as a wife, she must have been lonely and terribly disappointed, but I never heard her complain or question the sharp turn in her future. My father's insurance money was divided between donations for masses said in his name and my mother's share of a down payment on the house in which she and my aunt still live. Then, with the small monthly stipend from my father's military pension and social security to supplement my aunt's salary, my mother stayed home, devoting herself to the perfection of my childhood.

Before her marriage, according to uncensored snips of stories and to the evidence of the family photo album, my mother was infamous in her circle as a free spirit. She swam at midnight in the Ohio River, spent her vacations from Colgate Palmolive as a below-decks passenger on United Fruit Company boats in the Caribbean, even once sang on a local radio station as part of a trio that included Dale Evans. In the snapshots from her early twenties, she often has flowers tucked in her long, curly black hair or sports an off-the-shoulder blouse. With her strong brow and deeply lidded eyes she has the look of a youthful Loretta Young, with a smile as wide as Lena Horne's.

There wasn't much money during the depression for store-bought clothes, and early on my mother taught herself to sew—she needed a wardrobe for the fun she intended to have. In my favorite picture of her from the period, she has glamorized a cloth coat with epaulets fashioned from pieces of an old carpet, meant to resemble pressed fur. Her expression is bold, interested to see what comes next.

I personally first encountered this adventurous side of my mother when I was nine years old. A friend of my Aunt Ginny's, Henry Lea, had a job as assistant stage manager at the Memorial Coliseum downtown, the theater where nationally touring Broadway plays were presented. One January day Henry called to offer my mother and me passes to see a matinee of *The Dark Is Light Enough*, a drama starring Katherine Cornell and my mother's all-time favorite actor, Tyrone Power.

My mother took a long time to get ready that morning, and when she finally appeared, perfumed and made up, she was transformed in my eyes into a movie star herself. She seemed almost distant, enveloped in a cloud of graciousness, as if her enthusiasm had reached some plateau of calm from which she could review all that followed with serene detachment. The day, for her, was an occasion, an opportunity to step out of the role she normally played and into a brighter, less constricting version of her possibilities.

The last thing my mother did before we departed was to write a few words on a piece of note paper, stare at it for a moment, make a correction or two, then slip it into her purse. When I asked for an explanation, she would only say, mysteriously, "Just in case, Honey."

I don't recall a single detail about the play—its dialogue was far over my head—but I do remember that my mother sat at attention for the whole performance, her back straight, her full concentration on the rhythm of the lines and the flow of the action on the stage. During intermission we remained in our seats, didn't talk much. I looked at the program, and once or twice my mother checked the paper she had stuck in her purse—but she still refused to let me see the words. There were curtain calls, many of them, yet we didn't leave when the house lights went up.

"A surprise," my mother whispered. "Henry's going to

sneak us in backstage." Her voice was tense, and she seemed less thrilled than terrified by the prospect. I followed her to a small door near the orchestra pit, and our friend met the knock.

"It'll have to be quick," Henry warned us. "He's beat. I'll put you in wardrobe and he'll try to drop in to say hello."

We waited in a room filled with wonderful costumes in brilliant colors, drawers overflowing with masks and capes, the props from many productions stacked upon every surface. But instead of exclaiming at each new thing I pointed out, my mother dug once again into her purse and found the now familiar paper. She was still looking at it when we heard someone at the door, and quickly she crumpled it in her fist.

Tyrone Power was the first famous person I ever met, and what I remember about him were his eyelashes: unnaturally long. I shook hands when we were introduced, but I hung my head, tongue-tied with shyness, incapable of uttering a sound.

"Ty," Henry said. "This is my friend Mary Besy and her little boy, Michael."

I glanced up to see my mother step forward without hesitation.

"Oh, Mr. Power." She spoke smoothly, confidently, each syllable enunciated, distinct and clear. "We missed you every moment you were offstage."

It was just the right compliment. Tyrone Power smiled—

that was the other thing he had besides eyelashes: teeth—
and lingered for a few minutes longer than I think he'd
planned.

It was a cold, raw winter dusk. My mother drove with
one hand on the wheel and with the other she absently
combed her hair. As we made our way down Frankfort
Avenue, she sang along with the music on the radio.
Somehow I knew that if she ever smoked, which she never
did, she would have had a cigarette.

At home, I ran ahead into the house, showed my grandmother and aunt the program, raved about our excursion
backstage, our hobnob with celebrity. My mother stood by
the door, listened, nodded, even reluctantly consented to
repeat her opening remark to Tyrone Power, but when she
went into the kitchen to fix supper she seemed returned to
the routine of her life, almost as though nothing out of the
ordinary had happened.

But next morning, there was evidence to the contrary. In
search of a glove, I went out to our car, parked in the alley
beside our house. The door on the driver's side was open
and the overhead light was still dimly lit, illuminating a
layer of gray frost that covered the inside of the windshield.
The turn signal blinked, my mother's winter coat lay abandoned across the seat, the keys were still in the ignition,
and the tank had run out of gas.

It must have been a year or two later when my mother
heard about a competition run by the local Singer Sewing

Machine outlet. Each registered contestant paid a $20 fee to enroll in an advanced class during which she would design and construct an outfit called an "afternoon ensemble." Eventually a fashion show would take place, with official judges. The grand prize was an airplane dream trip to Florida for two, all expenses paid.

The tuition put a strain on our finances, but my mother regarded this as an investment. Every Tuesday night for three months she went to her seminar, discussed the intricacies of basting and pleating and tucks with other women, and returned with ideas that she translated into sketches. She took me along when she shopped for her material, examining each flat bolt with an eye toward the cloth's drape and texture, as well as price.

On the big night, however, my mother wouldn't let anyone accompany her to the finals. She had made a blue linen sundress—ideal for Florida, she had decided—with an ivory bolero jacket. She even dyed a pair of shoes the same shade of blue and covered a pillbox hat frame to match. My aunt contributed her good white gloves, and my grandmother came up with a pair of pearl-drop earrings to complete the effect. My mother had gotten a beauty parlor permanent wave that afternoon, dressed early, and stood during supper so as not to wrinkle. We all applauded when she did a last twirl before walking out the door alone.

My mother has suffered many disappointments, big and small, in her life, and borne them all bravely, but that night was a triumph. She arrived home at ten o'clock with a red velveteen crown, a silver plastic scepter, and a certificate worth two airplane tickets, four days at the Belmar Hotel in Miami Beach, a cabana by the pool, and a welcome dinner that included shrimp cocktails and dessert.

I vividly recall that trip of thirty-five years ago—for I was my mother's chosen companion, the chief beneficiary as always of her labor. She found a pattern, made an orange plaid sports coat for me, along with a new pair of long pants, and she bought me a clip-on bow tie. After dinner, that first night in the tropics, we sat together on our private balcony, listening until well past my usual bedtime as the hotel band played tune after tune of the music from my mother's youth: "Harbor Lights," "Stormy Weather," "The Heart of a Fool." She was wearing the linen dress, of course, and her hair was blowing free in the ocean wind. Her head was back, her eyes were closed, and she was smiling, harmonizing the familiar words to herself.

Ladies' Home Journal
May 1993

FATHER'S DAY

My father, a career army officer, was twenty-seven when he was killed, and as a result, I can't help but take war personally. Over the years his image has coalesced for me as an amalgam of familiar anecdotes: a dashing mixed-blood man from the Northwest who, improbably, could do the rumba; a soldier who regularly had his uniform altered by a tailor so that it would fit better; a date, according to my mother, who "knew how to order" in a restaurant; the person whom, in certain lights and to some people, I resemble. He is a compromise of his quirkier qualities, indistinct, better remembered for his death—my grandmother still wears a gold star on her best coat—than for his brief life.

From the perspective of the present, my father was a bit player on the edges of the movie frame, the one who didn't make it back, whose fatality added anonymous atmosphere and a sense of mayhem to the plot. His grave, in a military cemetery near Tacoma, is located by graph paper like a small town on a map: E-9. He's frozen in age, a kid in a T-shirt, a pair of dog tags stored in a box in my closet. His willingness to die for his country may have contributed in some small part to the fall of the Nazis, but more in the way of a pawn exchanged for its counterpart, a pair of lives eliminated with the result that there were two fewer people to engage in combat. I was a few months old the last time he saw me, and a single photograph of me in his arms is the only hard evidence that we ever met.

The fact of my father's death exempted me, under the classification "sole surviving son" (A-IV), from being drafted during the Vietnam War, but it also obliged me to empathize with the child of every serviceperson killed in an armed engagement. "Glory" is an inadequate substitute, a pale abstraction, compared to the enduring, baffling blankness of a missing parent.

There was a children's book in the 1950s—perhaps it still exists—titled *The Happy Family,* and it was a piece of work. Dad toiled at the office, Mom baked in the kitchen, and brother and sister always had neighborhood friends sleeping over. The prototype of "Leave It to Beaver" and "Father Knows Best," this little text reflects a midcentury standard, a brightly illustrated reproach to my own unorthodox household, but luckily that wasn't the way I heard it. As read to me by my Aunt Marion—her acid delivery was laced with sarcasm and punctuated with many a sidelong glance—it turned into hilarious irony.

Compassionate and generous, irreverent, simultaneously opinionated and open-minded, iron-willed and ever optimistic, my aunt was the one who pitched a baseball with me in the early summer evenings, who took me horseback riding, who sat by my bed when I was ill. A fierce, lifelong

Democrat—a precinct captain even—she helped me find my first jobs and arranged among her friends at work for my escorts to the father–son dinners that closed each sports season. When the time came, she prevailed upon the elderly man next door to teach me how to shave.

"Daddy" Tingle, as he was known to his own children and grandchildren, was a man of many talents. He could spit tobacco juice over the low roof of his garage, gum a sharpened mumbly-peg twig from the ground even without his false teeth, and produce, from the Bourbon Stockyards where he worked, the jewel-like cornea of a cow's eye—but he wasn't much of a shaver. After his instruction, neither am I.

Aunt Marion, on the other hand, was a font of information and influence. When I was fifteen, on a series of tempestuous Sunday mornings at a deserted River Road park, she gave me lessons in how to drive a stick shift. A great believer in the efficacy of the *World Book Encyclopedia*— the major literary purchase of my childhood—she insisted that I confirm any vague belief by looking it up. To the then-popular tune of "You, You, You," she counted my laps in the Crescent Hill pool while I practiced for a life-saving certificate. Operating on the assumption that anything out of the ordinary was probably good for me, she once offered to mortgage the house so that I could afford to go to Mali as a volunteer participant in Operation Crossroads Africa. She paid for my first Smith-Corona typewriter in thirty-six $4-a-week installments.

For over sixty years Aunt Marion was never without steady employment: telegraph operator for Western Union, budget officer for the city of Louisville, "new girl" at a small savings and loan (when, after twenty-five years in a patronage job, the Democrats lost the mayor's race), executive secretary for a nationally renowned attorney.

Being Aunt Marion, she didn't and doesn't give herself much credit. Unless dragged to center stage, she stands at the periphery in snapshots, minimizes her contributions. Every June for forty years I've sent her a Father's Day card.

National Public Radio
June 1989

Hungry Mind Review
May 1991

THE NEW YORK HAT

My maternal grandmother was a small, heavy woman, born in Henderson, Kentucky, who wore her gray hair coiled in a bun at the base of her neck and had fierce hazel eyes and thick black brows behind the lenses of her rimless glasses. She was queen of our house, demanding no less than total respect from the rest of the world. If any visitor was so foolish as to come to call without bringing some small token of homage for her—a cutting from a special flowering plant, a lace handkerchief, a straw fan—she refused to emerge from her bedroom. The rest of us made small talk with the offending guest, hoping that the slam of dresser drawers, the loud play of a radio, the prolonged sighs broadcast through the closed door, would go unnoticed.

My grandmother had survived all but one of her eleven brothers and sisters and expected that now, in her late seventies, she was owed celebration, especially on formal occasions. Every Easter, my Aunt Marion's friend Mrs. Shreck constructed from flour and icing a large lamb reclining in a field of spiky green meringue. With wool of shaved coconut, raisin eyes, a smiling maraschino mouth, and—the most realistic touch—a pink strawberry cake interior, the lamb was ceremoniously displayed in the center of the dining room table.

"It's too pretty to cut," my grandmother annually pronounced, and so the lamb remained, growing stale and stiff, then fragile, as we went about our lives around it. The weather warmed and the grass softened. Humidity caused the coconut to swell and drop like an aura. Finally, sometime around Decoration Day, gravity would prevail and, with an audible thud, the creature's head would fall off.

My grandmother expected and received an azalea for the 4th of July, a new dress for her birthday, lily of the valley scent in commemoration of her wedding anniversary, and cash on Thanksgiving, but Christmas was the crowning feast, for on Christmas my Aunt Ginny took the train from New York and brought with her, among other things, a gift for my grandmother from Bonwit Teller.

I knew Aunt Ginny's story by heart: In 1945, at the end of her third decade and shortly before I was born, my mother's eldest sister, Virginia, took the train from Louisville to New York on a vacation with her friend, Linda Lee. They ate at automats in order to have enough money to stay at the Algonquin, locale of the round table they'd heard about on the radio. Out of curiosity they read the want ads in the *Times*, where Linda's eye was caught one day by "Reputable Theatrical Firm Needs Secretaries." Aunt Ginny had been a slave to the Louisville Little Theater for years, a star in its productions, a constant presence backstage, and so when Linda read her the ad she cried, "It's fate!" and went to be interviewed.

"I was so enthusiastic," she always added when reporting this part of the tale. "I told them 'I love the theater, I love it!' Only after they'd hired me did the boss remember to ask, 'Can you type?'"

Aunt Ginny intended to work a week, as a lark, at the United Booking Company, which scheduled Broadway shows for out-of-town performances, but from her first day she was in her element. She found an apartment in a five-story walk-up on Jones Street in Greenwich Village. To pay the rent, she put in a forty-hour week plus weekends and holidays and spent every spare minute at the theater, standing or seated in the highest balcony.

After World War II, business on Broadway boomed. The demand for tickets exceeded the span of a normal working day, so Aunt Ginny started moonlighting in theaters and was there when *South Pacific* hit big and the steady mail order stream became a flood. Each night she'd watch the show from behind the exit curtains; in three and a half years, she never missed her favorite number, "There Is Nothing Like a Dame." But when, around the same time, she met James Michener at a party, she refused his offer of a drink. Enzio Pinza he wasn't.

Over the years, Aunt Ginny gained a reputation as someone who knew the intricacies of selling blocks of seats to parties and groups. She knew the view of the stage from every seat, was familiar with the idiosyncrasies of each playhouse, and was mesmerizing—equally to the president of a Hadassah in New Jersey and to me, sitting at her feet in our living room—with her synopses spanning a seasonful of the shows she had seen or a new outline she had just read. She had leaped when an executive assistant position opened with the Shubert Organization.

"They wanted a man to handle it," she always added. "Well, P.S., I got the job. From then on it was a whole different ball game. I had responsibility, handled millions of dollars' worth of business. And I got a raise, too."

"How much?" I once asked her.

"Oh, honey, I don't know! The thing is, I didn't care." Aunt Ginny caught her breath, struck all over again by the perks. "I'd have worked for nothing because I got free tickets."

Then she paused. "There was a time I couldn't get along financially, so I thought I'd join the ushers' union. I had no fear of anything." She raised her fist, a familiar gesture. "I walked New York at any hour. But then I found out I'd have to start in second balcony, as an usher I mean." She shook her head, reflecting. "I couldn't do it. I'm scared to death of steps."

When Aunt Ginny talked about her employers at the Shubert Organization, they became real, characters in the drama of her life. I could see Mr. Lee, a small-boned gentleman in a dapper dark suit and brown derby, his hair blacked and face heavily made up to look tan. "He loved the theater, worshipped the stars. He and I were kindred spirits!"

In her work, which was on the order of a daily devotion, Aunt Ginny read scripts, argued with producers, arranged rehearsal space, saw every show at least once, and did her best to keep them playing through her monomaniacal attention to sales. She met and sparred with everyone from production consultant Eleanor Roosevelt (*Sunrise at Campobello*) to star Rosalind Russell (*Wonderful Town*).

She moved uptown, changed buildings as each was torn down or went co-op. She had strong, enduring friendships, but no time for romance, unless one counted her triumphant affairs with New York or the "other town" in her life, Paris, whose streets she walked on five vacation visits—with tears of happiness streaming down her cheeks.

By the time Aunt Ginny arrived on the train for her annual visit from New York, the box of gifts from my father's mother was under the tree. A red wool stocking with white piping sewed by my seamstress mother hung from the mantel of the fake fireplace, officially there for the cheer and pleasure of our dog, Jerry. Nothing was out of place, but for some reason on the Christmas I was fourteen I didn't take any permanence for granted. I watched each member of my family with the appreciation of distance, with the kind of homesickness one anticipates before ever leaving home. In the warm room flickering with colored lights from the tree, we gathered after dinner to sit around my grandmother's chair. We knew each other so well that every routine was practiced, a ritual, casually affectionate, and I caught a glimpse of that fragile, fleeting construction of blood and intersecting time, of family.

As the youngest member, I was given my present first—much more than what I'd hoped for: a secondhand office typewriter, tall and shiny black, its alphabet a careful, precise pica on yellowing white keys. Everyone was delighted at my surprise, took their thanks proudly. One by one, my mother and aunts opened their gifts—powders and scarves and rose sachets and Santa Claus earrings—each exclaiming that she had received exactly what she wanted.

My grandmother was last and she waited, patient and appraising, pretending that she had forgotten that her turn had not yet come. There was a moment of silent anticipation. Aunt Ginny left the room and then returned bearing the large violet-strewn container she had carried all the way from New York. We had pooled our Christmas funds and had heard described what was inside, but we hadn't actually seen it.

I remember that a flush spread along my grandmother's neck as she busied herself with layers of tissue paper, taking her time at unwrapping. Suddenly her hands froze, then lifted from the box a hat of purple crushed velvet. Around its border, at intervals, were pure white feathers arranged as half-wings. It was a hat from outer space, a hat of the imagination, larger than life—a hat so different from anything we had ever seen that we could only marvel.

My grandmother recovered first.

"Oh, my," she said. "My stars." She straightened her

shoulders, lifted her chin, kept her lips steady. Raising both hands, their skin fine and crossed with tiny wrinkles, she set the hat firmly on her head. Then, expertly aiming its matching pin, she fixed it in place and arranged the flowered net veil about her face. She posed, a lady about town, a dowager, for a moment the complete collection of all her aspirations. Her eyes, however, were masked. Perhaps they watched for our reaction, or perhaps, just for that one instant, they were closed.

Seventeen
December 1987

New York Woman
December 1986

THE TRAIN CAKE

In 1972, when Abel, my eldest son, was three and I was still an unmarried adoptive parent, I moved to Hanover, New Hampshire, to teach at Dartmouth College. My classes started immediately, so within days I enrolled Abel at a day-care center across the river in Vermont.

Still young enough to believe that all it took to juggle family and career was organization and good intent, I was aggressively confident, well versed in the literature of single parenthood, and prepared to quote statistics to prove that nurturing was a human, and not exclusively female, potential. I was ready for the doubtful glance or the skeptical eyebrow, I was ready to share recipes and remedies while folding clothes in laundromats or waiting in line at Sears to have baby pictures taken. I was not, however, expecting to vie with a population of high-achieving working parents—single or married—every bit as defensive as I was about being employed outside the home.

The competition, I soon realized, would not be easy. The other parents had read and taken notes on every how-to-be-perfect manual on the market. Their children arrived in the morning dressed in color-coordinated outfits with matching wristwatches and down-filled winter gear, sporting hairstyles that had to have taken an hour of dexterous labor to create. Every boy and girl had at least one famous trait—an aversion to synthetic cloth or an allergy to dust—that required special instructions.

Birthdays were the occasions for each child to be center stage, and so lavish had the festivities apparently become the year before we arrived that the day-care center now limited the gala spread to foods explicitly made by the actual parents in their actual homes. This seemed reasonable enough, but as fall turned into winter and I witnessed, at the end of the afternoons, the excessive remains of one extravaganza after another, I began to suspect that some people were cheating. How else to explain the ice-cream cupcakes, the individual hot-dog-and-baked-bean quiches, the fluted papaya cups filled with *crème fraise?*

Abel and I lived in those days in a small wooden house by a lake—two bedrooms and a tiny kitchen, not a fancy place, but the right price for an instructor's salary. It was there that I retreated to think and plan as Abel's January birthday neared. I had something to prove.

I considered briefly the family of cream puffs and éclairs but rejected them as too risky. I was not an experienced cook and my oven, although a dutiful heater, was not up to wild extremes or precise gaugings of temperature. I contemplated the possibilities of puddings, but ultimately judged them as too unorthodox, too frivolous. From every unconventional excursion, I came back to cake.

"What would be the best cake you could imagine?" I

asked Abel one night as he played on the carpet with our Siberian husky, Skahota. His reply was immediate and unsurprising. He was a boy of fierce attachments, and at the moment his passion was railroad.

"A train!" he announced, and went back to his game.

I took his idea seriously and called a friend who knew about such things. Culling through her recipe collection, she uncovered directions for specialized cake pans made from cardboard wrapped in aluminum foil. Boxcars and the caboose were a cinch, the coal car was a problem, and the locomotive was a challenge. But it was possible, it was Abel's wish, and done right, it could be the most spectacular dessert ever to grace the two-foot-high day-care table. I gave the project a week of my life.

Mounted on a single square of plywood, each of the six cars was at base an eight-by-four-inch-long rectangle of trimmed sponge cake, to which I attached paper wheels and connecting toggles made of taffy. No food colors at the local grocery seemed bright or impressive enough, so I traveled one lunch hour to a specialty outlet where, for $2 each, I purchased small vials of blues and reds and yellows and greens so vivid, so ceramic in their luster, that a mere drop was sufficient to tint a small bowl of white icing. But I was looking for more than a tint—I was after bold—so for good measure I mixed more and more edible dye into my palette until the hues that confronted me were dazzling. No caboose was ever so barn-red; no passenger car so grass-green; no plucky little locomotive, decorated with gumdrops, a hand mirror, and a cheerful expression, so sky blue. This was a little engine that *could,* and knew it. Black, for the coal car, was trickier but was solved with melted licorice that, when spread warm and then hardened, transformed the fragile sides into indestructible steel.

I got behind in my lecture preparations but finished the train at midnight before the day of Abel's party. All around it I had constructed toy houses, cutout happy families (more than one shepherded by a lone adult male), grazing cartoon animals, and before going to bed, exhausted but smug, I took photographs of my creation from every angle. Abel—and I—would have nothing to apologize for.

And it all happened just as I had imagined. When I carefully carried my creation from the car and negotiated the door of the center, the train montage was greeted with exclamations of delight and disbelief by staff and children alike. Other parents, peeling their sons and daughters from layers of mittens and boots and snowsuits, looked from the cake to me with deeply satisfying expressions of betrayal and chagrin. I had become the act to beat, the standard against which to be measured. With a spin of the mixer I had achieved the status of Ideal Parent, the adult for whom no task was too great, no child's whim too onerous to grant. Yes, I worked full-time, but did I let that get in the way of my fatherly duties? The train cake answered *that* question in a puff of spun-sugar smoke.

The party, which I returned to preside over later in the day, was memorable. In the flickering light of five candles (one to grow on), the children's eyes were glazed. The volume of their singing voices was urgent with greed, and once the clapping ceased they made fast work of all my labors. Within twenty minutes my carefully ordered platter had become a surrealistic swatch of colors. Only the indestructible coal car, chipped at but still whole, remained.

Abel, who in his excitement had eaten almost none of the cake, was momentarily everyone's best friend, the hero of the day, and when we got in our car to go home, he leaned across the seat with a smile so wide and happy it startled me.

"Thank you, Daddy," he said.

I looked at him, this little boy who really was, after all, what this was for and about. In his dark eyes there was one message only, one idea: his wish had come true. And I looked back with a single realization of my own: in him, my wish had come true, too.

"Happy birthday," I said.

The cake story should have ended there, with the train consumed and Abel content and me reacquainted with the true meaning of things, but there was one final chapter. About ten o'clock that night, I was at the kitchen table trying hard to organize the next day's class notes when the phone rang. It was the director of the day-care center, and her voice was frantic.

"What did you put in that damn cake?" she demanded.

"Why, nothing," I said. "Just flour and sugar and a few pieces of candy. Why?"

"The parents have been calling me all night," she said. "They're hysterical. They're ready to rush their children to the hospital."

"What's wrong?" Now I was scared.

"It's when they put their kids to bed," she said. "When they took them to the potty. They noticed before they flushed! The water in the toilet bowl was green! Or bright blue! Electric orange!"

I closed my eyes and saw again the jaunty cars, lined up and ready to roll. The train cake had made more of an impression than I had planned.

Days later, when every expensive color had passed safely but remarkably through the digestive system of each child, the day-care center inaugurated a new rule: henceforth, all birthday ingredients must be normal.

Working Mother
November 1987

A SECOND ADOPTION

There is one feature of single parenthood that any man or woman solely responsible for a young child knows, no matter how the arrangement evolved: dating is next to impossible. By the time a baby-sitter is found, picked up, given instructions, checked upon by telephone, driven home, and paid, your partner for the evening had better have been True Love. If not, you wonder: was it worth it? Furthermore, you become a kind of package deal: like me, like my child. Or forget it.

In 1974, with a demanding job, a six-year-old adopted son with special needs, and no fiancée on the horizon, I realized the time had come to recontact my adoption agency. If I was going to spend the next twelve or thirteen years of my life unpartnered—a distinct possibility—I wanted to do so with a larger family.

Denis Daigle, Abel's caseworker, was not encouraging. There were so many couples waiting for placements, he said, that it was unlikely that any agency would approve a second child for a single male, especially since this time I requested an infant or toddler. He would submit the paperwork, but I should not count on anything, not get my hopes up.

Okay, I promised, and pasted yellow wallpaper with a

small green-and-red teddy bear design in the spare bedroom of our house. I watched yard sales for cribs and
bassinets, and found a used rocking horse in mint condition. I put my name on the waiting list for a child-care center and arranged for a lighter teaching load.

When Denis called, his voice incredulous, I was ready.

"You won't believe it," he said. "There's a little Lakota
boy, just over a year old, who's available. They've approved
your application."

"When does it happen?" I felt the stirrings of the male
analog for labor.

"He's in South Dakota."

I did some geographic calculations. "I'm presenting a
paper at a one-day conference in Omaha next Tuesday," I
said.

"Could you be in Pierre on Wednesday?"

Could I? I had already chosen his name, Sava, after a
Native Alaskan friend who had taken me on as a salmon
fishing partner for two summers while I was doing anthropological fieldwork.

On Tuesday afternoon the Nebraska weather turned
nasty, grounding all planes, so I rented a car, called the
caseworker in South Dakota to tell her the name of my
motel in Pierre, and drove all night. I checked into my
room exhausted, unbathed, and bleary-eyed at 9 A.M., but
before I had a chance to unpack my suitcase there was a
knock on the door. I opened it to a smiling young blond
woman bundled in a green parka.

"Hi, I'm Jeanine from SDDSS," she announced. "Are you all set to meet your son?"

"Can you wait a few minutes? I want to take a shower, change my clothes, maybe pick up a present for him somewhere."

An uneasy expression crossed her face.

"Not a good idea?" I asked.

"Well . . . *actually* he's waiting in my car right now." Jeanine glanced to her left and, following her look, I saw in the backseat a baby carrier and the top of a purple knitted cap. I didn't want to give the impression of the slightest hesitation, so I said, "Great! Bring him right in."

The instant she turned her back I dashed to the bathroom, splashed water on my face, and dabbed some aftershave on my neck. First impressions are important and at least I could smell good.

When I emerged, Jeanine was standing in the room holding a solid-looking baby whose dark, intelligent eyes regarded me with raw suspicion.

"He's very friendly," Jeanine assured me. "He's been so anxious to meet you."

I held out my arms, savoring the tender moment of first encounter. He was no lightweight. I cradled him in my arms and lowered my face close to his to get a good look. "Hello Sava," I whispered.

His eyes widened, then closed tightly. Simultaneously his jaws opened and opened and opened, revealing a space more like the Grand Canyon than a mouth. I felt him draw a long breath into his lungs, and when he released it in a howl, my mind pictured a cartoon image of pure sound, strong as a hurricane, blowing everything—furniture, hair, trees—in its wake.

Jeanine made a step toward us, but I shook my head and spoke more confidently than I felt.

"Give us an hour or so." I nodded encouragingly to underscore my words, and she reluctantly departed.

Sava's yells did not abate but he didn't struggle as I sat down on the bed, jiggled him on my lap. He was not in the slightest afraid but was simply registering a protest, a critique of my grinning face. I unsnapped his coat, removed it, spoke softly in what I hoped was a comforting tone, and after a few long minutes he opened one eye and gave me a second appraisal.

He was a beauty: feathery straight black hair, a sensuous mouth, a strong, broad nose, a clean, sweeping jaw. His torso was wide and his hands were square-shaped with thick, tapering fingers. He opened the other eye and, as abruptly as he had begun to cry, he stopped. We stared at each other, amazed in the sudden silence.

"Hello Sava," I tried again. This time, speculatively, he only blinked.

Late the next day we boarded a plane back to New Hampshire. By then, I knew Sava's favorite food—mashed green beans mixed with cream of mushroom soup and canned fried onions sprinkled on top—and that he hated to have his hair washed. I knew he was a sound sleeper, that he had a long attention span, and that he was ticklish just below his rib cage on his right side. I knew that he and Abel were profoundly different in their personalities—Abel would leap headfirst into any strange lake, while Sava would always test the water—but I trusted that they would be compatible brothers. And I knew all over again, as if for the first time in human history, the experience of becoming a parent. Within twenty-four hours of meeting my son, I had already forgotten what it felt like not to be his father.

Generations
1987

GROWING UP

The picture I developed of my late father was a collage of stories I heard from family members who had known him and of my musings upon a series of his photographs—him, at attention in an army uniform, him marrying my mother, him standing arm in arm with two buddies on a Hawaiian beach—as well as from impressions gleaned from observing the fathers of friends and from watching the dads on television.

I knew as fact that my father had a wide-ranging military career, always seeming to be at the wrong place at the wrong time. He survived being awakened from sleep in his Pearl Harbor barracks by the Japanese attack in 1941, then came through the Battle of the Bulge without an injury. His only major physical wound was sustained at a baseball game in Texas when another soldier, in excitement over a home run, accidentally shot him in the leg. He was an eldest son, popular in high school. He prized a ruby ring, which failed to come back with the rest of his things from the town in Germany where, at age twenty-seven, his life ended on an icy mountain road.

The father of my imagination, however, took me to the places I hated to go without him—to "males only" grade school sports banquets and to public swimming pool locker rooms. He taught me how to bat one-handed. He advised me how to handle bullies, how to do a box-step, how to impress a date. He was Ward Cleaver, Jim Anderson, Dr. Stone, the Rifleman, and Ricky Ricardo, and when I became a man, I promised myself I would be just like him.

As it turned out, it was not impossible to master the arts of changing diapers, kissing scratches, exclaiming at each appropriately timed defecation, and buying increasingly sized—and priced—sneakers. I took pride in my ability to schedule regular physical exams for my two sons and daughter Madeline (whom I had adopted at ten months when Sava was four), to listen to their tales of day-care woes.

When my older children were, respectively, thirteen, nine, and five, Louise Erdrich and I got married, and she did her best to be patient with me as I gradually relaxed those solitary prerogatives of decision making and rule setting that are among the advantages of single parenthood. When the time was right, she, too, legally adopted our children, and in a few years we had two more babies. With a total of five offspring, I was technically more of a father than I had ever imagined I'd be.

But something was missing, some vestigial fantasy from Hollywood or literature, some sense of bridging an archetypal gap. None of our children had ever seemed to require

me in quite the vital, aspecific way I had imagined needing
my own father.

Then one day Sava, just twelve, waited until I was alone
and approached me with a body language and verbal hesitation that broadcast that a significant event was about to
transpire.

"Dad," he said, his voice low, slightly embarrassed.
"Would you help me with something?"

Instinctively I knew this was it, and prepared myself to
don the mantle of true paternity. Every boyhood daydream
flooded back: maybe he wanted me to take him for a nature
walk in the woods, maybe he desired to know something
arcane about human biology, maybe he had been cut from
the football team and yearned for a pep talk, maybe he was
in love for the first time and feared rejection. I prepared
myself to dispense a mixture of wisdom and compassion no
matter what the question.

"It's like this," he continued, talking to the floor. "A lot
of guys in my class got their ears pierced, but . . . I don't
really want to go to a jeweler and I'm kind of nervous to do
it myself, so . . . would *you* do it for me?"

My mouth remained open as I searched for a reply. What
would Ward say to the Beaver?

"I don't know how," I answered, pedaling as my brain
spun calendar pages through the sixties and seventies,
scanning for precedents. Of one thing I was certain: if I
tried to be reasonable, to talk him out of his plan, he
wouldn't soon trust me enough again to ask for something

when it wasn't guaranteed that I'd say yes . . . and I didn't want to preempt the opportunity to counsel him on an issue that really mattered.

"I found this," Sava offered, and pulled from his pocket a much folded piece of newspaper. It was a "Hints" column that recommended a procedure entailing ice cubes, a sterilized needle, and a raw potato placed directly behind the numbed anatomical part. The piercer was instructed to think of sticking only the potato, not the piercee's skin before it. The result was promised to be an operation painless for both parties.

What could I say? "I'll give it a try."

Sava had all the tools assembled. I brushed aside his dark hair and held his left lobe between two slivers of ice. His skin was soft to the touch, a pale tan. His ear was so familiar, so cherished, that I could have picked it out of a lineup.

Impatient, Sava lit a match, held the point of the needle into its flame until it turned black, then quickly offered it to me. I dropped the ice and fit the brown potato beside my son's head.

"Are you sure?" I asked, and our glances met.

He was.

I followed the Hint and pushed the needle into the potato. I expected a cry of pain, a drop of blood, something dramatic, but Sava didn't flinch, and when I withdrew the needle, a neat puncture remained in his earlobe, perfectly centered.

"Did it work?"

I nodded, steered him to the bathroom mirror. Sava had a gold post soaking in alcohol, which he fitted into the hole before turning his head left and right to admire the effect.

"Thanks, Dad," he said, and was out the door, headed for the telephone.

I sat alone, thinking that life was never as you expected it to be, never the same for anyone else as it was for you, never as strange in the imagination as it often turned out to be in reality. But as I overheard Sava bragging to his friend, "My Dad did it. Yeah, my *Dad*," that elusive piece of fatherhood I thought I had missed fell square into place.

Parents
June 1989

MICE

With the birth—in 1989—of Louise's and my third biological daughter, our family life explored new territory. From our collective gene pool (Chippewa-Cree-Modoc-Irish-German-French) had emerged a trio of personalities so disparate as to define the limits of diversity within the species.

Persia, now seven, is pure heart. Even as a baby, she was empathic, looking up at us in mutual condolence when she needed a midnight change or feeding. She's an actress, a ballerina, a would-be equestrienne. She weeps equally for joy and sorrow, and always with great gusto. Her dolls are dressed in the latest styles, told stories, and bathed daily. Persia has the look in her eye that the French Lieutenant's Woman must have sported as a child: romantic, enigmatic, mesmerizing.

Pallas, just turned six, is all mind. As a toddler she insisted upon sleeping each night not with a teddy bear but with a red block of wood. Her passion is spiders, and her delight is that one tiny brown arachnid has spun a delicate web in an eave above her bed. When we asked what she wanted for her birthday this year, she said, wistful and despondent: "I have a dream, but I know it can't come true."

"Try us," her mother and I implored.

"Well," she said. "I've decided I want to be a carpenter. Do you think I could have a tool chest?"

Compared with her older sisters, Aza, already at two, is iron will, Gertrude Stein's soul transmigrated. Before the age of one she had taught herself how to instantly dismantle, from within, any crib or other restraint devised by modern technology. Her first words were, emphatically, "Good girl," and she has seemed ever afterward immune to self-doubt. The other day, as I was zipping her jacket, I said, "You're a sweetie pie."

"No," she corrected me. "I'm a woman."

It's no accident that whatever Louise and I write, whether fiction or nonfiction, there always seems to be a baby getting born and being cared for. When you're typing with one hand while aiming a bottle of juice at an open mouth with the other, you take your inspiration where you find it.

As parents, we try to be ever vigilant lest our girls limit their horizons because of sexist stereotyping. Each one, we vow, should aim for whatever her talents and inclinations dictate—be it president or Nobel Prize physicist, Supreme Court justice or space shuttle pilot.

So what did we do, a few years ago, when, for their special Christmas present, Persia and Pallas's collective wish was for the complete Minnie Mouse kitchen? Despair. Despite all of our gender-neutral picture books, our daughters had clearly been molded by the subtle messages of media and popular culture. White aprons, not lab coats, loomed in their future.

How about a chess set? we suggested. A magic kit? An ant farm?

No. Persia was firm, Pallas obdurate: it was Minnie Mouse or nothing. Tucked under the pillow of their imaginations was the page torn from a Sears Wish Book in which two future mommies happily baked miniature angel food cakes, washed tiny plastic dishes, and planned the week's menu by perusing their pantry of brand-name products.

Early December became the time for an unstated battle of wills, a contest of aspiration over who knew best what two of us wanted. Louise and I made of the issue a symbol that spanned from suffrage to the Equal Rights Amendment. Our daughters, however, remained steadfast in their inclination toward Home Ec, though ultimately they seemed to resign themselves to the inequities of power. Their rages would be saved, no doubt, for some future psychoanalyst.

Then on Christmas Eve, as I was preparing my grandmother's special sweet-potato balls (whipped, flavored with brandy, formed around a marshmallow, and dredged in cornflake crumbs) and Louise was making a family favorite, wild-rice stuffing for the turkey, a string of startling insights simultaneously occurred to us: we loved to cook. We spent lots of time doing it. *We were Minnie Mouse.*

Yikes! It was almost 4:00 P.M., and the stores would soon close.

A gentle snow had begun to fall, and here and there as I drove along the road toward town, colored Christmas lights twinkled through the windows of houses with smoking chimneys. New England in winter can, at such moments, seem like one giant Hollywood set, a Currier and Ives scene ready for a heartwarming story to unfold. In this version, my part would have been played by Jimmy Stewart: awkward, stalwart, the honest gallumpf who carried the American dream like a red-white-and-blue banner. He was out to do a deed, to accomplish one of those minor miracles that make life wonderful and annually brings a tear to Donna Reed's eyes.

The problem was, every store within a hundred miles was sold out of the Minnie Mouse kitchen.

"The last one went ten minutes ago," the local Sears salesman noted, driving a stake through my heart as I finally stood at the head of a long line of shoppers.

A poor excuse for a father, I looked from right to left in search of any idea . . . and there it was, suspended by wires from the ceiling: every one of Minnie's treasures—stove, sink, and "frigerator," its doors invitingly ajar.

"How about that one?" I pleaded.

"Oh, no," the man said. "That's the display model."

"It's not for me," I argued, perhaps unnecessarily. "It's for my little girls." I paused theatrically, then fired my best shot: "It's Christmas Eve."

The man hesitated as Minnie teetered between us: rules, or little girls' dreams come true?

"Sell it to him," the grandmother behind me snarled menacingly. "What are you, Mr. Scrooge?"

"Call the manager," protested a man waiting to buy a snow shovel.

"Climb up there and take it down," demanded a very pregnant young woman with an ominously quiet voice. "Or I will."

There were holes in the plywood facades of Minnie's jaunty, red major appliances where the hooks had been inserted, but no matter. Jimmy Stewart drove home singing carols with the radio.

After our daughters were in bed, Louise and I arranged the kitchen beneath the tree, amid the puzzles and books and telescopes. We rose early to witness the girls' reaction, and right on cue they ran into the room, stopped still, and stared. What would each do first? Cook? Scour a pot? Clean out the freezer? Anything was possible.

Persia and Pallas held hands for what seemed a long time. Then, as one, they turned to where we sat and ran to squeeze between us.

"We knew you would," Persia said.

And Pallas nodded in agreement. "We knew it all the time."

We Americans are tempted to distinguish ourselves from other current and former inhabitants of this planet by assuming that we are ruled by "progress." Last year's passion—in clothing style, music, literature, or food—

instantly fades before the latest trend. National magazines inform us that yuppies will soon be consigned to the same scrapbook as hippies and flappers, and we seek to dispose of rather than recycle everything from diapers to slang. Newness is interesting, exciting, full of promise. Old is, well, used.

When we think of non-Western societies, we often imagine that they are different, bound to boring repetitions of tradition, with each generation replicating the lives of its parents. As they are depicted in popular media, tribal societies appear static, frozen in the past, remote and forbidding.

Anthropologists report that some nonliterate peoples go so far as to preserve an archaic version of their language exclusively for the education of their young, guarding against the slightest syllabic alteration lest something precious in the ancient wisdom be lost forever. Since there are no libraries, no videocassette archives in which to store excess knowledge, information must be compressed, packed in an easily transmitted dramatic format and passed on. Only the most streamlined, most universally understandable stories survive—"The Girl Who Brought Light to the World," "The Boy Who Found Fire"—and they, in time, become myth.

Yet are we really so different? This thought occurred to me recently as I sat on the couch reading the newspaper while Persia, Pallas, and Aza waited for their currently favorite program to appear on the Disney cable television channel. Promptly at 4:00 the familiar fanfare of The Mickey Mouse Club anthem began, and I found myself humming along. Thirty years had passed for me, but, as if from a time warp, out danced Jimmie and Bobby and Doreen and Annette and especially (sigh) Darlene. They were wholesome, enthusiastic, brimming with the excitement of being child stars, the envy of hundreds of thousands of other baby boomers, before we had acquired the name. "As we continue through the years / We won't forget the Mouseketeers," they promised, and they were right. They introduced Spin and Marty, still embroiled in the adventures of their dude ranch camp; they talked earnestly about their hobbies, their ambitions for the future; and then, their voices reverential and serious, they adjourned with song, "The Club That's Made for You and Me."

Of course, time does count for something. I know what happened to Annette's career, for instance—a few hit records, a few campy beach movies, then peanut butter commercials, chronic illness, and courage; yet knowledge didn't detract from my nostalgia for the youthful exuberance she and the others projected. For me the show was a bridge, a visit to an uncomplicated era when I was not forced to worry about income taxes and deficit spending, before I knew enough to notice that there were no minority Mouseketeers, before domestic terrorists and assassinations and AIDS.

But for Persia, Pallas, and Aza, Cubby and Karen and the gang were absolute contemporaries, children whom they could, as I used to do, measure themselves against, imitate and critique. So familiar was my daughters' conversation about the program, so similar to one I probably had with my cousin Frank after watching the identical episode, also at 4:00, in the 1950s, that it was almost as if I remembered rather than overheard their remarks.

And we weren't over yet. Before dinner, with the magic of a satellite dish and a limitless variety of stations from which to choose, we aimed at the point in space where at 4:30 Lassie still barks instructions at obtuse human beings.

"Just wait," I advised my girls, like some wizened prophet or witch doctor. "One of these days Jeff is going to disappear and Lassie will belong to a new little boy named Timmy." They looked skeptical, so I didn't tell them about the eventual forest ranger. Let them be surprised.

Mister Ed still talks good horse sense. Samantha can still clean a messy kitchen with a twitch of her nose (and Darrin still, maddeningly, irrationally, doesn't want her to). Mighty Mouse still saves the day.

One definition of cultural continuity might be that each generation participates during its childhood in a comparable learning process and then retains and reinterprets those lessons throughout a lifetime. As our perspective matures, we penetrate layers of meaning, enjoying the same tales at a greater moral depth and intellectual complexity. The specifics may change—a calculator may replace the abacus and the map of the world may display more or less color as the boundaries of nations are altered—but within the context of a healthy society some concepts must remain core. The necessity of loyalty between friends, the responsibility that the strong owe the infirm, the illusion of ill-gotten gain, the rewards of hard work, honesty, and trust— these are enduring truths glimpsed and judged first through the imagination, first through art.

And whether these values are initially transmitted by a tribal seer reciting fables around the fire, by parents reading their favorite fairy tales to their offspring before bedtime, or by Persia, Pallas, Aza, and me donning mousekeears together for half an hour, the result is what matters: each method creates a shared set of formative impressions, a common cultural shorthand that collapses the barriers of time and experience, a bond that permits old and young to harmoniously inhabit, however fleetingly, the same world.

Vogue
September 1991

Parents
December 1990

TV Guide
May 28, 1988

RITES
OF
PASSAGE

ON THE ROAD

I've always hated departing on a journey. The night preceding a trip, I walk through familiar rooms, memorizing the organization of old furniture. I stand outside recording the particular sounds, the quality of coolness in the air, the circle of vision as if seeing it for the first time.

Each of the many homes I've surveyed on those emotional occasions seemed absolutely the best, preferable to any that might follow. Despite precedent, despite the fact that I almost always eventually like where I land, at the prospect of forsaking the known for the unknown my imagination can't stretch to the concept of "better." I say good-bye by vowing undying connection. I console the necessity of change only by forswearing alteration.

Then, of course, I alter.

A familiar place is always new—bigger, smaller, better, worse—upon return. Intervening experience blurs the edges, forgetfulness inspires surprise, new perspectives bring insight. Home is home as long as it's home, and after that it's memory or imagination, wish or regret. It's the taken-for-granted base one must quit in order to harbor the dream that it might be recovered. It's the last place before the next, the starting point and the goal.

THE QUEST FOR PIE

One of the seminal books of my childhood was *Mickey Sees the U.S.A.*, a travel extravaganza in which Mickey, Minnie, and the two nephews, Morty and Ferdy, set out in a red convertible and traverse the country. Every place they pass offers adventure, new sights, tasty treats—the ultimate all-American family vacation on wheels.

That was awhile ago—so far in the past that Disneyland didn't yet exist as a promotional destination—but the high concept of that fictional journey took root in my imagination and informed each subsequent family outing. We had relatives scattered from Tacoma to Miami, from New York to San Francisco, from Tensed, Idaho, to Henderson, Kentucky, and every summer my mother, my aunt, and I managed to visit some of them. (Occasionally my cousin Frank would join us, but not for the long hauls. He had a tendency to become carsick, and once my aunt had to bathe his forehead in milk from the thermos just to distract him until we reached a picnic grounds.)

I was too young to drive, of course, so I became the navigator. In deep winter I would begin to clip coupons from the *National Geographic*, soliciting maps and lodging brochures from the tourist bureaus in states along our potential routes. These packets, as they were invariably labeled, arrived in impressively lumpy envelopes, extolling the "enchantment" of New Mexico, the "surprises" of Missouri, the "discovery" potential of New England. Sometimes, once I had learned to type, I wrote letters to accompany the clippings, broadly hinting that I had more than just a passing interest in this or that region and was in fact contemplating relocation. This line of correspondence yielded even more substantial harvests of mail when the respective state offices of economic development got into the act. For one heady week in 1959 I received, absolutely free, a daily subscription to the Fort Worth *Star-Telegram*, forever establishing in my mind a loyalty to that plucky city in its underdog rivalry with Dallas—which was apparently above wooing my business.

Over the spring I would cull through my colorful stash, making shortlists of state parks, petting zoos, and inexpensive motels that promised heated, kidney-shaped swimming pools. I mail ordered a wonderful little device that looked like a cross between a ball point pen and a thermometer—by merely adjusting a setting to correspond to the scale of a map and running the creaking metal wheel on the tip along the route of any highway, one got an instant reading of the approximate mileage involved. Then it was a matter of simple arithmetic. The distance from starting point A to destination B divided by fifty miles an hour (my family's average speed) times eight hours a day (their joint endurance capacity behind the wheel) equaled the range of my accommodations search.

There was a limit, however, to the discretion I enjoyed. I was, after all, a child, a passenger, and my mother and aunt—the women who drove the car and paid the bills—had their own priorities that any proposal of mine necessarily had to incorporate. And those were, in a word, pie.

Looking back, I realize now that each of our journeys could quite accurately be described as a quest for pie. For instance, like experienced surfers who chart odd itineraries (Laguna to Capetown by way of The Big Island) in order to snag a reliable wave en route, I always had to include Paoli, Indiana, in any cross-country trip. There was a café off the square in that placid hamlet where was served, according to my mother the connoisseur, a lattice crust like no other. Woven in intricate patterns across a sea of blueberry or peach, each segment was crisp and melting, studded with just the right amount of sugar, laced with a subtle jolt of almond extract, and browned to perfection. If I brought us through Paoli too soon after a major meal, we might order our twenty-five-cents-apiece slices for the crust alone, reluctantly leaving the fruit on the green plastic plates.

An innocuous-looking lunch counter in New Ulm, Minnesota, was the polar opposite: a decent pastry, nothing to complain about, but a truly spectacular chess or lemon or coconut cream within. The baker wouldn't tell, but my grandmother back home, upon hearing my aunt describe the airy yet smoothly substantial and satisfying volume of the filling, put her money on whipped egg whites and a dash of mace. No amount of research was too exhaustive in pursuing the solution to so important a mystery, and that was fine with me.

(New Ulm was also the site of my favorite motel in the world: a swimming pool, a playground, and a fully made bed that folded down from a door in the wall—for eight dollars a room. I always finagled it so we hit town just as the sun was about to set, and consequently in New Ulm we ate pie for dinner and then again for breakfast.)

The pie map of the United States bears little resemblance to standard demographics. The New Yorks and Clevelands and Milwaukees are mostly etched in light print, marked with tiny dots, while the big black circles and capital letters are reserved for BRATTLEBORO, Vermont, TYLER, Texas, SHELBY, Montana, and HAYS, Kansas. There are other features as well: on the west side of an invisible line, running roughly correspondent to the Appalachians, people prefer their doughnuts with icing. The South is The South when you leave a restaurant and instead of "good-bye" the waitress pleads, "Come back," unless it's New Orleans and she croons, "Enjoy." The hallmark of the Midwest is "Have a good one," answered by "You betcha," and an all-you-can-eat salad bar with at least one hundred items, most of them encased in Jell-O. The Rocky Mountain states feed in pure volume, no matter what the course—the byword there is "Refill?"—whereas the Pacific Rim overdoes it with fruit, as in a wedge of orange on the plate next to your pizza.

A culinary relief map of the country pretty much inverts the standard topological zones. Rather than the vaguely camel-back shape of North America (the humps represented by the two major north–south mountain ranges), portion size translates into more of a hammock effect. Sea level becomes the highest instead of the lowest part, and major sags and droopings are found inland from the coast. The state of Utah, for instance, constitutes the sleeping giant's hip, for it's a place that compensates an arid and rather Spartan environment by distributing ten-cents-a-pop soft ice cream machines at the exit door of most restaurants with large parking lots. Nebraska, home of a particularly high-density food called potato meatloaf (offered at rest stops beckoning from the endless Interstate 80), accounts for the mid-depression of the continent, and the old South—arbitrarily centered in Gadsden, Alabama, birthplace of the bottomless grit—is its lolling head, which, as any chiropractor will tell you, is the heaviest part of the body.

European tourists, with their effete tradition of teeny-tiny glasses of no-ice Coca-Cola, must be flabbergasted by the proffering of "20 oz. Thirst Busters" at each K-4 convenience store in the western steppes, and Japanese honeymooners, coming from a context of hundred-dollar steaks, must believe they've found paradise in the hefty "full-pound burgers" of rural Texas. Dietary largesse is patriotic, an entitlement protected, coterminal with individual ownership of automatic weapons, by the Constitution. We fought Iraq for the right to drive-thru an emporium boasting thirty-six oil-based flavors of frozen nondairy dessert. We celebrate Christmas with Federal-Expressed boxes of the world's weightiest Oregon pears or Idaho potatoes or California onions, or by sending each other baskets, their overflowing contents of dense Edams and Goudas barely contained by protective cellophane, shipped from Wisconsin—a state whose highway signs proclaim, more often than historic markers or scenic vistas, simply CHEESE. Less specific, but no less commanding, is the banner permanently over-hanging Tower City, North Dakota, visible for miles in any direction, shouting FOOD, and followed by an enormous arrow pointing straight down to the rich, loamy landscape.

For Americans of a certain age and class, food is the punctuation of life, a commercial break between those bothersome segments of work or play that require the use of our hands, thus prohibiting their availability for unwrapping, unpeeling, or defrosting. Eating certifies leisure, the coffee 'n' Danish break a defiance of the time clock, the snack a voluntary intrusion into a routine not of our own making. And yet eating is also a kind of defensible duty, a recreation we can shrug off as a need, excuse ourselves for, indulge in with some righteousness. Researchers tell us that diners' pupils narrow to pinpoints when plates are set before them. Our beings concentrate, focus, rivet to the task at hand. We need to eat, we tell ourselves. Our parents mandated it, and they were happy when we complied. Food made us good. It made us grow.

Unlike masturbation or pleasure reading or a midmorning nap, determined consumption carries a cultural cachet of respect, equaled only, on occasion, by refraining from eating, an appositive ingestive practice during which, if anything, our minds are even more firmly fixed on what's not for dinner. We read cookbooks as literature, copy and exchange exotic recipes, devote on the average (if we can afford it) one technology-laden room of our homes for the sole purpose of food storage and preparation, and another, plus deck or patio, for its display prior to disappearance. We support an entire industry of pressure-sealed leftover containers because we invariably prepare more of everything than we need.

What is this obsession with jumbo helpings? Is it the aftershock of the Great Depression, a kind of chipmunk drive to hoard unto and into ourselves so that in the event of lean days we can feed off our own stored fat—the ultimate convenience: we don't even have to leave home or microwave! Is it an assertion of Manifest Destiny, the ultimate reward for the transoceanic migration of our starving ancestors? Do we eat "because it's there"? Certainly for most of us the urge to stuff normally arises from habit, not from hunger. Early on we were initiated into the clean-plate club by a ritual that culminated in a swipe of every eating surface with Wonder bread, a final lip-smack cleansing of each utensil, the lick of fingertip so that no available morsels escaped our digestive tract. Is it an instinctive urge toward bulk-signifying power, a thumbed nose at death, an insistence on closure before the hunt begins afresh?

Once food has been elevated to the category of symbol, it begins to serve other, quasi-existential functions. Pie, for my mother, is much more than pie. It's the icing on the doughnut of a life challenged with disappointments in love and expectation, an affordable, slightly illicit luxury, a thing for which her addiction is coyly confessed. Pie has served as a staple of barter in her dealings with the universe—raised, as she was, in a complex Roman Catholic economy of indulgences and leveraged buyouts. The standard microsystem was fairly straightforward: three hundred days' grace in the afterlife for the trifling price of a whispered ejaculation, more for a whole rosary or a novena. Attending mass on the first Friday of each of nine consecutive months purchased an insurance policy that guaranteed a happy death. Remaining resolutely still during the reading of the long gospel of Palm Sunday or Easter sprung the soul of your choice from purgatory on early parole.

Good works produced results, and there was no more potent form of good works than sacrifice, no sacrifice more expensive than one involving abstention from the thing most cherished. Abraham anted up Isaac. St. Elizabeth of Hungary abdicated her royal throne. St. Teresa, obviously on my family's wavelength, forewent all nourishment save a daily communion wafer.

It's little wonder that my mother's devotion to pie became a valuable commodity, her own personalized bar-

gaining chip with a shrewd divinity so omniscient that no
over-weighting of the scale or inflated price gouging would
ameliorate. Pie, like the coin of the realm, came in various
denominations, depending on my mother's sliding prefer-
ence. Value was purely subjective, and all contracts were
accepted or rejected on a single best-bid basis—no hag-
gling allowed. In my mother's metaphysical accounts
payable department, apple and cherry were nickels and
dimes, the stuff one threw on (or, more accurately, took off)
the table in exchange for the finding of lost car keys, but
God *knew* how much she loved her pecan. When she negotiated to forego it voluntarily for, say, six months in recipro-
cation of my receipt of a college scholarship, it was a serious offer He couldn't ignore. My aunt once saved herself
and an entire busload of other tourists from vaulting over
the guardrail of a twisting Mexican highway by eliminating,
curve by treacherous curve, every type of liquor, nut, and
cake from her future diet. There was something my grandmother wanted enough to warrant her giving up all candy—
for life—at the age of forty-two, but she would never tell
me what it was. Obviously, "no publicity" was part of the
deal.

At the other end of the spectrum from deprivation lies
submission, and my family, in extremis, has been known to
combine the two: not eating potato chips, for instance, is all
the more negotiable when supplemented by a contract to
consume salad without dressing. For every declined satin
negligé among the major food groups, there's a hairshirt

waiting to be donned, and doing with can easily double the value of doing without. But if comestibles are the hard currency of immortal transaction, they're also clearly the reward for virtue. Dinner is to a day what dessert is to dinner.

Such philosophizing is a perfectly respectable way to wile away the minutes between breakfast and brunch. Think about the issue intensely enough, however, and the automatic biological response is hunger—an insight that is no stranger to the fast-food industry, whose roadside advertisements must convey, in staccato shorthand, a metalanguage that can be scanned, judged, and braked for by people hurtling past at seventy miles per hour. Inevitably in transit, where having enough fuel is an ever-present concern, there's a spillover from gas tank to stomach, and thus the vocabulary of a menu must communicate more than simple information, especially to a target audience. No type of vehicle is more desirable than a station wagon or van, preferably one that carries a suction-cupped yellow window message announcing "Child on Board." Not only do such chariots transport multiple hungry passengers, but they are likely to be in the thrall of juveniles who experience no hesitation in making a snap decision. In casting their net for such prey, restauranteurs lay a double bait. To the recently literate young they dangle, "Fried!" and to the long-suffering parents they whisper, "Relief."

"Homemade" is a basic code word of such establishments, along with "Family Style" and "E-Z Access," but these phrases are subtle substitutes and stand-ins for their true meanings: doubleburgers, grilled cheese, and peanut butter. "Don't worry," parents are assured. "They won't gag. And we won't complain when they spill their drink." In many of these establishments, pictographs replace writing on the laminated menus. Standardized, no-surprises photographs beckon diners seeking the reassurance of a homogenized national cuisine. Adults are lured by the supposed economy of "platters," with their suggestion of balanced nutrition coupled with volume, and proprietors compete against each other with ingenious "extras." "Boy Have We Got Chicken!" brags a Country Kitchen in Great Falls, Montana, whereas a Denny's in Bellevue, Washington, simply exclaims, "Canadians!" Certain nouns, masquerading as other grammatical forms, are especially in evidence—*country, purveyor, family, kitchen, dining*—and ersatz icons implanted into decor ("antiqued" or quilted wall hangings, oak-grain coat hooks, and wood-burned slogans) also contribute to a sense of the predictable and familiar "away from home."

Exceptions to this type of lingo often signal promising gastronomic finds, for even as a chef might err on the billboard, being slightly off the mark in comprehending the lowest common denominator, so too might the side dishes retain a regional or individualistic signature. "Egg Roll and Barbecue Take Out" could spell disaster, but at least it will probably be a memorable one. "Live Bait and Ice Cream" indicates a particular sensibility. The old-fashioned word "cafe" is often a plus, especially when it lacks an accent mark, is preceded by the cook's first name, and graces a cement block building surrounded, at 6:00 A.M., by a semicircle of parked police cruisers and pick-up trucks bearing in-state license plates. Once inside, listen for a bell attached to the door, look for day-of-the-week specials listed on a blackboard in illegible penmanship, and keep an eye out for real plants in the windows. If actual herbs or tomatoes are growing outside, settle yourself upon a round stool at the lunch counter. And if the owner confesses, with some pride, that the well-scrubbed stains on the baby high chair upholstery were made by her very own grandchildren, contemplate permanent residence. You may have stumbled into an eatery where children are regarded as people with smaller appetites and not as a separate, cholesterol-crazed subspecies.

It's the kind of joint Mickey and Minnie were always pulling into during their journey of forty years past, the Americana of Frank Capra faces, bottomless cups of coffee, and in-the-booth jukeboxes with selections drawn from local favorites rather than MTV. It flourished when geography meant more than a printout of bills from the same motel chain, when the Mississippi River divided—except for Pittsburgh—the radio stations whose call letters began with a "W" from those that started with a "K," when every small town produced its own version of a newspaper reporting its own slant on the news.

And it still exists.

In 1986, Louise and I drove a Dodge Caravan across the country with one son and four daughters to visit my grandmother. We probably appeared to be the ideal demographic—the nuclear family feeding group—but in our hearts we were Kerouac, ready to be transformed by the bizarre, the offbeat, the unknown. We eschewed major highways and fine family dining that provided crayons with the placemats, and we set our radar detectors for homemade curtains in the windows of establishments with names like "Betty's." We spent a night in the Atlasta Motel because it advertised "in-room clock radios" and "heat."

Late one afternoon we came by chance upon the cafe of our dreams in an otherwise undistinguished little town in the Pacific Northwest. A mimeographed sheet, tucked between the salt and pepper shakers, informed us that a "pie war" was presently under way with a rival establishment, one block down Main Street, and as a result a slice from any of the sixteen varieties made fresh on the premises that morning could be had for only thirty-five cents. So confident was the baker that he invited us to sample the competition (naturally, at the same price), then return and get our money back if his was not better. For me, it was Paoli squared—Parsifal had found the holy grail.

Antæus
Spring 1992

THE SENTRY

You can go from and you can go toward. There's a photograph, taken by Louise, in which we are on a roundtrip boat ride, forever doing both. If our car journey from New Hampshire to Washington State—out via U.S. 2 and back on Canada 1—was marked with string, this meandering ferry voyage from Anacortes, Washington, through the Channel Islands our farthest point west, would be the bow.

Five years later I look at this picture and both see what's in it and notice what's not. In my bones, I remember the exhaustion of three thousand miles logged in a small van with a toddler and a three-year-old strapped in car seats and two preadolescents in the far back. It's a weariness best measured in cracker crumbs, powdered milk, whispered conversations and observations between adults. Relatively speaking, Persia and Pallas were very good companions, but at the moment of this snapshot they are standing up because they're tired of sitting. The tender skin of their backsides has become impressed with the patterns of cushions. I, on the other hand, am sprawled on the deck in the loose-limbed embrace of a moment of peace: salt air, temporarily contented children, an expanse of beauty undisturbed by duty. There is a grill-backed guard-rail, so I don't have to worry about anyone falling in the water and my thoughts can stray, pause on a cloud, antici-pate the miles to come.

When we arrived at my grandmother's small house in Tacoma after finally bidding good-bye to Route 2, we found her in the backyard, out of breath.

"I had to climb every one of these apple trees," she announces to us indignantly, "before I found the caterpillar nest. But I got it!"

At nearly ninety, living alone and independently in a house of memories, my grandmother has survived the loss of two of her sons, the oldest of them my father, and yet can reminisce with equanimity, the old stories ever new and changing in her retelling. I've heard of her early years on the Coeur d'Alene reservation, of triumphant ballroom dance competitions in which she was partnered with my streetcar-driver grandfather, of disappointments forgotten by everyone on earth save her. There are scandals that hap-pened in her mother's time, in her grandmother's, she still tells in whispered tones, and confided recipes full of secret ingredients, their special cooking instructions dictated and copied on lined paper.

I've shot many photographs, my grandmother alone with each of her great-grandchildren, posed in the spot beneath the same grape arbor where she once held me in her arms. Now, as I lie on the sun-warmed boards of the ferry boat, I am not yet completely gone from her house.

What else is not in this picture—or rather, who's not— are two of our older children, Sava and Madeline, then early teenagers. When the snapshot was taken they were below deck in the ship's arcade, playing video games and eating French fries. The summer of that trip—this day in particular—was the last interlude before the confusing, disruptive onset of their adolescences, and I recall it was a halcyon time of trust, when old patterns of interaction between us worked, when they were yet content to be driven where we wanted to take them, when they, to an extent, still agreed to look at the world through our eyes.

I held the camera for another photograph, the companion to this one in our family album. In it, my son and daughter sit in deck chairs on either side of Louise. She's reading from a book and they incline toward her voice, eager and receptive, ready to laugh.

The thing about a photograph is that a present is fixed, mute and preserved, and so it becomes in retrospect a doorway from the past to the future—a doorway passed through, open once, one way.

The day we rode the ferry was windy. The ship's motor was surging, and the children had to shout above its roar to be heard. All was forward motion, noise, the sweep of the second hand too swift to measure. But looking back through the lens from image to eye, the instant is as solid as a stone monument. Persia watches something out of the frame, attracted and anxious for us to see it. I'm sure I sat up, followed the direction of her gaze to the horizon, strained to understand her questions. She was keeping watch, the sentry of our little band, alert on behalf of us all for what might happen next.

EVERYBODY'S
CHILDREN

THANKFULNESS

As we grow older, we tend to celebrate much of our good fortune in the past tense, savoring the circumstances that brought us satisfaction, the people who informed our lives for the better. Through such a process, we make a conscious inventory of highlights, balance the ledger of our disappointments and fears with a precious, necessary list of pleasures.

As Americans, we've arranged an annual holiday for this ritual of affirmation, signaled by the assembly of family and friends around a festive table, centered on a brown, cooked bird, bred for this precise purpose. The stuffing cools, the gravy thickens, our appetites whet while we tick off our bounties, congratulating ourselves for being together, for our collective and mutual appreciation.

Formal commemoration is an important element of any culture, commercialized and clichéd though its trappings may become. Too often, rushing through the chaos of daily activities, we fail to see the tree for the forest. We inhabit a world where problems of environment, social injustice, hunger, and indifference are prevalent, pervasive, and apparently implacable. We lack the time for solutions that take too long, we argue, and then we become discouraged, paralyzed. We're systematically deprived of all illusions we may harbor about the character of our heroes; we read that El Niño, the warm current of air that gave us all such a mild winter last year, has caused drought in Africa, and we throw up our hands in helplessness. Worst of all, we forget the power, the beauty, of small accumulations, of private treasures.

And yet, when emphasis is placed on the particular, when the focus rests without hurry on the single flower, the one good deed or manifestation of selflessness, the impact can be staggering. We may pretend to take permanence for granted, but we know empirically that continuity is, in the long run, only temporary. The triumphs of the past extend into the present, much less so into the future, but briefly.

The reverie of what was inevitably reminds us of what no longer is. The Thanksgiving table is large as life, the potential seating spacious enough to welcome every new arrival, yet the vacant spots proliferate with the passage of years. From our fragile vantage, we nod to private shadows as well as to invited guests. We find ourselves astride a continuum, and grace is fleeting, light as air, bright as a candle at midnight. We miss what we had, even as we rejoice that we ever had it.

Thankfulness, combined with reminiscence, constructs the only permanent monument that can travel with us. Complicated and frustrating, it alone establishes that remarkable events and beloved people matter, that their impact endures.

The long table stretches through time, its cloth intricately woven. The guests represent many generations, their song a chorus, their feast a cornucopia's spill.

Parents
November 1992

FETAL ALCOHOL
SYNDROME

A National Perspective

At the time I adopted my oldest son, Abel, in 1971, I knew that his birth mother had been a heavy drinker, but even the medical textbooks in those days stated that exposure to alcohol could not damage a developing fetus. I knew that Abel had been born small and premature, had "failed to thrive," and was an initially slow learner, but for ten years as a single parent I convinced myself that nurture, a stimulating environment, and love could open up life to my little boy.

It wasn't true. At the University of Washington and elsewhere, biochemists and psychologists now confirm that for some women even moderate doses of prenatal exposure to alcohol can permanently stunt a human being's potential. According to the U.S. surgeon general, *no* level of ethanol is guaranteed to be "safe."

My grown son has a full range of physical disorders: seizures; curvature of the spine; poor coordination, sight, and hearing. But his most disabling legacy has to do with his impaired ability to reason. Fetal alcohol syndrome (FAS) victims are known for their poor judgment, their impulsiveness, their persistent confusions over handling money, telling time, and in distinguishing right from wrong.

Since the publication of *The Broken Cord* last August, I have received an outpouring of wrenching letters from literally hundreds of readers—rural and urban, religious and agnostic, of all ethnic and economic backgrounds—who share experiences of heartache, grief, and frustration uncannily identical to my wife's and mine. Their sons, daughters, or grandchildren have been repeatedly misdiagnosed with the same amorphous labels: retarded, sociopathic, attention-deficit, unteachable troublemakers.

A majority of full-blown FAS victims are adopted or in state care, but many children who are less drastically impaired (i.e., with fetal alcohol effect [FAE]) remain with their natural parents. Depending on the term of pregnancy in which the harmful drinking occurred, these individuals may look perfectly healthy and test in the normal range for intelligence, yet by early adolescence they show unmistakable signs of comprehension problems or uncontrollable rage. It is currently estimated that in the United States some eight thousand babies are born annually with full FAS and another sixty-five thousand with a degree of FAE. Nothing will ever restore them to the people they might otherwise have been.

And it seems that's far less than the half of it. An additional three hundred thousand babies prenatally bombarded with illegal drugs will be born in this country in 1990. Recent studies indicate that crack cocaine, if

smoked during pregnancy, causes learning deficits in offspring similar to those caused by alcohol. The "first generation" of children from the 1980s' crack epidemic is about
to enter public school, and these children are consistently
described as "remorseless," "without a conscience," and
passive, apparently lacking that essential empathy, that
motivation toward cooperation, upon which a peaceful and
harmonious classroom—and society—so depends.

No curriculum or training program has so far proven to
be completely effective for people with this totally preventable affliction, and a Los Angeles pilot education project costs taxpayers $15,000 a year per pupil. However, the
price of doing nothing, of ignoring the issue, is beyond
measure.

Nothing like crack—a baby shower gift of choice in
certain populations because it is reputed to speed and
ease labor—has occurred before. According to one survey,
upwards of 11 percent of all U.S. infants in 1988 tested
positive for cocaine or alcohol the first time their blood was
drawn. A New York City Health Department official estimated that births to drug-abusing mothers had increased
there by about 3,000 percent in the past ten years.

Why? Some explanations have to do with a paucity of
available services and support. Too many fathers regard
their baby's health as solely their partner's concern. Only
one residential treatment program specifically for chemically dependent pregnant women exists in New York City,

where the State Assembly Committee on Alcoholism and Drug Abuse estimates that "twelve thousand babies will be born addicted . . . in 1989, and the number of children in foster care has doubled in two years from twenty-seven thousand in 1987 to more than fifty thousand today, mainly because of parental drug abuse." The system has broken down. Sixteen percent of all American mothers have had insufficient prenatal medical attention—increasing to 33 percent for unmarried or teenage mothers, 30 percent for Hispanic women, and 27 percent for black women.

At last, thanks to a 1989 act of Congress, liquor bottle labels must include a warning, and signs posted in many bars proclaim the hazards of alcohol to unborn children. But what happens when public education doesn't work as a deterrent, when a pregnant woman herself is a victim of FAS or prenatal crack and therefore cannot understand the long-term disastrous consequences for the life of another resulting from what she drinks or inhales? It isn't that these women don't love the *idea* of their babies. They just can't foresee the cruel realities.

The conflict of competing rights—of protecting immediate civil liberty versus avoiding future civil strife—is incredibly complex, with no unambiguously right or easy answers, but as a nation it's unconscionable to delay the debate. If we close our eyes we condemn children not yet even conceived to existences of sorrow and deprivation governed by prison, victimization, and premature death.

My wife and I think of these tragedies as we wait for our

son to have brain surgery that may reduce the intensity of his seizures, though not eliminate them. At twenty-two, despite all of our efforts and his best intentions, he remains forever unable to live independently, to manage a paycheck, or to follow the plot of a TV sitcom, and we worry about the very fabric of society when hundreds of thousands of others with problems similar to his or worse become teenagers, become adults, beyond the year 2000.

Newsweek
June 18, 1990

FETAL ALCOHOL SYNDROME

A Parent's Perspective

Unlike so many good people—scientists and social workers and politicians—who have chosen out of the kindness of their hearts and the dictates of their social consciences to become knowledgeable about fetal alcohol syndrome and fetal alcohol effect, to work with their victims, to demand prevention, I was dragged to the subject blindfolded, kicking and screaming. I'm the worst kind of expert, a grudging, reluctant witness, an embittered amateur, and, above all else: a failure. A parent.

I'm a living, breathing encyclopedia of what hasn't worked in curing or reversing the damage to one child prenatally exposed to too much alcohol. Certain drugs temporarily curbed my son's seizures and hyperactivity but almost certainly had dampening effects on his learning ability and personality development. Fifteen years of special education—isolation in a classroom, repetitive instruction, hands-on learning—maximized his potential but didn't give him a normal IQ. Psychological counseling—introspective techniques, group therapy—had no positive

results, and may even have encouraged his ongoing confusion between what is real and what's imagined.

Brain surgery hasn't worked.

Anger hasn't worked.

Patience hasn't worked.

Love hasn't worked.

When you're the parent of an FAS or FAE child, your goals
change with the passing years. You start with seeking solutions: ideas and regimens to penetrate the fog that blocks
your son's or daughter's ability to comprehend rules, retain
information, or even be curious. You firmly believe—because
it has to be true—that the answers are "out there." It's just a
matter of locating them. You go through teachers and their
various learning theories like so many Christmas catalogues
received in the mail, determined to find the perfect gift, the
right combination of toughness and compassion, optimism
and realism, training and intuition. Once you find a likely
prospect, you badger her (in my experience, most teachers of
"learning disabled" [LD] children seem to be women),
demand results, attempt to coerce with praise or threat. You
become first an ally, then increasingly a pain in the neck, a
judgmental critic, an ever-persistent, occasionally hysterical,
nuisance. When the teacher, worn out and frustrated, eventually gives up on your child, decides he's beyond her ability or
resources to help, she's as glad to see *you* go as she's relieved
that your son won't be back to remind her of her limitations.
"With a crazy, irrational parent like that," you imagine her
saying to her colleagues, "no wonder the kid has problems."

Do I sound paranoid, cynical? I wasn't always this way, but I'm the product of a combined total of fifty years of dealing with alcohol-damaged children—for not only does the son I wrote about in *The Broken Cord* suffer from fetal alcohol syndrome, but his adopted brother and sister are, to a lesser and greater extent, victims of fetal alcohol effect.

For years, my wife and I and our extended families had no choice but to become a kind of full-time social service agency specializing in referrals, the admissions policies of various expensive institutions, the penalties meted out under the juvenile justice system, the nightmares of dealing with uninformed, often smug, bureaucrats given by default responsibility for people who can't make it on their own in contemporary America. We were forced to progress from attending increasingly sour PTA meetings to learning the intricacies of intelligence testing—hoping that the score will come in below 70 and thus qualify a child for legal disability. We've had to become acquainted with the admissions policies and maximum length of stays at institutions like Covenant House, Boystown, and the Salvation Army. We've paid out well over $150,000, not counting what our insurance has covered, for our children's primary and secondary special school tuitions, counseling, doctors of every sort, experimental medical procedures, Outward Bound for Troubled Youth, and private camps for the learning disabled. We have managed to try every single avenue that's been suggested to us by well-meaning people who should know what might benefit our sons and daughter, and nothing—*nothing*—has consistently worked for more than a few months.

Our older children, now all adults or nearly so, often cannot function independently, cannot hold jobs, tell the truth, manage money, plan a future. They have all at one time or another been arrested or otherwise detained for shoplifting, inappropriate sexual conduct, and violent behavior. Despite all our efforts to protect them, they have periodically come under the influence of people who, for instance, worship Satan or take advantage of them physically, mentally, and/or financially. They maintain no enduring friendships, set for themselves no realistic goals, can call upon no bedrock inner voice to distinguish moral from amoral, safe from dangerous.

Okay: maybe it's us. Maybe we're incredibly dysfunctional parents. We've spent years feeling guilty and inadequate, holding on to the belief that if only we could become better, more resourceful, more sympathetic, more enlightened in our expectations and requirements, we could alter the bleak future that seems to lie in store or have already arrived for our adopted children. Like every self-reflective father and mother, we can recall our failures, our lapses, our losses of temper, and time after time we have added up these shortcomings to see if they balance the devastating total of our sons' and daughter's current situations. *The Broken Cord* was written, at least in part, to further this process, to assign guilt—if not wholly to us, then to somebody, something—to make not just sense of a senseless waste, but a difference. If every avenue of investigation were explored, maybe something would be discovered that could reverse the fate of not just any anonymous afflicted fetus, child, or adult, but of *our* children.

But what the book yielded was worse than the least I had expected. Not only was there no magic trick, no scientific breakthrough that could produce a "cure," but from the out pouring of letters that have come from around the country it is clear that our family's private sorrow is far from unusual. In the year and a half since *The Broken Cord* was published, we have heard from more than two thousand parents of FAS and FAE victims. All love their children, and almost none have given up hope. But none of them knows what the hell to do next.

The hardest group to answer are the parents of very young children, children who seem from the symptoms described to be clearly fetal alcohol affected. I recognize these parents: in the early stages of denial, full of the surety that answers exist. They want practical advice, experts to consult, books to read, innovative doctors to visit. They want to head off the unpleasant disappointments chronicled in my book, to save their child—and themselves—from such a miserable chain of events. If *The Broken Cord* had been written by somebody else, I would have mailed just such a letter to its author. I would have been skeptical of his pessimism, sure that I could do better, last longer, be smarter, succeed where he had failed. So when I answer the letters I receive, I root for those parents, applaud their confidence, ask them to write back and tell me when things improve. So far, there has been no good news.

Almost equally difficult to absorb is the mail I receive from parents whose FAS and FAE children are older than ours. They write with the weary echo of experience, the products of many cycles of raised expectations followed by dejection. They tell of their "fifty-two-year-old child," or their FAE adult daughter who's just given birth to her third FAS baby and is pregnant again and still drinking. They tell of children serving twenty-year prison terms or, in one case, of a "sweet" son sentenced to the death penalty for an impulsive murder for which he has never shown the slightest remorse. They tell of children raised in privilege who are now lost among the homeless on a distant city's streets, of children once so loving and gentle who have been maimed from drug use or knife fights, or, as is so often the case, who have been raped. They tell of innocents become prostitutes, of suicide attempts, and always, always, of chemical dependency. They tell of children whose whereabouts are unknown, or who are dead at twenty-five. This is not the way it was supposed to happen, these parents cry. It's not fair. It's not right.

We read these letters and wonder: is *this* in store?

I've even heard from adults diagnosed with fetal alcohol effect—one of them with a Ph.D. from Harvard and several others with master's degrees. These are highly intelligent people, the Jackie Robinsons of FAE, who have had to become specialists on themselves. Through years of observing their own trials and errors, of watching how "normal" people behave in a given context and analyzing how that contrasts with their own uncertain reactions, some of them have worked out complicated formulas to simulate a greater connection to the world than they in fact possess. One woman carries in her purse a card on which is typed a series of questions she explicitly asks herself in an attempt to gauge the consequences of her possible responses to an unprecedented situation: What would so-and-so do in this instance? What will people probably think if I do x, y, or z? She's compensating for life in a universe that's slightly, almost imperceptibly alien, and trying to speak a language whose idiom and nuance are forever just beyond her automatic reach.

The correspondence we've received from around this country, and lately from around the world, has magnified exponentially our particular family experience, but hasn't contradicted it. The letter I've waited for but which has yet to arrive is the one that begins, "I've read your book and you're dead wrong," or "My child was diagnosed as having FAS but we fixed it by doing the following things and now, five years later, he's perfectly fine."

To what extent does this preventable scourge affect American Indian people? The answer, like so much about FAS, is ambiguous. On the one hand, prenatal exposure to ethanol impairs a fetus in exactly the same ways whether its mother is a member of a country club in Greenwich,

Connecticut, or an ADC mom on the White Earth reservation. Every human being during development is vulnerable,
fragile, easy to poison; ethnicity acts as neither a shield nor
a magnet. Yes, "drinking age" matters, diet counts, smoking and other drug use will exacerbate the damage done by
alcohol, but all things considered, no woman is physically
destined to give birth to an FAS baby.

The factors that really make a difference have to do with
ephemeral things: strong family and community support for
abstinence, access to good prenatal care and chemical
dependency treatment, clear and widespread information
on the dangers of drinking during pregnancy. And it's here
that Native American women are at a severe disadvantage.
Health programs on reservations have been among the first
things cut when the federal budget gets tight; clinics are
shut down, counselors laid off, preventive educational cam-
paigns scrapped. Access to organizations like Planned
Parenthood is, in many tribal communities, impossible.
Poverty, unemployment, despair—familiar elements in the
daily lives of too many Indian people—lead to alcohol and
other drug abuse. The causes of the problem, and the solutions, are so much bigger and more complex than just saying no.

When you factor in to the statistics on FAS and FAE those
having to do with prenatal exposure to crack cocaine—
which seems to produce in children many of the same learning disabilities as too much alcohol—we are looking at hundreds of thousands of impaired babies born in this country

annually. In ten years that's three million people. By the time the first generation counted is twenty years old, it's six million, and that's assuming a stable rate—not the current geometrically accelerating one. How does our society handle this onslaught, on either a local or a national level? How do we make laws that apply equally to those of us who can understand the rules and to a significant minority who, through no fault of their own, can't? How do we preserve individual liberty, free choice, safe streets, mutual trust, when some members of society have only a glancing grasp of moral responsibility? How do we cope with the growing crime rate among young people, with "wilding," with trying to teach the unteachable?

The thorny ethical issue that has troubled me most in thinking about the social impact of FAS and other such lifelong but preventable afflictions concerns responsibility. When, if ever, are we, one-on-one or collectively, obliged to intervene? It's becoming increasingly clear that FAS victims beget more FAS victims: a pregnant woman who can't calculate the long-term consequences of her decisions is a hard case for prenatal counseling. It is difficult if not impossible to convince her to defer an immediate gratification because nine months or nine years later her hypothetical child might suffer from a night of partying. That child is an abstraction, a hazy shadow at best, and the argument is a great deal less compelling than the draw of another drink or fix.

Some studies have suggested that compared with the "average" woman, female FAS and FAE victims start having children younger, continue for a longer period of years to produce them, and ultimately conceive and bring to term more offspring. They are less likely to seek prenatal care, to abstain from dangerous activities during their pregnancies, and to keep custody of their babies. Statistically a woman who's given birth to an FAS baby has almost an eight out of ten chance to do so again, if she continues drinking, and subsequent siblings are likely to be even more impaired than the first.

These often abandoned or removed children, whether adopted or institutionalized, are ultimately our culture's victims and therefore are its responsibility. How to cope? At the absolute minimum, how do we—especially in a tight economy—pay the medical bills, build the prisons, construct the homeless shelters? How do we train special education teachers to function indefinitely with no hope of success, or ordinary citizens how to forgive behaviors that are irritating at best, threatening or dangerous at worst? How do we teach compassion for a growing class of people who are likely to exhibit neither pity nor gratitude, who take everything society has to offer and have almost nothing constructive to give back? How do we maintain the universal franchise to vote, the cornerstone of our political system? How do we redefine "guilty or not guilty" to apply to heartless acts committed by people who are fundamentally incapable of comprehending the spirit of the law?

To me these questions can be understood if not answered by a simple analogy: Imagine we saw a blind woman holding a child by the hand attempt to cross a busy street. The traffic was fast, she guessed wrong, and before our eyes her child was struck by a truck and killed. A tragedy we would never forget. Then a year later we come by the same intersection again, and again there's the woman, but with a new child. The light is against her but she doesn't see and tries to cross to the other side. The child is hit, terribly injured, as we stand by helplessly and watch. The next year it happens again, and the next, and the next. How many times must it happen before we become involved? Before we take the woman's arm or hold up our hand to stop the cars or carry her child or at least tell her when the signal is green? How many children are too many? When do their rights to safe passage assert themselves? And how long before the mother herself is killed?—for remember, she's a victim and at grave risk, too. It does no good to blame her, to punish her for the result of her blindness. Once the street is crossed the child is dead. The mother needs help and we need to find a decent way to provide it. If we turn our backs, we stop being innocent bystanders and become complicit in the inevitable accident, accessories after the fact.

Despite all his recent fame since *The Broken Cord*'s publication, Abel continues to be fired from menial jobs, to lose places to live. He hasn't made a single lasting friend, hasn't received a friendly personal phone call, hasn't read a book unless you count *Garfield*. He's twenty-three and lonely, without being able to think of the name to describe that emotion or figure out and persevere in any action to alleviate it.

My wife and I had to go out of town on business last week. When we returned we called Abel's new residence and were greeted by the chilling report that he had apparently "forgotten" to eat from Thursday through Sunday and had lost a considerable amount of weight.

Abel isn't considered to be sufficiently impaired to qualify for a state-run facility for the disabled, so his only option is to board in a private home close enough to walk to the truck stop where he works part-time. As it happened, the perfectly nice husband and wife who maintain this home had a family emergency that necessitated that they be gone the same weekend that Louise and I were away. They left Abel's food, clearly marked for each day, on a special shelf in the refrigerator, but in their absence—that is, without the cue of their direct, repeated instructions at meal time—it had not occurred to our adult son that the hunger he had to have felt could be sated simply by feeding himself.

And Abel is the easy one, the most fortunate of our three adopted children, because he is at least unambiguously diagnosable. The state of New Hampshire, financially strapped as it is, has no choice but to examine him and conclude "LD." Minimal services are provided: a social worker takes him to the dentist and checks on his living situation a couple of times a month. He's finally eligible for social security and Medicaid benefits, providing he doesn't earn more than $500 a month. Strangers and friends who interact with him think, "Ah, retarded," instead of "stupid," "rude," or "dangerous." They make allowances.

Our two other older children, however, are another story. Their respective birth mothers drank in sprees while pregnant—not heavily enough to produce full FAS symptoms in their offspring, but . . . heavily enough. Almost certainly fetal alcohol affected, our son and daughter are now nineteen and almost sixteen, respectively, and they have fallen apart, right on the FAE schedule. My son has been on the street since, at seventeen, he chose to quit the last of the many special schools and treatment centers we found for him, starting at age fourteen. That final place was the only one that didn't kick *him* out. He's intellectually capable of a normal life, but he often lacks judgment, empathy, perspective, the patience to set long-term goals and then work to accomplish them.

Our daughter, at Boystown for the last two years after having been expelled from three "regular" schools for shoplifting or for failing to pass any courses since the sixth grade, has recently discovered satanism. She has carved an upside-down cross into her arm with a ballpoint pen, twice. After seeing *Dances with Wolves* she's become convinced that the reservation where she was born (and where her birth mother is currently in jail again for drunk and disorderly conduct) is like the happy community in the movie, and so has refused to cooperate with her house parents in any way because she hopes to be sent to South Dakota. Helpful people from the Omaha Indian Center, as well as Louise and I and a dozen others, have tried to explain to her the huge gap between fantasy and fact, between antiseptic fiction and the ragged poverty of Rosebud reservation, but it doesn't penetrate.

Every parent is helpless, that's a given, virtually a cliché. The children of hippies become CPAs or join the army, rural kids move to the city as soon as they can buy a ticket, passing on their way the teenage urban cowboys en route to the wide open spaces. But the utter helplessness of an FAS or FAE parent is of another magnitude. We stand by, throwing one temporary impediment after another into the path of boys and girls seemingly bent upon engineering their own destruction. Many of us hear at one time or another the standard advice of the stumped psychological counselor: let your kids sink to the bottom, then they'll start to work their way back up. Well, we come to discover that in the case of our "special" children, the bottom is very deep indeed. At each plateau, a new descent is immediately sought, and if the levels of Dante's *Inferno* spring to mind, it's not inappropriate. For an FAS or FAE child who doesn't understand rules or morality, honesty or loyalty (except as applying to the exigencies of the moment), the drop is that of an elevator once the cable has been severed.

Louise and I are not the persons to consult for a benign or inspirational message. Hope has become our enemy—a trickster who lies in wait, who reappears in dreams and then pulls the rug from under us time after time. Our afflicted children are beyond placebos, beyond the reach of platitude. Our sons and oldest daughter were brainwashed by alcohol before they were born, casualties in this battle. We have fought the aftereffects of their prenatal exposure to ethanol for twenty years—tried every tactic we could think of or that was suggested to us by specialists—and we barely made a dent in their fates.

When one son calls me from a reservation phone booth and speculates about how he might steal a car and drive to Seattle, it's not much consolation to think that the sum of all our efforts may have merely forestalled this moment in his life by a year or so. We know that buried within the brooding adult Abel resides a sweet little boy, capable of responding with affection if the right buttons are pushed— but try to convince his co-workers when he forgets to punch in on time.

Let us make no mistake about one point: we're not *facing* a crisis, we're *in* one, though official statistics can be deceiving. A couple of years ago South Dakota, a state with at that time no resident dysmorphologist (the only doctor, except for a geneticist, fully trained to diagnose FAS or FAE), reported a grand total of two FAS births—during the same period in which my friend Jeaneen Grey Eagle, director of Project Recovery in Pine Ridge, estimated that somewhere between one-third and one-half of the infants born in certain communities of her reservation were at high risk due to heavy maternal drinking. Underdiagnosis, unfortunately, does not equal small numbers.

But what can we do about it? Each person must provide his or her own answers. Some of us—the scientists—can study the biochemistry involved in fetal damage from drugs, learn to predict which women are most at risk and when, figure out how much ethanol, if any, is tolerable. Others—advocates and politicians—can address the issue of prevention: get out the word, make pests of ourselves, speak up even when it makes our friends uncomfortable, fight for the future of a child not yet even conceived. Still others—social workers, psychologists, and educators—can tackle the needs of the here and now, of the tens of thousands of FAS and FAE men, women, and children who exist on the margins of society. We can devise effective curricula, learning regimens, humane models for dependent care.

If we, today, put our minds to it, if only we did our part, we might not obliterate fetal alcohol syndrome on a global level, but, in all candor, we could save many lives, many mothers, many babies. All it takes is nine months of abstinence, a bit longer if a mother breast feeds. Three hundred thousand separate and discrete solutions, three hundred thousand miracles, and it's a clean year.

And finally some of us, the parents into whose care these children have been given, whether by birth or adoption, can try to get through another day, to survive the next unexpected catastrophe, to preserve a sense of humor. We

laugh at things that really aren't funny—quite the contrary—but we laugh, without malice, for relief. When Abel
went with me last fall to his annual case management meeting, he was asked to list all the accomplishments in the
past twelve months about which he felt especially proud.
He drew a blank.

"Then, tell us what you've been doing since we met here
last year," the man directed—and Abel complied.

"Well, I went down the stairs and I opened the door," he
began. "Then I got into the car and my father took me
home. For supper we had . . . " Abel tried to remember that
anonymous meal he polished off some 365 days before,
stalled, and looked to me for help.

"Next question," I suggested, and the social worker consulted his list.

"Tell me what things you really *don't* like to do," he
invited.

Abel's eyes lit. This was an easy one. "I don't like to dig
up burdocks," he stated.

I blinked in surprise. Abel hadn't dug up burdocks in
three years. He was simply using a response that had
worked in the past.

"Wait a minute," I said. "Abel, thousands of people all
over the country have read your chapter at the end of the
book about how you dug up those burdocks to help us.
People liked that part so much I think that's why they gave
our book that prize you have sitting on your dresser. People
are very proud of you for what you did. I know it wasn't fun

to dig up those plants, but you should feel good that you did it."

Abel was having an especially polite day. He smiled at me, cocked his head, and asked: "What book would that be?"

The grind doesn't get easier and it doesn't go away. FAS victims do not learn from experience, do not get well. Louise keeps a diary and a while ago she glanced back over the past four years. That can be dangerous, because there are some things you don't notice until you take the long view. It turned out that as a family we hadn't had a single period longer than three consecutive days in all that time when one of our alcohol-impaired children was not in a crisis—health, home, school—that demanded our undivided attention. It often seems to us that their problems define our existence as well as their own, and in that respect perhaps we are in a small way the forecast of things to come for this country. How many children of chemically dependent parents have perished in house fires, from malnutrition, from lack of medical care, from exposure? Are these, also, options protected under the rubric of an adult's right to choose to drink or take drugs beyond the point of responsible self-control? Who are these lost babies but the victims of "victimless" crime? Certainly if they survive, the penalties they suffer are ongoing. The prisons to which they are confined exist without the possibility of parole.

FAS is not a problem whose impact is restricted to its

victims. It's not just a woman's issue, not just a man's. No one is exempted. These are everybody's children.

I am descended from the Modoc tribe on my father's side, and I can't help but think of a historic parallel to my present circumstances. In the late nineteenth century the Modocs were engaged in what history calls "the Last Indian War." It consisted of about fifty hungry men, women, and children leaving the Oregon reservation to which they had been assigned—a reservation owned and operated by their traditional enemies, the Klamath—and returning to the Northern California lands they had previously occupied. As was the custom in those days, they were pursued by the cavalry and a full military force—who had a terribly hard time locating them, since the Modocs were hiding in a moonscape of lava beds. But find them they eventually did.

A few of the captured leaders were executed without trial, but what to do with the rest? A group of about twenty adult Modocs were given a choice: either be shipped to a cholera-ridden prison camp in Indian Territory (now Oklahoma) or work the vaudeville circuit with A. B. Meacham, the former Indian agent who had been the source of many of the tribe's troubles. Meacham, you see, had a dynamite idea: America had read in newspapers about the savage Modocs, now the public must be allowed to see them in person.

For more than a year, in cities and towns throughout this country, between a troop of jugglers and a knife-throwing act, the final agonized moments of the "war" were restaged. The Modoc POWs were assigned new, more "Indian-sounding" names, costumed in the kind of fringe-and-feather outfits the audience expected Indians to wear, and commanded to re-create, twice a day, six nights a week, plus two additional matinee performances, the moment of their final defeat.

I know how they must have felt.

People have asked me whether it was "cathartic" to write *The Broken Cord* and then see it have some impact on national awareness. The answer is no. There's no catharsis when you're the parent of an FAS or FAE child or adult.

On my book tour, I one day found myself on a Seattle TV talk show. During the commercial break the hostess chided me for not revealing enough of my *feelings* about the plight of my oldest son. "You want feelings, get Barry Manilow," I told her, but it did no good. The next time I looked at the monitor, there was my face, and lest anyone miss the point, it had a caption: *Tragic Dad.*

That's hardly the identity I expected when I became a father. I speak out publicly today as a living anecdote, a walking warning label, a Chatty Cathy doll who spews forth a version of the same cautionary tale whenever the string is pulled. Our unhappy personal chronicle, the struggle of many well-intentioned and initially optimistic people to alter for the better the life of one damaged little boy, has to the great surprise of my wife and myself become a kind of flagship sound bite for prenatal sobriety, and yet mostly my role is not to warn but to mourn—and that's easier done in private. To be best known for one's saddest story is not the road to notoriety anyone would willingly choose.

Centers for Disease Control
1992

(a partial version appears in the 1993 Medical Supplement of the *Encylopædia Britannica*)

CROSSING THE LINE

A writer of fiction is in disguise, wearing the clothes and speaking the words of somebody else. Stories and novels are elaborate puppet shows where, if the ruse works, the enlivening hands are invisible. There's a protocol, even in the most baldly autobiographical works, by which readers agree to pretend that everything on the page derives from imagination. It's impolite to impute the motives or to confuse the actions of a character with those of the "artist."

What could be more liberating? To the extent one manages to be convincing, one can be anyone, go anywhere, say anything, and escape unscathed. Don't blame me for those men and women in *Yellow Raft* who lie and fail and fool themselves—that's *them*, though I chose to write about some in the first person. Speculate—please—about the unspoken secrets of the people in my books. But as for me, I take the Fifth.

What, then, was I doing on the roof of a Denver TV station last summer, chatting with the hostess of the noon variety show about some of the saddest moments I have ever experienced? She was maximizing her time slot, this curly haired, smiling young woman: we were outdoors in order to observe the first annual hot air balloon race, and I was in town to tell a bleak tale of what could happen to a child if a mother drank alcohol during pregnancy.

By the time I arrived in Colorado, the juxtapositions no longer surprised me. I was almost done with a fifteen-city author's tour to publicize *The Broken Cord*. I had done the morning network news shows, my segment sandwiched between lady weight lifters and Lassie (who was making a comeback). I had stood on a platform in the central walkway of a glitzy Minneapolis shopping mall and read passages aloud that a few years ago I would have had trouble admitting to myself. Via telephone, I had been gloomy company for St. Louis drivers on their way to the office, and in person I had bantered with dozens of DJs who had not even opened my book. "So," scrambled one of them, trying to fill up a long hour in Detroit. "I see you're part Indian." He looked me up and down. "What part?"

A very hip black call-in host in Cleveland allowed that *of course* everyone knew that Indians couldn't hold their firewater, but became annoyed when I asked him if he was a good tap dancer. In Los Angeles I sat before a microphone in a studio with a glass wall front. Shoppers rested on benches only feet away, ate fast food, and listened as the silver-haired popular personality asked if writing the book had restored my faith in the Lord.

I had crossed the line with a vengeance. A personal tragedy was translated into sound bites, interspersed every ten minutes with commercials. Newspaper reviewers, for the most part generous in their comments about the work, still felt free to complain when they thought I hadn't told enough. "Why did Dorris adopt a child as a single parent?" the *Los Angeles Times* writer pondered. "Was it some unresolved sexual thing?"

In a very real sense, my family and I have forfeited the rights to a portion of our own lives. We have lost precious anonymity. By becoming characters in print, we have to a degree sunk our heels in buckets of cement. Like fictional personae, we are expected to be consistent and immutable, as if all the complexities, mixed emotions, and accumulations of two decades could be encapsulated in three hundred pages. We are all, psychologists tell us, bound to and directed by our individual histories, but by particularizing a set of events, trying to make plot out of life by selective editing, we seem to have narrowed the vista from which we travel. By imposing beginnings and endings on the flow of the days, certain key moments have become barnacled with anecdote, arranged like scenery on an empty stage—with no possibility of a proscenium curtain or a revamped revival.

I've never had much patience with people who seek something and then complain when they get it, with rock stars who bemoan the road tour or with politicians who resent public scrutiny. Certain consequences go with the territory. When an author writes a book, he or she hopes it will be read.

I simply wish *The Broken Cord* wasn't about us. I wish Abel (whose name, at least, I changed to "Adam" in print to preserve him some privacy) had been born healthy and whole. I wish, when he began to have problems, I had found a book in the library that informed me about FAS on a level that I, as a nonscientist and as a parent, could have comprehended, so that I would have been off the hook in writing my own. I wish the nature of Abel's impairment was so rare, so esoteric, that only a handful of readers had identified with its tragedy and waste.

This November, by congressional mandate all liquor bottle labels contain a warning that drinking alcohol during pregnancy may endanger the fetus. This law took effect a month after the announcement of a new national statistic that suggested that the blood levels of more than 10 percent of all newborns in the United States tested dangerously high for alcohol or cocaine—a drug that may very well turn out to produce the same long-term learning disorders as does alcohol. Our son's story is the tip of a very large iceberg.

Now that *The Broken Cord* is behind us and Louise and I are back to dreaming up fiction, I can't help wondering why anyone would choose to attempt an autobiography unless there were an underpinning political motive. There seems to me no inherent pleasure or satisfaction in—no excuse for—the announcement, "Look what I've done," unless it's followed immediately by the proscription: "Don't make the same mistake!"

New York Times
February 2, 1992

CRAZY HORSE MALT
LIQUOR

People of proclaimed good will have the oddest ways of honoring American Indians. Sometimes they dress themselves up in turkey feathers and paint to boogie on fifty-yard lines. Sometimes otherwise impeccably credentialed liberals get so swept up into honoring that they beat fake tom-toms or fashion their forearms and hands into facsimiles of the axes European traders used for barter and attempt, unsuccessfully, to chop their way to victory. Presumably they hope that this exuberant if ethnographically questionable display will do their teams more good against opponents than those rituals they imitate and mock did for nineteenth-century Cheyenne or Nez Percé men and women who tried, with desperation and ultimate futility, to defend their homelands from invasion.

Everywhere you look such respects are paid: the street names in woodsy, affluent subdivisions, mumbo jumbo in ersatz male-bonding weekends and Boy Scout jamborees, geometric fashion statements, weepy anti-littering public service announcements. In the ever popular noble/savage spectrum, red is the hot, safe color.

For five hundred years flesh and blood Indians have been assigned the role of a popular culture metaphor. Today, they evoke fuzzy images of Nature, The Past, Plight, or Summer Camp. War-bonneted apparitions pasted to football helmets or baseball caps act as opaque, impermeable curtains, solid walls of white noise that for many citizens block or distort all vision of the nearly two million contemporary Native Americans. And why not? Such honoring relegates Indians to the long ago and thus makes them magically disappear from public consciousness and conscience. What do the three hundred federally recognized tribes— with their various complicated treaties governing land rights and protections, their crippling unemployment, infant mortality, and teenage suicide rates, their often chronic poverty, their manifold health problems—have in common with jolly (or menacing) cartoon caricatures, wistful braves, or raven-tressed Mazola girls?

Perhaps we should ask the Hornell Brewing Company of Baltimore, manufacturers of The Original Crazy Horse Malt Liquor, a product currently distributed in New York with packaging inspired by, according to the text on the back, "the Black Hills of Dakota, *steeped* [my italics] in the History of the American West, home of Proud Indian Nations, a land where imagination conjures up images of blue clad Pony Soldiers and magnificent Native American Warriors."

Whose imagination? Were these the same blue-clad lads who perpetrated the 1890 massacre of two hundred captured, freezing Lakota at Wounded Knee? Are Pine Ridge and Rosebud, the two reservations closest to the Black Hills and, coincidentally, the two counties in the United States with the lowest per capita incomes, the Proud Nations? Is the "steeping" a bald allusion to the fact that alcohol has long constituted the number one health hazard to Indians? Virtually every other social ill plaguing Native Americans—from disproportionately frequent traffic fatalities to arrest statistics—is related in some tragic respect to ethanol, and many tribes, from Alaska to New Mexico, record the highest percentage in the world of babies born disabled by fetal alcohol syndrome and fetal alcohol effect. One need look no further than the warning label to pregnant women printed in capital letters on every Crazy Horse label to make the connection.

The facts of history are not hard to ascertain: the Black Hills, the *paha sapa*, the traditional holy place of the Lakota, were illegally seized by the U.S. government, systematically stripped of their mineral wealth—and have still not been returned to their rightful owners. Crazy Horse, in addition to being a patriot to his people, was a mystic and a religious leader murdered after he voluntarily gave himself up in 1887 to Pony Soldiers at Fort Robinson, Nebraska. What, then, is the pairing of his name with forty ounces of malt liquor supposed to signify?

The Hornell brewers helpfully supply a clue. The detail of the logo is focused on the headdress and not the face; it's pomp without circumstance, form without content. Wear the hat, the illustration seems to offer, and in the process fantasize yourself more interesting (or potent or tough or noble) than you are. Play at being a "warrior" from the "land that truly speaks of the spirit that is America."

And if some humorless Indians object, just set them straight. Remind them what an honor it is to be used.

New York Times
April 1992

THE POWER OF LOVE

At different stages of our lives, the symptoms of love may vary—dependence, attraction, contentment, worry, loyalty, grief—but at heart, the source is always the same. Human beings occasionally have, among our multiple amazing talents, the capacity to, against every odd and despite any pull otherwise, connect with each other. Like functional crafts that dock in deep space, we blindly reach, touch, and, if we're fortunate, form synapses through which air and light and communication rush. We hurtle, bonded by blood or desire, into the question of "what next?"—our discrete futures temporarily one, our pasts conjoined in unlikely, fragile alliance. Love transforms: it simultaneously makes us larger and limits our possibilities. It changes our history even as it breaks a new path through the present. It may, through accident or inattention, through expediency or necessity, cease, but once in place it can never afterward not have been. Once we love, we are permanently in that love's thrall, caught in its wake, a part of its flow.

On the first year's anniversary of our oldest son's death, I collected the dense cube of his ashes at the funeral home where they had resided during our mourning. It was a quiet, overcast September day. Fall was coming, and the grass along the familiar road from Hanover to Cornish had mostly gone to yellow seed.

Twelve months before, Abel had as usual risen from his single bed, shaved badly, dressed in a favorite Garfield T-shirt, and eventually made his way to the truck stop where he worked. At twenty-three, he had recently survived a rough transition in his life: two experimental brain surgeries that had at first partially and then ultimately completely separated the left and right hemispheres of his brain so that when he experienced a seizure on one side the other might remain alert. For him, the worst element of each hospital stay—the most dreaded and worried-over procedure—was the implantation of an IV, but for the rest of us who realized the risks, the dangers were far more drastic. Our son could lose memory, the use of limbs, continence, mobility.

Since Abel was over eighteen and legally an adult, albeit mentally handicapped as a result of fetal alcohol syndrome, the question of consent had necessitated that my wife and I appear in court to argue that his operations were vital. His seizures had become so frequent and severe, whether due to the natural evolution of his condition or to his chronic failure to remember his various required daily medications, that the chance of his collapse in a hazardous context was increasingly likely. Our petition to act, in this limited capacity, as his legal guardians was granted by the judge, and a week later he underwent the first surgery. It didn't solve the problem.

On the morning of the second and more radical operation, a few months later, I picked up Abel at his apartment at dawn and drove him to the hospital. He seemed sluggish from too little sleep, confused and resentful at the idea, I assumed, of having to go through many more weeks of confinement and rehabilitation. At least, I consoled myself, he doesn't completely comprehend what's happening to him. At least his limited imagination doesn't stretch to include the concept of mortality. And then, stopped at a traffic light, I glanced at his face. On his beautifully sculpted cheeks, illuminated by the red glow, there were tears. I had mistaken his silence for fog when, in fact, it was the purest bravery.

I was always either over- or underestimating Abel— expecting too much or settling for too little. I had fluctuated for the twenty years since his adoption between the extremes of disappointment and surprise. On the one hand, he possessed traits so rare as to be remarkable: utter loyalty, complete good will, the impulse for wholehearted forgiveness. And yet, on the other, he could often be maddening in his incapacities for sustained motivation, curiosity, and spontaneous intellectual growth. He absorbed without critical thought the dumbest stereotypes and attitudes, the most teeth-grinding vocabulary and obsessions. He stubbornly believed in things that weren't real even as he scoffed in superior doubt at facts that indisputably were.

He didn't dream. He didn't complain. He didn't aspire. He didn't despair.

Especially during Abel's childhood, before the full magnitude of his learning block was undeniable, I indulged in the persistent fantasy of his brain as a kind of messy room. If I could somehow get inside his head, sweep out the cobwebs, straighten up the clutter, open the windows, organize the files, turn on the lights, suddenly he would become normal. But whether I tapped on it gently, banged at it with a ram, clawed at it with my fingernails, the door stayed firmly, mutely locked. Finally I gave up, let Abel rest. For me, it was defeat. For him, I'm sure it was a great relief.

When at last I accepted that I could not affect my by now grown son's life, I elected, instead, to document it. If he could not contribute to society by his actions, then, I reasoned, let him act as example, as a flesh and blood object lesson against the dangers of drinking alcohol during pregnancy. Abel was passively agreeable to this idea, just as he would have been if I had proposed we move to Mars, eat only peanut butter, or go live in a cave.

And so together, Abel, Louise, and I wrote *The Broken Cord*. It was published, won a literary prize, and was optioned for a network film. And on the day I arrived in Hollywood to discuss its production with famous actors and directors, I received word that Abel was in critical condition, the victim of a driver who hadn't seen him as he crossed a street at night.

After flying the red-eye back to New Hampshire I arrived at his bedside to find him unconscious and bandaged. He had broken bones, a collapsed lung, and unknown internal injuries. Machines assisted his breathing, monitored his pulse, drained his fluids, maintained his temperature. He had suffered no pain, the intensive care doctors promised. Any awareness he might have had after being struck would have been cushioned by shock. He might have heard the trucks on the highway, seen the moon above where he lay, but his mind would have been calm, stunned, almost blank.

It was not hard to talk to Abel, even though I didn't know if he could hear me. I had put words in his mouth so often over the years that the process came naturally. I supplied the questions, and I provided the right answers. I knew the skeptical tone his voice would take, the way his mouth would pull down at the ends in a desultory grin. "Here I am," he would half-confess, half-joke. "What a mess, Dad."

In the two weeks before Abel's body finally wore out and stopped living, I had many such one-way conversations. I kept apologizing for my constant failures of kindness or understanding, and he, as he surely would have done, kept forgiving me. I kept exhorting him to get better, he kept promising to try his best. He kept slipping away, I kept refusing to let him go. And then he died.

Losing a child is an unimaginably painful experience, a moment that calls for privacy and quiet, and yet, through our book, Abel's life had become something of a public cause. His death was reported in *People* and *Time,* and we received many letters of condolence from strangers as well as from friends. We required time for our grief, time to heal, to accept, and so as a family we followed a tribal tradition and waited for a full year before conducting a memorial service.

At last—too soon and not soon enough, as such events inevitably turn out to be—the day arrived. Only seven people were present: Louise and I, three of our daughters, Abel's primary doctor and his wife. We had chosen a spot Abel loved, a little knoll above our pond, and Louise had selected a strong young maple tree to plant as his marker. After the simple ceremony, we stood by the tree in silence for a long time, each reading in the movement of its leaves a different memory. We burned cedar, fanned the smoke upon each other and upon the tree in blessing, and finally each of us in turn, using words Abel would have understood, quietly said good-bye.

Because of who our son was, how he was, our sorrow got mixed with humor, for no one could tell a story about Abel that didn't, in one way or another, have a funny twist, a non sequitur, a punch line. He took nothing very seriously, except love—from which he was not for an instant of his existence divided by doubt or meanness of spirit. Spontaneous and direct, love was his true power, the reaction he inspired in others, and love, for those who knew him or read about him or benefited—without ever realizing the source—from the essence of his life, is his legacy.

New Choices
December 1993

INDIANS

"I" ISN'T FOR "INDIAN"

"I" isn't for "Indian," but it is often for "ignorance." In the never-never land of glib stereotypes and caricature, the rich histories, cultures, and the contemporary complexities of the diverse indigenous peoples of the Western Hemisphere are obscured, misrepresented, and rendered trivial. Native Americans appear not as human beings but as whooping, silly, one-dimensional cartoons. On occasion they are presented as marauding, blood-thirsty savages, bogeys from the nightmares of "pioneers" who invaded their lands and feared for the consequences. At other times they seem veritable angels, pure of heart, mindlessly ecological, brave and true. And worst of all, they are often merely cute, the special property of small children.

A society that chooses to make a running joke of its victims embalms both its conscience and its obligations, relegating a tragic chronology of culture contact to ersatz mythology. It's hard to take seriously, to empathize with, a group of people portrayed as speaking an ungrammatical language, as dressing in Halloween costumes, as acting "wild," as being undependable in their promises or gifts. Frozen in a kind of pejorative past tense, these make-believe

Indians are not allowed to change or in any other way be like real people. They are denied the dignity and dynamism of their history, the validity of their contributions to modern society, the distinctiveness of their multiple ethnicities.

Let "I" be for somebody else.

Introduction to
Indian Stereotypes and Children's Literature
1982

INDIANS ON THE SHELF

While on my way to do research in New Zealand several years ago, I stopped in Avarua, capital of the Cook Islands. To my tourist's eye it was a tropical paradise right out of Michener: palm trees, breadfruit and pineapples, crashing surf, and a profusion of flowers. Most people spoke Maori, and traditional Polynesian music and dance were much in evidence; there was no television, one movie theater, one radio station, and few private telephones.

There were, of course, gift shops, aimed primarily at people like myself who wanted to take with them some memento of a vacation spent sitting in the sun, eating arrowroot pudding, and smelling frangipani on every breeze. And so I browsed, past the Fijian tapa cloth dish towels, past the puka shell necklaces, past the coconut oil perfume, and came face-to-face with an all-too-familiar sight: perched in a prominent position on a shelf behind the cash register was a tribe of plush monkeys, each wearing a turkey-feather imitation of a Sioux war bonnet and clasping a plywood tomahawk.

The Rarotongan salesperson replied to my startled question that, yes, indeed, these simian braves were a hot-selling item. She herself, she added with a broad smile, had played cowboys and Indians as a child.

More recently, I entertained in my home a young man from Zaire who was spending the summer at Dartmouth in order to teach Swahili to students who would travel the next winter in Kenya on a foreign environmental studies program. My guest spoke very little English, a good deal more French, and three East African languages.

He was homesick for his tiny radioless, roadless, remote village on the west shore of Lake Tanganyika, and the Santa Clara pueblo chili I served reminded him of the spicy stews he had eaten in Africa as a child. He listened with rare appreciation to recordings of southwestern Indian music. He had never met "real" Indians before, he reported, and was interested and curious about every detail. But it was not until I brought out a nineteenth-century eagle-feather headdress, a family heirloom, that his eyes lit up with true recognition. Sweeping it out of my hand, and with an innocent and ingenuous laugh, he plopped it on his head, assumed a fierce expression and, patting his hand over his mouth, said "Woo woo woo."

Generations of Germans have learned to read using Karl May's romanticized novels about imagined Apaches who live in Arkansas; Hungarian intellectuals dressed in fake buckskins cavort each summer, playing Indians for a week on a Danube island, an unpleasant, puerile student newspaper in Hanover, New Hampshire, tries to make some "conservative" point by peddling "Indian-head" doormats for $15 each. Far from vanishing, the First American seems if anything to be proliferating as a cultural icon.

As folklore, Indians seem infinitely flexible. They can be tough and savage, as in the Washington Redskins football team, or, starring in environmental commercials, turn maudlin and weepy at the sight of litter. In advertising, they are inextricably linked with those products (corn oil, tobacco) the general public acknowledges as indigenous to the Americas. Indian motifs have inspired hippies, Ralph Lauren designs, and the Boy Scouts of America. But flesh and blood Native Americans have rarely participated in or benefited from such commercial exploitations, though their recognition factor, as they say on Madison Avenue, outranks, on a world scale, that of Santa Claus, Mickey Mouse, or Coca-Cola.

For most people, the myth has become real and a preferred substitute for reality. The Indian mystique was designed for mass consumption by a European audience, the fulfillment of old and deep-seated expectations for "the Other." Yet, many non-Indians, prepared as they are for a well-defined, carefully honed legend, literally would not know a real Native American if they fell over one. Ordinary human beings, with widely variable phenotypes and personalities, defy the mold. Unless they talk "Indian" (a kind of metaphoric mumbo jumbo pidgin of broken English), ooze nostalgia for bygone days, and come bedecked with metallic or beaded jewelry, many native people who hold positions of respect and authority within their own communities are disappointments to non-Indians whose standards of ethnic validity are based on misperceptions of Pocahontas, Squanto, or Tonto.

For five hundred years Indian people have been measured and have competed against a fantasy over which they have had no control. They are compared with beings who never really were, yet the stereotype is taken for historical truth. Last week the local mail carrier knocked at my door and announced that he was taking his Boy Scout troop into the woods where they intended to live "like the Iroquois" for two days. Did I have any advice?

I suggested that they bring along their mommies, pointing out that in a matrilineal society, properly behaved children would be bound by the dictates of their respective clan mothers. This was not what the postman wanted to hear, for it ran counter to his assumption of a macho Indian culture where men were dominant and women were retiring and ineffectual "squaws."

Such attitudes are difficult to rebut persuasively, grounded as they are in long traditions of unilateral definitions. In the centuries since 1492, a plethora of European social philosophers has attempted to "place" Indians within the context of a Judeo-Christian tradition that never suspected the existence of a Western Hemisphere, much less an inhabited one. It has been the vogue for hundreds of years for Europeans to describe Native Americans not in terms of themselves, but only in terms of who they are (or are not) vis-à-vis non-Indians. Hardly a possible explanation—from the Lost Tribes of Israel to outer space or Atlantis refugees—has been eschewed in the quest for a properly rationalized explanation. Puritans viewed Indians as temptations from the devil; historian Frederick Jackson Turner, when he noticed Indians at all, saw them as obstacles to be overcome on the frontier; and expansionists, from President Andrew Jackson to Interior Secretary James Watt, have regarded Indian tribes as simply and annoyingly in the way.

American history, as taught in public schools, omits mention of the large precontact Indian population, much less its rapid decline. Instead, students are given the erroneous impression that the few people who did live in the Americas before European contact were quickly dispatched to the Happy Hunting Ground by conflict with stalwart pioneers and cavalrymen. Such a view of the past, clearly at odds with well-documented facts, not only serves to reinforce the myth of Indian aggressiveness and bellicosity but it further suggests that Indians got what they deserved. In addition, by picturing Indians as warlike and dangerous, Euro-American ancestors reap honor by having vanquished them.

The pattern of Indian-European negotiation for land title in the seventeenth, eighteenth, and nineteenth centuries is also misrepresented. Though students learn about the fifty states, they remain unaware of the ongoing status of close to two hundred domestic, dependent nations subsumed within the country, and regard reservations, if they are conscious of them at all, as transitory poverty pockets "given" to the Indians by philanthropic bureaucrats. In many respects living Native Americans remain as mysterious, exotic, and unfathomable to their contemporaries at the end of the twentieth century as Powhatan was to John Smith over three hundred fifty years ago. Native rights, motives, customs, languages, and aspirations are misunderstood out of a culpable ignorance that is both self-serving and self-righteous.

Part of the problem may well stem from the long-standing tendency of European or Euro-American thinkers to regard Indians as fundamentally and profoundly different, almost not human, motivated more often by mysticism than by ambition, charged more by unfathomable visions than by intelligence or introspection. Since the whys and wherefores of Native American society are not easily accessible to those culture-bound by Western traditional values, there is a tendency to assume that Indians are creatures of either instinct or whimsy.

This idea is certainly not new. Rousseau's noble savages wandered, pure of heart, through a preconcupiscent world, never having had so much as a bite of the fruit from the "tree of the knowledge of good and evil" (Gen. 2:17). Since native people were assumed a priori to be incomprehensible, they were seldom comprehended. Their societies were simply beheld, often through cloudy glasses, and rarely probed by the tools of logic and deductive analysis auto matically reserved for cultures prejudged to be "civilized." And on those occasions when Europeans did attempt to formulate an encompassing theory, it was not, ordinarily, on a human-being-to-human-being basis, but rather through an ancestor–descendant model. Indians, though obviously contemporary with their observers, were somehow regarded as ancient, examples of what Stone Age Europeans must have been like.

It's a great story, an international crowd pleaser, but there is a difficulty: Indians were, and are, *Homo sapiens sapiens*. Though often equipped with a shovel-shaped incisor, an epicanthic fold, or an extra molar cusp (or the absence of type-B blood), Native American people have had to cope, for the last forty thousand or so years, just like everyone else. Their cultures have had to make internal sense, their medicines have had to work consistently and practically, their philosophical explanations have had to be reasonably satisfying and dependable, or else the ancestors of those we call Indians truly would have vanished long ago.

The reluctance in accepting this tautological fact comes from the Eurocentric conviction that the West holds a monopoly on science, logic, and clear thinking. To admit that other, culturally divergent viewpoints are equally plausible is to cast doubt on the monolithic center of Judeo-Christian belief: that there is but one of everything—God, right way, truth—and Europeans alone knew what that was. If Indian cultures were acknowledged as viable, then European societies were something less than an exclusive club.

It is little wonder, therefore, that Indian peoples were

perceived not so much as they were but as they had to be, from a European point of view. Whisked out of the realm of the real and into the land of make-believe, Indians became either super- or subhuman. They dealt in magic, not method. They were stuck in their pasts, not guided by its precedents.

Such expedient misconception argues strongly for the development and dissemination of a more accurate, more objective historical account of native peoples—a goal easier stated than accomplished. North American societies were nonliterate before and during much of the early period of their contact with Europe, making the requirements for piecing together an emic history particularly demanding and, by the standards of most traditional methodology, unorthodox. The familiar and reassuring kinds of written documentation found in European societies of equivalent chronological periods do not exist, and the forms of tribal record preservation available—oral history, tales, mnemonic devices, and religious rituals—strike university-trained academics as inexact, unreliable, and suspect. Western historians, culture-bound by their own approach to knowledge, are apt to declaim that next to nothing, save the evidence of archaeology, can be known of early Indian life. To them, an absolute void is more acceptable and rigorous than a reasonable, educated guess.

However, it is naive to assume that any culture's history is self-perceived without subjective prejudice. Every modern observer, whether he or she was schooled in the traditions of Rarotonga or Zaire, of Hanover, New Hampshire, or Vienna, was exposed at an early age to one or another form of folklore about Indians. For some, the very impressions about Indian tribes that initially attracted them to the field of American history are aspects most firmly rooted in popular myth and stereotype. Such scholars may have first come to "like" their subject because they believed Indians to be more honest, stoic, and brave than other peoples . . . and forever after must strive against this bias in presenting tribal societies in an evenhanded fashion. Or, when they eventually discovered to their disillusionment that all Indians were not pure of heart, they may have had to suppress, consciously or unconsciously, an abiding resentment and disenchantment.

Serious scholarship about Native American culture and history is unique in its approach, for it requires an initial, abrupt, and wrenching demythologizing. Most students do not start from point zero, but from minus ten, and in the process are often required to abandon cherished childhood fantasies of superheroes or larger-than-life villains.

Those historians and anthropologists who also happen to themselves be ethnically Native American may have an advantage here, especially if they grew up in the context of tribal society. They, at least, have always known other Indians as just "people." Furthermore, through relatives or inheritance, they may have better access to traditional sources of record keeping and thus may be more comfortable with taking analytical risks, basing their assumptions upon subtle but persuasive clues surviving in their own cultural experience.

Revisionist native scholars, of course, are assumed by some colleagues to be hopelessly biased in favor of their subjects. Though Europeans and Euro-Americans who deal professionally with the histories of their national ancestors are not automatically accused of self-aggrandizement, native scholars are presumed by some to be incapable of impartiality.

In any case, whoever attempts to write Native American history must admit in advance to fallibility. There is not and never likely will be any proof to support a conjecture based on deduction. David Bradley, in his novel *The Chaneysville Incident,* writes wistfully of a firmly fixed chamber in historians' heaven in which all things are clear. "And we believe," Bradley says, "if we have been good little historians, just before they do whatever it is they finally do with us, they'll take us in there and show us what was *really* going on. It's not that we want so much to know we were right. We *know* we're not right (although it would be nice to see exactly how close we came). It's just that we want to, really, truly, utterly, absolutely, completely, finally *know*."*

Indian history hardly even offers limbo. It depends upon the imperfect evidence of surviving artifacts; upon the barely disguised, self-focused testimony of European

---

* David Bradley, *The Chaneysville Incident* (New York: Avon, 1982), p. 277.

traders, missionaries, and soldiers; and, lastly and most radically, upon common sense. The making of cross-cultural, cross-temporal assumptions is enough to send every well-trained Western academic into a state of catatonia, yet there is no avoiding it. If the only two stipulated givens are that Indian societies were composed of people in the normal range of human intelligence and that human beings, wherever and whenever they may live, share some traits, then we can dare, once having amassed and digested all the data available from usual sources, to imagine the world through the eyes of our historical subjects. We can attempt to make sense of practices, beliefs, and reactions that do not conform to a Western model but must, within the configurations of their own contexts, have some explanation. We can stop treating Indians as sacred European myths and begin the terribly difficult and unpredictable task of belatedly and permanently taking them off the shelf.

from *The American Indian and the Problem of History*
1987

REWRITING HISTORY

History is rewritten, revised constantly and incrementally to explain and justify the present. In attempting to piece together a pattern of events that leads from any random "then" to a specific "now," there is an inevitable assortment of objective facts, subjectively selected. In postulating a sequence, we seek to discover underlying order, an unfolding story that not only documents the way things worked in the past, but that also, as an instructive precedent, anticipates what might yet happen—thus providing us with at least the illusion of control, the whiff of accurate prediction.

History, of course, comes in all sizes, in every scope and span. When we mentally reconstruct our day or our year, any segment of our personal existence, we term the process *autobiography*. In my nonfiction book *The Broken Cord*, I sought to untangle the threads of just three lives— my own, my wife's, and especially our oldest son's—in order to impose some meaning on events that, superficially, seemed simply arbitrary and unfair. Why, in both the narrow and the broad picture, had Abel been born permanently damaged by alcohol? What could we do to assist him, or, if he was beyond all help save sympathy, what could we do to prevent his impairment's being visited upon others?

Over the course of a year I struggled in the hours before each dawn to retrieve and organize incidents only dimly recalled, searching out the telling details, the odd departure from the ordinary, the clues whose weighted accumulation balanced the conclusions we inescapably reached. I strove to be scrupulously honest, even at the cost of embarrassment, endeavored to tell the whole truth, to extrapolate theory only from established knowledge—but at best the result was merely a shorthand and overly neat version of multiple causes and effects. A human life is not a plot to be teased out and critically analyzed in retrospect, and though each of us might be regarded as the stars of our own particular drama, we are but bit players or extras in the epics of other people.

History always deceives when it pretends to be universal or to have overcome bias. Someone was its ultimate author or editor, identified certain key elements and eliminated others from consideration because they were overly complicated, distracted from the operative thesis, or outright disputed it. Traditional Western history, if not an intentional lie, is invariably a distortion, a nearsighted tracing useful in answering a few key questions (What in the world did powerful European males do next?) but irrelevant to others (What was everyone else up to?). Even the most thorough educational flow charts—those that dare to interweave the invention of the Maya calendar or the birth of Buddha with the usual chain-reaction parade of pyramids-Fertile Crescent-Alexander the Great-Rome-Jesus-Middle Ages-Renaissance-Columbus-Reformation-American Revolution-colonialism-world wars . . . us——categorically leave out primary mention of women, statistically at least half the species in any society, plus sub-Saharan Africa, most of Asia, and the precontact Western Hemisphere, to name only three immense geographic arenas that are usually all but ignored.

Standard history is based upon the notion that some elite lives, some favored types of people, some supposedly blessed places are ipso facto more important than others. As a result, the argument goes, they are more deserving of rapt attention, scholarly study, and wide allegiance. But isn't it really a matter of the shifting nature and definition of context? There's necessarily an escalating degree of generalization as the saga is expanded from the chronicle of one individual, to that of the person's family, community, nation, region, continent, or era.

As long as we accept the obvious limitations, as long as we keep perspective on what traditional history actually reveals, it's no worse than any similarly self-serving enterprise. Trouble ensues only when a single group claims unto itself, intrinsically and forever, the comprehensive planetary narrative. If a cabal of orthodoxy presumes to monopolize and manipulate the interpretation of the pasts of even those who are or have been systematically excluded from membership in the inner circle, all save a minority are

denied a sense of legitimacy, a theoretical centrality to a
vision whose contemporary manifestation coincides with
their own existence, and in whose unfolding culmination
their efforts play a substantive role. A population displaced
of its rightful temporal depth is instantly transformed into
an assemblage of interlopers, beneficiaries, guests at a
stranger's table. Even if they've lately been welcomed to
the feast, their participation is hampered by the message
that they've made no valuable contribution toward its
preparation. The implication is that dinner is a sit-down,
formal affair and not a potluck where everyone brings his
or her own special creation, the product of secretly per-
fected recipes, handed down through generations.

A people's self-history writes its own invitation. It vali-
dates continuities, credits earnings, marks investments. It
binds the members of a society into a unit with commonly
held causes and aspirations. It functions to emphasize the
hard-won base of shared values, and acts to mitigate individual jealousies and conflicts. We all descend from the
same primordial roots—no living human boasts a lineage
more ancient than another's and, conversely, all living
human beings are equally "modern." We are each of us,
one way or another, survivors whose ancestors, through
good fortune or wise choice, formed an unbroken relay: we
but carry the baton in the current lap. And we're none of
us, in the drop of begats, independent of the influences of
countless others, known and unknown, gratefully acknowledged, vociferously denied, or patently ignored.

It is the nature of all cultures to change, grow, evolve, sample among earlier options in exploring solutions to new situations. There are as many microhistories as there are people, as many macrohistories as there are self-identifying clusters. But the fact remains: if we concede the explication of our past, on any level, to those who have no investment in its accurate and sympathetic portrayal, we are giving up much more than the exploration of roots. We are abandoning the future to which we are uniquely entitled.

How does all this work in practical terms? How do we plumb a plundered past without condescending, romanticizing, or fabricating? How do we revivify and make provocative in its own right a legacy relegated to the nooks and crannies of museums? Let me propose but one example.

No known group has been rendered more invisible—in an anniversary year in which their prominence should have been assured—than those Native American inhabitants of Caribbean islands first visited by Europeans five hundred years ago. Nonliterate and all but wiped out by successive infestations of Old World diseases, the Taino are sketchily approachable through archaeology, through analogy with other small hunting and gathering groups, and through the journal entries of Christopher Columbus himself. In the latter case, especially, a conscientious reader must filter out ethnocentrism to find dependable data lodged within a cloud of opinion. In short, we have access to certain classes of information—what foods people ate, what types of houses they lived in, what the weather was like, how social groups were organized, and the way people reacted to the sudden appearance of oddly dressed visitors—but little sense of three-dimensional men and women.

To rewrite history, to suggest voices and personalities for the Taino and other groups peripheral to a European world-view, the protagonists need their own faces, their own stories—even made-up stories, so long as they don't violate or exist outside the perimeters of objective truth. Fictional characters must be treated with respect but not undue reverence, must be actors, not reactors, must be granted the dignity of their own agendas, even if these vary from Western priorities. In depicting the Taino we can dare to exercise that trait essential to all history but so often denied by most historians: creative imagination. By merely imparting to them the expectation of cross-culturally shared responses, by recognizing that they were as human as we, we instantly shatter the static stereotype.

Nowhere is this process more possible—and more plausible—than among our children. Young minds are not yet schooled to screen out paradox, not yet programmed to gauge significance on the basis of establishment imprimatur, not yet fixed with absolute judgments. Most children would not contend, as did a Dartmouth English professor— at least not with his know-nothing self-assurance—that there could *be* no Asian, African, or Native American Shakespeares, Platos, or Thomas Jeffersons. If there had been, my former colleague assured me, *he,* as an educated man, would surely have heard of them.

Unfortunately, when we present the non-Western world to young readers or listeners, we often waste the opportunity of their innocence and fall into counterproductive patterns. In the world of contemporary children's books dealing with American Indians, the road to the unhappy hunting ground is paved with good intentions but few rewards. Perhaps in reaction to a previous generation's broad categorization of native peoples as savage, dangerous, or just plain odd, the accepted approach to tribal societies seems a curious mixture of distance and caution, with a heavy dollop of mysticism thrown in for ethnic flavor. The reader must search hard for portraits of aboriginal men and women, boys and girls, that afford a complex view or a matter-of-fact attitude toward everyday life, past or present.

Storybook Indians seem always teetering on the verge of extrasensory perception. Their dreams prognosticate with an eerie accuracy any weather reporter would envy. They possess the convenient ability to communicate freely with animals and birds, and they demonstrate a knack for nature-based simile. In the politically correct vocabulary of multiculturalism, Native Americans of whatever tribe or period tend to be an earnest, humorless lot, stiff and instructive as museum dioramas.

In other words, boring.

As a child, I seldom identified with Indians in books because for the most part they were utterly predictable.

They longed for days gone by, were solemn paragons of virtue—were, in short, the last people I would choose to play with. Those pretend Indian kids seemed far too busy making pots out of clay or being fascinated by myths about the origin of the universe to be much fun. They didn't remind me of anyone I knew, especially my cousins on the reservation.

Why were those Indians so wooden? Typecast in advance of introduction in a particular story, they were set in concrete, the antithesis of dynamic, the opposite of surprising, the denial of real life, and though children who heard or read such tales might not be able to articulate this drawback, they often validated it by their nightly reading choices. If you really don't want to go to bed, you don't choose a book guaranteed to put you to sleep.

In fact, portraying non-Western peoples as dull is worse than bad entertainment: it's counterproductive to the intent of most parents and teachers. We seek to expose our children to other cultures in an effort to encourage tolerance, to pique a lively curiosity, and to promote an appreciation for diversity. This is all fine, as long as the encompassing story is full of nuance and subtlety, as long as our attention is earned, not smugly presumed, and as long as the basic common denominator that underlies all individuals—the delight and dilemma of being fully alive—is not lost in the effort. Indian children in fiction must be children as much as they are Indian, for without some primal sense of identification, some attraction toward vicarious emotion, some invitation to shared imagination that spans all the obvious points of distinction between "us" and "them," what began as merely foreign winds up as dutiful, even forbidding.

I admit, my first impulse in writing my young-adult novel, *Morning Girl*, had to do with justice. When Louise and I were researching *The Crown of Columbus*, one of our frustrations was the virtual anonymity of the Taino. "They should make good and intelligent servants," was Columbus's initial and overriding impression. Among the first people he says he met was "one very young girl," and I wondered who she was, or rather, who she was prior to that encounter.

In fact the Taino didn't make any kind of servants. Susceptible to the diseases whose germs Columbus and his crew were carrying along with glass beads and red caps, they were virtually wiped out within a generation or two, and have since been treated—in textbooks and in popular imagination—as a minor footnote, more famous for what they weren't—hostile—than for what they had been, could have been, or were. The Taino's experience was, in the extreme case, a precursor for what happened to native peoples throughout the Western Hemisphere over the past five hundred years. So I thought, in this year of national birthday parties and the celebration of "discovery," they, as the first to say hello, deserved at least an imagined voice, a whisper that suggested that they were more than a passing welcome wagon.

Of course, for a writer, good intentions can be dangerous, even lethal, because they tend to subvert the business of telling a story. Starting with the premise of "a message" is a lot like beginning a joke by announcing, with a wide grin, "You're really going to laugh at this one!" Therefore, when I began the book, I put my political reasons out of my head and tried to conceive a pair of characters, hear and translate their feelings. The only departure from the method I've used in adult novels was that in this instance the protagonists lived a long time ago and were a twelve-year-old girl and her ten-year-old brother. Writing in the first person, one must pay attention to various contextual and linguistic limitations: I could only "know" what each character possibly knew and could only express that knowledge—of self or of the world—in language and metaphors that each might reasonably employ. If the suspension of disbelief were done well, the story should be accessible to younger readers and listeners. Furthermore, I had to dream a place and a time very remote from my own experience, a world that was infinitely smaller, safer, and consequently had the illusion of being better understood and more trusted by its inhabitants.

Yet, a work of fiction—whatever readership is primarily intended—is truly, at its heart, the product of an author's personal history. We can only draw with authenticity upon emotions we've known and tasted. In the case of Morning Girl and Star Boy, in trying to flesh out their shadowy outlines, I naturally returned to the questions I've had to ask in my own life, and to the hypotheses I've tentatively formulated in connection with my late eldest son, in many respects as incomprehensible to my wife and me—due to his prenatal exposure to alcohol—as any imaginary character could be. A victim of fetal alcohol syndrome, our son manifested actions and reactions to ordinary events that often forced Louise and me to fill in certain blanks, to suppose the boy he might have been, could have been, should have been, but for the insult of the manner in which he entered the world. He, like the mysterious Taino, was and remained vulnerable, at the mercy of more powerful others who quickly categorized him. He, like the Taino, was exploited, misunderstood, his history dismissed as inconsequential. He, like the Taino, lacked a song of his own.

And so, with Morning Girl and Star Boy I allowed myself to speculate freely, to invite onto the page two fully invested children—curious, independent, self-analytical, strong, moving toward independence—whose flaws were the flaws of youth: redeemable with wisdom and maturity. They are not brilliant or precocious, but merely normal, typical, likely, if circumstances had been different, to grow into decent, responsible adults, people who could hold their own. In my experience, if that can happen, it seems the most marvelous of miracles.

Too often, when we reflect on the sweep of history, we fail to see the individual tree for the forest. The people who met Columbus become "The Taino" instead of, possibly, Morning Girl and Star Boy, their parents She Wins the Race and Speaks to Birds, the grandfather who they remember fondly, the new sister who never got to be born.

All distinctions, for convenience, are swept aside in favor of the lump category: learning disabled, good servants, homeless, primitive. Invisible. Without a past. Without a future.

It's an efficient solution, and we value efficiency, but happily it's not a rule that a writer must follow. Alone before a page, in the quiet of early morning, anything seems possible. Dream children can come to life, talk to each other in argumentative, demanding voices, assert themselves, expect to be heard. A history interrupted or interfered with can be momentarily restored, celebrated. It's been a thrill for me to listen, to allow a pleasure that real life does not permit, and if, as I'm sure is the case, I haven't gotten it completely right, perhaps, in the reciprocating imaginations of those who read my little book, my mild rebuttal to the booming microphones of quincentenary self-congratulation, my write of a possible history, two not-implausible Taino children will at least be recognized as capable of bearing names.

Booklinks
1992

DISCOVERIES

Multiculturalism as a topic has become almost cliché, a bow to each federally recognized ethnic population, a dutiful list of their respective accomplishments and contributions to the modern world. The word *mosaic* is often used, or, in Canada, the homier *patchwork quilt*. However, perspective, in discussing the various patches, is problematic, for it presumes a kind of omniscience that only God or objective history can achieve. An individual, ultimately, speaks *from* a patch, *as* a patch. There is a way of viewing the mishmash of America from an African American point of view, or from a Chicano or Puerto Rican or Russian émigré. Each vantage has its own *ad*vantage, its own unique illumination.

Half a millennium ago, my ancestors on my father's side, Modocs who lived in the lava flats of northern California, were going about their lives—hunting, fishing, falling in love, mourning their dead, completely unaware of an Atlantic Ocean, much less any human beings on the other side of it. Irish peasants—my mother's people—toiling the rocky fields of the western county of Roscommon, speaking Gaelic and worrying when the next attack from the sea might come, had little notion of Spain, much less the possibility of America. Somewhere in the tree of my particular lineage there were French farmers, Swiss shepherds, German professors, Coeur d'Alene salmon fishermen, all innocent of the complications of contact, oblivious of each others' priorities and concerns, insular, ethnocentric, proud . . . and unfathomable to a contemporary person.

These were men and women whose world was infinitely smaller, easier, but ultimately, I would argue, less interesting in its homogeneity than our own. When their worlds inadvertently collided, well into the eighteenth and nineteenth centuries, they were probably at least as confused as they were enlightened, as terrified by newness as they were fascinated by it. They no doubt mistrusted the strange, yearned for the security of the "old days," often wished each other gone. But somehow, fortuitously (for me), there were among them people who dared to look beyond the boundaries of their own birthplaces, who not only accepted but embraced the possibilities of difference, who joined together to forge something new.

In contemporary America we are assembled from many lands and diverse backgrounds, and seem alternately to periodically examine and celebrate, criticize and revise, maybe even learn from the process of our ongoing union. At our best, we seek the truth, and through that lens to avoid the mistakes and blindnesses of our respective forebears. We commemorate, we remember, we say Kaddish, we hope. We are the unlikely survivors of an inexorable process beyond any of our controls, and we feel an odd mixture of shame and pride, relief and regret. We are the chain of dancers on the beach at the end of Federico Fellini's *8½*, and we are, potentially, in our thoughtfulness, our willingness to listen to each other, our curiosity and our mutual compassion, the best chance for a better and more harmonious next five hundred years of world history.

There are, among Native American people I know and respect, many who were angry at the attention lavished on the 1992 quincentennial. These individuals profess an aversion to Columbus and all that he stands for; they're embittered descendants of tribes whose lands were stolen, whose populations were decimated, whose religions were outlawed and held in contempt, whose books were burned, whose skin color reviled. And they are right to be angry. Mythologizing and glorifying—or deprecating—a complicated past does no justice to anyone. It buries, in its fear of clarity, hard facts and sad realities. It absolves without any confession of guilt, and it does not heal.

There are, among my non-Indian friends, those who resent any cloud cast over the international orgy of self-congratulation, of blissful dismissal of every history save that of the conquerors. "To the victors belong the spoils," they crow. And they are wrong, wrong as the extollers of Manifest Destiny, wrong as those who would remake the world in the image of a single culture or society or faith. Our diversity, as a species, has always been our salvation.

Why do we struggle to deny and suppress it? And what do we forfeit in so doing?

Who were, after all, the societies that greeted Europeans five, four, three hundred years ago? What were their motives, their important elements, their contrasts with the norms of Old World nations that attempted to dominate and destroy them?

Imagine the scene: it is an autumn day in the late fifteenth century. On a beach with rose-colored sand, somewhere in the Caribbean, two groups of people, the hosts and their visitors, are about to meet for the first time. Emerging from a small landing boat is a group of men exhausted from a long and frightening ocean voyage. They didn't trust where they were going and now they don't know where they've arrived—but it doesn't look at all like the India described by Marco Polo. They come from Spain and Portugal and Genoa, are Christian and Jewish. The more superstitious and uneducated among them feared that, by sailing west across the Atlantic, they would fall off the edge of the planet.

The men seek treasure and adventure, fame and glory, but the people who greet them—if in fact they are "people" at all—seem, though handsome, quite poor. They are not dressed in fine brocade encrusted with precious jewels, as one would expect of subjects of the great Khan. They are, in fact, not dressed at all, except for a few woven skirts and dabs of ochre. Are they demons? Are they dangerous? Do they know where the gold is hidden?

Watching the boat draw near is a cluster of men, women, and children. They speak a dialect of the Arawak language and are delighted to receive new guests, especially ones who aren't painted white—signifying death. Strangers arrive often, anxious to barter parrot feathers or new foods or useful objects made of stone or shell. These particular visitors look rather strange, it's true: their bodies are covered with odd materials, not at all suited for the warm climate, and they communicate with each other in a tongue as indecipherable as Carib or Nahuatl.

Up close there are more surprises. The group includes no women and some among the hosts speculate why this may be the case. Have their clan mothers expelled these men, banned them to wander alone and orphaned? Has their tribe suffered some disaster? And another thing: they have the strong odor of people who have not had their daily bath. Are they from some simple and rude society that doesn't know how to comport itself?

But all this notwithstanding, guests are guests and should be treated with hospitality. They must be offered food and shelter, must be entertained with stories and music, before the serious business of trade begins.

The earth was much larger than Christopher Columbus imagined, its human population far more diverse. The land mass he encountered on his transatlantic voyages was thoroughly inhabited by more than one hundred million people, from the frigid steppes of Patagonia at the farthest extremity of South America to the dark arboreal forests of New-foundland. In the inhospitable Arctic, Inuits foraged for much of the year in small nuclear or extended family groups, assembling sporadically to carry on the necessary business of marriage, remembrance, or collective action, and only when the availability of food was at its peak. In the lush and verdant jungles of Yucatán and Guatemala, the Mayas had invented agriculture, writing, and an accurate calendar fifteen hundred years before the birth of Christ. Organized in complex, class-oriented societies, they subsisted on a nutritionally balanced diet based on maize, squashes, and beans. In the Andes of northwestern South America early Quechuas domesticated the potato, engineered an intricate system of roads and bridges, and formed a nation in which the state owned all property except houses and movable household goods, and taxes were collected in labor.

The Western Hemisphere was home to literally hundreds of cultures whose people spoke a multiplicity of dialects and languages derived from at least ten mutually exclusive linguistic families. Many societies had well-developed traditions of science and medicine—some 40 percent of the modern world's pharmacopoeia was utilized in America before 1492—and literature, visual art, and philosophy flourished in a variety of contexts. Yet beyond a shared geography, there were few common denominators; due to the haphazard nature and long process by which in-migrating peoples distributed themselves throughout the conti-

nents, the Western Hemisphere thrived as a living laboratory of disparate lifestyles, linguistic variety, and cultural
pluralism.

Obviously, no single group was directly aware of more
than a fraction of the other extant societies—and there was
no conception of an overarching group identity. "We" was
the family, the community, the tribe, and "they" were everyone else, known and unknown. The fact of cultural diversity,
however, was manifest. Within a day's walk of virtually
every indigenous population could be found at least one and
probably more than one unrelated community whose inhabitants, relative to the visitor, spoke a totally foreign and
incomprehensible language, adhered to a unique cosmology,
dressed in unusual clothing, ate exotic foods, and had a dissimilar political organization with peculiar variations on age
and gender roles.

A native person in most regions of precontact America
could and undoubtedly did believe that he or she belonged
to the smartest, most tasteful, most accomplished, and most
handsome human constellation in the universe, but clearly
not the only one. Pluralism, in whichever way it was construed and explained, was inescapably the norm.

It is little wonder, therefore, that for Europeans of the
fifteenth and sixteenth centuries, America proved to be
much more than a single new world: it was an unimagined
universe. The sheer heterogeneity of Western Hemisphere
societies challenged every cherished medieval assumption
about the orderly nature of human origin and destiny. It

was as if a whole new set of potential operating rules were revealed—or, even more disconcerting, the cultural hodge-podge of America was an ego-threatening intimation that there were no dependable rules at all. Imagine the shock! To have believed for a thousand years that everything and everybody of consequence was known and neatly categorized and then suddenly to open a window and learn that all along one had been dwelling in a small house with no perspective on the teeming and chaotic city that surrounded one's accustomed neighborhood—no map or dictionary provided. How did Cain and Abel fit into this new, complicated schema? Which Old Testament patriarch begat the Lakota or the Chibcha? How did the Comanche get from the Tower of Babel to Oklahoma?

The contrasts between the Old World and the Americas were staggering. With only a few minor exceptions, virtually all Europeans spoke languages that sprang from a single linguistic family. Moreover, in the larger context, Europe's vaunted religious and philosophical divisions were basically variations on a concordant theme. Everyone from the Baltic to the Balkans to the British Isles professed belief in the same divinity or, in the case of European Jewry, His father.

As side effects of this theological unity, Latin became a lingua franca for intellectuals from all sectors, and the Mosaic code formed the basis for practically every ethical or legal philosophy. The broad assumption of male dominance reigned uncontested, from individual marriage contracts to the leadership hierarchy of emergent nation-states. The Bible—in particular, the book of Genesis—was regarded as a literally true and factually accurate accounting of the origin of everything.

Significantly, in the Adam and Eve story, creation is intentional; a personalized, anthropomorphic God formed a man in His image and then threw in a woman, made out of a nonessential rib, for His company and pleasure. His word was law and His only token competition came from a fallen angel, also of His manufacture. After devising, in six days, a universe whose primary purpose was to exist as a backdrop and amusement park for man, the Divinity set up a test for the objects of his invention—a test that the Divinity, being omniscient as well as omnipotent, must have known all along man would fail.

Man did.

A nonbeliever attempting to analyze this saga might well find parts of it, while interesting, a bit bizarre. Why were men and women so disproportionately blessed? Why did God go to all the trouble? For all its paradox, however, the Genesis story did fulfill a function for the Hebraic culture to whom it was initially addressed. It authenticated divine sponsorship for the law of the land and proffered the explanation, so necessary for a poor, threatened minority population, that life was supposed to be pain, that man deserved what he got, and that the only true happiness and peace would come to the just after death.

The disparate creation stories Native Americans believed

about themselves—be they emergence myths or earth-diver tales, divine births or great floods—are every bit as pregnant with particular meaning for their specific audiences as was Genesis for the Israelites. Take, for example, a tale found in several Northwest Coast repertoires: According to legend, one day Raven, the androgynous culture hero/Trickster, spies a bush containing a new kind of berry. They are purple and luscious, bursting with sweet juice, and Trickster can't resist. He/she begins to gobble them up and doesn't stop until every one is consumed. His/her breast feathers are stained and his/her belly is bloated, but Raven staggers to the side of a cliff, spreads his/her wings, and careens off into the air.

Suddenly Raven is seized by terrible stomach cramps and immediately experiences the worst case of diarrhea in history. It's terrible: everywhere Raven flies, his/her droppings land, until finally the attack is over, the pain subsides, and with a sigh of relief Raven looks down at the earth to see the mess he/she has made. And there we are, come to life: human beings! Raven beholds these ridiculous creatures, made out of his/her excrement, and laughs. And the ridiculous creatures squint up at Raven—and laugh back!

A society with this irreverent coda has a very different self-concept than one with solemn Genesis as its primary referent. The Raven tale is supposed to be funny, is aimed to entertain and thus be memorable. Creation itself, the story implies, was a totally random act—a fluke. Additionally, the first encounter between creator and createe is maddening for both. Theirs is a relationship without mutual culpability, without guilt, affection, or even clear purpose. As a matter of fact, subsequent chapters in the cycle demonstrate that the joking relationship between Raven and humanity persists and becomes even more perverse over time.

The universe based on such stories was conceived in large part as irrational, not a product of cause and effect, stimulus and response. Events occurred without great purpose and had to be dealt with on their own terms— pragmatically and intelligently. A plague of locusts, an earthquake, a misfortune did not take place because an individual or a people failed to satisfy a demanding and ambiguous Zeus or Jupiter or Jehovah, but rather were regarded as haphazard disruptions in the inevitable course of existence. Humor and fatalism, as opposed to responsibility and recrimination, were the appropriate attitudes toward misfortune. The gods, like everything else, were inscrutable. Harmony, in human communities or in nature as a whole, was best preserved through balance and established custom, and both people and divinities were but elements in a grand, interrelated panorama that encompassed all things.

Practically speaking, prior to the so-called Age of Discovery, Europeans had little contact with populations substantively dissimilar to themselves—certainly not enough to shake their entrenched ethnocentrism. Relations with central or eastern Asia, or sub-Saharan Africa, were rare, and usually filtered through the Islamic societies occupying the southern and eastern perimeters of the Mediterranean. Although Arabs were regarded in certain respects as exotic and the polar opposite of Christians, they were, nevertheless, comprehensible; generally similar in terms of skin pigmentation, patriarchal orientation, and even religious derivation, their customs fell within the range of at least plausible behavior. They were ideal "heathens" because they tended to embrace skewed versions of the values revered by Europeans: messianic and orthodox monotheism, territorial conquest, the accumulation of material wealth. In so doing, they provided a neat and precise contrast that, point by point, helped both groups define themselves (i.e., "this," not "that"). Throughout the Middle Ages, Europeans regarded rumored tales of a world beyond Granada or Cairo or Damascus, be they authored by Herodotus or Pliny, as odd to the point of science fiction and largely irrelevant to the daily lives of ordinary people.

This reassuring order suffered a severe blow when the first boatloads of Spanish and Portuguese sailors failed to topple off the edge of the world—pinpointed, predictably, just beyond the sight of Christendom's western shore—as they ventured far to the south and east. Verifying the immensity of Africa and the Orient, each continent bursting with undeniably non-European peoples and cultures, was traumatic enough news, yet not altogether a surprise. Alexander, after all, had been to India, and the spice route to Cathay was well worn. But with the dramatic materialization of the Western Hemisphere, the dazzling implications of global heterogeneity could no longer be avoided.

The argument for the centrality of Europe was forced to alter its traditional rationalizations in order to account for all else that turned out to exist. An initial solution, analogous to that of the ostrich sticking its head into the sand at the first sign of trouble, was abject denial. If new data didn't fit into old orthodoxy, then it couldn't be accurate. Later as the diversity of humanity became increasingly manifest, the working definition of "true human being" became more rigid, more narrow, and long theological debates took place on such esoterica as whether or not natives of America and Australia even had souls.

This condescending approach was hard to maintain in the face of the intelligence and industry evident in New World cities, bountiful agriculture, science, art, and, especially, wealth reported by conquistadors like Cortés and Pizarro. Indeed, the empire civilizations of Meso- and Latin America—those of the Aztec and Inca, especially—were probably easiest for Europeans to appreciate. Though the customs varied and the religions were unfamiliar to the early Spanish explorers, at least the motivating goals were recognizable: a thirst for conquest, the accumulation of wealth, a consolidation of political power in the hands of a single leader and his coterie. The larger nation-states must have been reminiscent of Moorish analogs, with their swarthy-looking populations, exploitable treasure, and grand capitals. Their wealth was obvious and marketable, their existing labor force was already organized and ready to be co-opted, and their belief systems posed familiar challenges for Christian conversion.

Smaller, tribally based cultures of North America, on the other hand, must have struck Europeans as utterly bizarre upon first encounter. By and large these groups maintained no standing armies, practiced a mind-boggling variety of inordinately flexible religions, were nonliterate, vague regarding the precise boundaries of their territory, and very often passed property and authority through a female line of descent. Few North American societies sought to impose ideology on neighboring cultures, insisting that the freedom of the individual predominated over the power of the state. Leadership tended to spring from expertise or proven ability rather than from dynastic heredity, and in any given tribe there might exist a multiplicity of "chiefs"—each a specialist in a limited arena of group life and none of them supreme over all others.

Furthermore, most native North American peoples considered land to be an abstract commodity similar in kind to air or water or fire—something necessary for human survival but above personal ownership. While the notion of a group or a person's rights to use a certain piece of property was widespread, there was almost no corresponding idea of "title," or land owned exclusively and permanently by those who didn't directly work it. Concepts of accumulation varied widely, from those who held all nonpersonal items in common, to Northwest Coast "potlatch" societies like the Kwakiutl and Nootka where family status depended on formal giveaways of property—to the point of temporary impoverishment.

Armed conflict could occur between tribes, parts of tribes, or individuals for a variety of reasons, but usually the hostilities lasted no longer than a single season or encounter, and loss of life was minimal. As a rule, there was no insistence upon "total victory" or the complete annihilation of an enemy. Battles were fought for personal reasons—revenge, honor, or greed—and once these limited objectives had been achieved, the reason for a prolonged hostile action no longer existed. Last year's antagonists might be next year's hunting partners.

As competition with European invaders became increasingly intense, few indigenous societies mounted effective resistance, and those that did were soon vanquished. Not only had most Native American cultures by and large failed to invent effective weaponry or support standing military forces, they were almost immediately devastated by an unseen foe that, according to some demographers, wiped out 95 percent of the precontact population. A pandemic of diseases that had long existed in the Old World but never previously in the New—influenza, smallpox, measles, tuberculosis, and cholera prime among them—was inadvertently carried to the Western Hemisphere by the first European visitors, and in a matter of several generations virulent bacteria spread throughout the indigenous population. Often by the time the first Spanish or British arrived in the interior of the continents, most Indians were already dead, the straggling survivors traumatized and in despair. The lands that, in their naivete, some European chroniclers called "empty," were in fact only recently depleted of their previous inhabitants.

Early European explorers in America, continually confronted with the unexpected, soon began to seek the miraculous, as well as the familiar, in their journeys. They sent home reports of the Seven Golden Cities of Cibola, of fountains whose waters restored eternal youth, of warrior queens who rode upon giant armadillos. Feudal-type agricultural societies, like those of the Cherokee or Creek, were labeled "civilized," and those whose dress, customs, and lifestyles seemed most foreign were "savage."

Rather, they were simply "different," part of the mosaic of human possibility and potential, the laboratory of cultural experiment, that characterized the America of 1491. Collectively, its tribes offered legacies of tremendous contribution to the contemporary world, from cultivated crops (corn, beans, squash, tomatoes, potatoes, manioc) to political structures (models of representative government, gender equality) to philosophical approaches toward environmental conservation and peaceful coexistence. Many of the ideas and ideals first developed among its native peoples remain viable, sane options for a world that becomes, through technology, increasingly small, increasingly homogeneous. Diversity, that multifaceted reflection of human ingenuity, has become something of an endangered commodity—just when, perhaps, our stripped and exhausted planet needs it most.

Let us return, at last, to that hypothetical first meeting with which we began. In historical retrospect, is it unambiguously clear which group was "advanced," which was "primitive"? *Barbarous*—a term many Europeans and their Western Hemisphere descendants eventually used to describe Native American societies—is a relative, superficial designate, as it has been since the days when ancient Greeks judged the sophistication of foreigners on the basis of whether or not they grew beards. The Arawaks of the Caribbean never went to the moon or built a telephone, but they also never waged a war, never depleted the ozone layer with fluorocarbons. They were not saints, but neither were they devils. History remembers them most as beautiful, gentle, and impossible to enslave, not as conquerors or missionaries or industrialists.

Yes, the boys from the boat obviously fulfilled their ambitions: they "won." But in the long run, if we as a species delimit our imaginations, forget or lose touch with the thesaurus of our marvelously diversified past, did *we?*

In conclusion, the plaster stereotypes must be abandoned, not only because they are simplistic and ill informed, but more so because they are far less intellectu-

ally engaging, less interesting, less stimulating, and less
challenging than the living, breathing, often exasperating,
and always complicated reality.

Georgia Review
Fall 1992

THE GRASS STILL GROWS, THE RIVERS STILL FLOW: CONTEMPORARY NATIVE AMERICANS

Federal Indian policy, without precedent or parallel anywhere in the world, is unique and complex for two reasons. First, the United States inherited in 1776 and then developed over the next two hundred years a singular legal relationship with American Indians. Second, the formulation and implementation of Indian policy derives from often conflicting sources: ethnocentric preconceptions, misunderstandings, and expectations; racism; treaties; congressional acts and statutes; federal, state, and tribal court judgments; programs evolved within such federal bureaucracies as the erstwhile Department of War and the Departments of the Interior and of Health, Education and Welfare (now Health and Human Services); the findings of the Indian Claims Commission; and even the social theories inherent in the American and tribal constitutions.

Anyone attempting to grasp the practical realities of Indian rights, claims, and title continually encounters paradox, confusing historical digressions, and untruth. Over the years, there have been dozens of seemingly contradictory non-Indian strategies for dealing with scores of separate Native American tribes—each described in its relationship to the federal government by a distinct treaty with specific goals and objectives.

Even well-meaning and highly educated scholars are befuddled by a question like "What do Indians want?" and to those unfamiliar with the ethnohistorical context, tribal assertions of sovereignty, land title, and what amounts to privileged status appear presumptuous, capricious, and annoying. Ordinary citizens not versed in the subject may read a map issued by the American Automobile Association unaware that, whereas state and often even county and city boundaries are delineated, reservation lands are omitted altogether—though their status is patently superior to any of these geopolitical classifications.

CULTURAL BACKGROUND

Whatever explanation of origins one accepts—be it the independent and intentional creation of most mythic and religious systems or the more quantifiable archaeological record of migrating populations—it is a fact that the ancestors of those people who are today known as American Indians have continuously inhabited North America for upwards of thirty thousand years, and possibly for much longer.[1] Furthermore, it is currently estimated that in the fifteenth century at least four hundred identifiable tribal cultures flourished north of the Rio Grande. Their populations included a vast array of physical types, language stocks, and political configurations. Indigenous peoples thoroughly, if not densely, inhabited this continent, adapting to temperature extremes from subarctic to desert, exploiting environmental opportunities from deep-sea fishing to intensive cultivation of hybridized crops. However, for tens of centuries prior to Columbus's voyages, Native American societies were, for all practical purposes, isolated from, and out of touch with, groups in Europe, Asia, and Africa. Though most tribal communities maintained far-flung, dynamic sets of trade and cooperative (or hostile) relations with their neighbors, no single group was dominant over a majority of the others.

Naturally, the attitudes Native American peoples brought to their contacts with European settlers in the fifteenth, sixteenth, and seventeenth centuries were shaped by the fact that tribes had long existed in a plural world where foreign cultures were assumed to differ from one's own. This is not to imply that all cultures were regarded as equally good or worthwhile; like people the world over, each Native American probably felt confident that his or her people were the raison d'être of creation and the most enlightened,

1. Estimate of thirty thousand years per Thomas C. Patterson, *America's Past: A New World Archeology* (Glenview, Ill.: Scott, Foresman, 1973), pp. 22–27.

interesting, tasteful, and humane society imaginable. But no sense of superiority, however secure, could contradict the inescapable observation that other groups, whose ways and beliefs may have appeared odd and inexplicable, similarly felt themselves to be the center of the universe.

Little wonder, then, that for Native Americans, initial contact with strangers was a rather mundane occurrence. The historical record indicates that Europeans were often treated as neither more nor less exotic than other Indian groups. Native people seem not to have been either especially intimidated by, or impressed with, most of the novelties offered as trade goods; on the contrary, they regarded the transoceanic newcomers with a mixture of curiosity and concern: though Europeans looked like adults, they seemed to be perpetually on the brink of starving to death.[2]

The history of Europe prior to the Age of Exploration contrasted sharply with that of North America. For all of its tradition of interethnic strife and turmoil, Europe was, relative to the rest of the world, culturally fairly homogeneous. With only a handful of exceptions, every language spoken from Ireland to the Dardanelles derived from a single family, the Indo-European. Furthermore, virtually every man, woman, and child in the Europe of 1491 was cognizant of the basic tenets of a Christian belief system, already a millennium and a half old. Its Ten Commandments were the foundation and validation of both moral and common law;

2. See, for instance, Wilcomb E. Washburn, *The Indian in America* (New York: Harper & Row, 1975), pp. 67–110.

its papal leadership was international and powerful; and its official language, Latin, formed the lingua franca of learned and precise communication. Europeans formally professed belief in the same cosmology and the same divinity, and shared fundamental assumptions concerning the meaning of life itself. In large part, they were unaware that, except for Islam, alternative or viably competing worldviews existed.

Finally, certain important political and social conventions were widespread, particularly in the developed western quadrant of Europe. Males were nominally accorded dominance over females in every arena from marriage to property rights to power in both secular and spiritual spheres. Regardless of class, it was commonly accepted that one person or a small group of persons could govern the actions of many, that rulership was hereditary, and that allegiance or loyalty was owed an individual simply because of his rank or station. The concept of "nation-state" was beginning to emerge in many areas. Beyond familiar borders, the world was regarded either as a place infested with dragons, barbarians, and infidels or as not existing at all; in the popular superstition, the ocean and everything else simply stopped somewhere west of Portugal.

The lack of any strong traditions of cultural pluralism or respect for extracontinental societies left Europeans poorly equipped to deal with a "new" world, and initial reactions to the presence of populations whose looks, beliefs, or disposition did not fit the familiar molds ranged from awe to outrage.

The very humanity of indigenous peoples was seriously questioned by some, and quickly there developed the notion of a natural hierarchy of "civilization," with Europeans at its apex. As the contact frontier expanded, it was at first presumed and eventually mandated by European administrators that all native peoples would unremittingly exchange their own languages, mores, and beliefs for imported substitutes.

Hence, from its earliest beginnings, the politics of social interaction between indigenous and immigrant peoples in North America was based on a self-perpetuating confusion. Neither side knew what to make of the other, though each searched its own known and mythic histories for explanations or analogies on how to deal with unfathomable beings. Native societies invented a wide assortment of hypotheses to identify and predict the behavior of Europeans, ranging from the Nahuatl "Maybe it's Quetzalcóatl" idea, to the belief of the Southern Cheyenne that mountain men—the early European trappers in the Rockies—represented the return to the world of a class of long-departed excrement-eating clowns.[3]

Europeans postulated an equally dazzling set of improbable conjectures to explain the origin and true nature of the Indians they encountered. Puritans concluded that New England tribes were manifestations of the Devil, sent to test

3. I am indebted to Prof. Henrietta Whiteman, a Southern Cheyenne and former chairperson of the Department of Native American Studies at the University of Montana, for this tale.

their will for The Good.[4] Others concluded that they had at last met the wildman-of-the-forest bogey—well known in Teutonic folklore. Cultural evolution proponents speculated that Indians exhibited a level of social development antecedent to that of contemporary Europe, with retardation laid to any number of possible causes, from a separate and more recent creation to the stress imposed either by reduced mental capacity or restrictive environment. The idea went that it was just a matter of time until Indians caught up—as far as they were able. Still other theorists imagined that the natives had come from outer space, Phoenicia, or Atlantis.

In general, cultural interactions take place on at least two levels, the imaginary and the real. North America, at its most metaphorically dramatic, was the setting for the contest between The Indian and The White Man. In this realm of heightened meaning, races confront each other—individual people are nowhere to be found. One can only guess at the plethora of interpretations made by Indian societies to account for the appearance and behavior of The White Man, but there is certainly no lack of data to document the fantasies traditionally used by Europeans to predict Indian behaviors.

In a composite of the popular and persistent folk beliefs, The Indian was, among other things, macho, red skinned, stoic, taciturn, ecologically aware, and a great user of

4. Louis Hanke, *Aristotle and the American Indians: A Study in Race Prejudice in the Modern World* (London: Hollis & Carter, 1959), pp. 1–27.

metaphor. Or, he was cunning, mercurial, wild, lusty, and a collector of blond scalps. At nightfall he silhouetted himself in the sunset, or danced, shrieking, around his campfire. Before vanishing forever, he was prone to skulking, sneaking, and sundry other double dealings. Rather than defend himself, he "uprose"; rather than resist the occupation of his land, he "outbroke"; rather than defeat a foe, he "massacred." The one major commonality uniting beliefs about this schizophrenic persona was a general agreement that, whomever and whatever he was, for better or worse, he was no more. The Indian, by and large, was a motif embedded in the Americana of days gone by, not perceived as part of the present or future.[5]

CONTACT STRATEGIES

American Indians have been consistent in their foreign policy objectives for the past five hundred years: simple survival has been the ambition of every major tribal or pan-Indian campaign vis-à-vis Europeans and their cultural descendants. During some periods of history the threats to that goal have been obvious; during others, more subtle.

The lack of immunity Native Americans exhibited to many Old World diseases, for example, resulted in an aboriginal population devastated within a generation or two

5. For an excellent discussion of this topic, see Robert F. Berkhofer, Jr., *The White Man's Indian: Images of the American Indian from Columbus to the Present* (New York: Alfred A. Knopf, 1978).

after biological exposure, directly or indirectly, to germ-carrying Europeans. It is currently estimated that as many as nineteen out of twenty members of many Indian societies succumbed to smallpox, cholera, measles, or any number of other contagious infections not found in the Western Hemisphere prior to 1492.[6] The pandemic was so extensive and drastic that resident non-Indians forecast the complete extinction of native peoples.

Those few native people who, by genetic chance, survived the onslaught not only had to watch most of their families and friends perish but had to simultaneously attempt to hold together the fabric of their kin-based political systems, all the while trying to respond appropriately to a growing and increasingly aggressive invading force.

Intentional genocide, though documented in certain instances in North America, was not carried out with any prolonged determination.[7] This may have derived in part from the common assumption that natural attrition would solve the "Indian problem," rather than from any ethical sensibility. Many Americans in the eighteenth and nineteenth centuries viewed the prospect of Indian disappearance with a philosophic, if somewhat cold-blooded, equa-

6. For a full examination of the effects of Old World diseases on American Indians, see Alfred W. Crosby, Jr., *The Columbian Exchange: Biological and Cultural Consequences of 1492* (Westport, Conn.: Greenwood Publishing Co., 1972).

7. Wagner Stearn and Allen E. Stearn, *The Effect of Smallpox on the Destiny of the Amerindian* (Boston: Bruce Humphries, 1945), pp. 44–45; also, Robert M. Utley and Wilcomb E. Washburn, *The Indian Wars* (New York: Simon and Schuster, 1977).

nimity. "Irresistibly held in the vise of evolution, [Indians] filled their niche in destiny and departed to their happy hunting ground."[8]

Though the indigenous precontact population was reduced from an estimated 12–15 million north of the Rio Grande in 1491 to a low of 210,000 in the 1910 census, a significant number of Indians did survive to pass on their chance predisposition to immunity to their offspring.[9] Each succeeding generation experienced relatively fewer fatalities as a result of disease;[10] and today, with an estimated aggregate population approaching two million nationally, Indians constitute one of the fastest growing ethnic groups in the United States. However, the expectation of their en masse demise profoundly affected the nature of early European perceptions of and official dealings with Indians, and had a lasting impact, on the provisions and language of the accords that established legal relationships between Indians and Europeans—and by extension on all consequences that derived from their models.

In actual, as opposed to hypothetical, culture contact

8. Eva A. Speare, *The Indians of New Hampshire* (Littleton, N.H.: Chester Printing Co., 1936).

9. For a thorough discussion of the methodology of Native American demographic estimation, see Henry Dobyns, "Estimating Aboriginal American Population: An Appraisal of Techniques with a New Hemispheric Estimate," *Current Anthropology* 7 (1966): 395–416; also, Wilbur R. Jacobs, "The Tip of the Iceberg: Pre-Columbian Indian Demography and Some Implications for Revisionism," *William and Mary Quarterly* 31 (1974): 123–132.

10. Indians still contract diseases such as tuberculosis and cholera at a disproportionately high rate.

situations, all parties endeavor to reach accords that regulate and define their eventual as well as their contemporary modes of interaction. Generally, there is a period of mutual testing and appraisal before understandings are established, then one of two possible outcomes prevails: either the two (or more) groups will coexist (or expect to coexist) in a relatively equitable power relationship, or they will settle into a dominant–subordinate hierarchy.

By the time a substantial number of British colonists arrived in North America, several major issues had already been settled. After years of debate among Spanish intellectuals, the pope had ruled with finality that Indians did, in fact, have souls and therefore were true human beings.[11] It was also evident that there were sufficient numbers of Indians to make a precipitous European conquest untenable. Finally, international law (i.e., the rules of mutual conduct shared by European nations) now expanded to include stipulations concerning "right of discovery." The minimum interpretation of this doctrine suggested that a superior legal jurisdiction fell to the European nation first landing on and officially claiming territory not formerly held by other European powers. As it came to be commonly understood, right of discovery awarded to that specific European nation the exclusive authority to negotiate with the native inhabi-

11. Wilcomb Washburn, *Red Man's Land/White Man's Law: A Study of the Past and Present Status of the American Indian* (New York: Charles Scribner's Sons, 1971), p. 10.

tants for the extinguishment of their claim and the transfer of absolute ownership to itself. This procedure enabled various exploring European nations to "legally" divide among themselves, at least in theory, dominion over the non-European world. If through conquest or cession one European nation succeeded the other in the control of a land area, right of discovery was transferred along with other prerogatives.[12]

During the sixteenth and seventeenth centuries, Europeans had no clear idea of either the extent of the North American continent or its total aboriginal population, but in word, at least, the British in particular recognized the prior sovereignty of any large Indian tribes they encountered, conceding that the indigenous populace had an inherent authority both to govern themselves and to claim possession of their land on the basis of "time immemorial" use and occupancy. Such claim could be quit only by high-level negotiations or formal warfare on a national level.

As the British understood it, an Indian treaty, aside from its other functions, ratified a cession of native territory in exchange for a clear and abiding recognition that Indians retained title to any portion of their formerly claimed lands that was not part of the deal. The British crown would own outright (with the power to assign and dispense at will) only

12. For a full discussion of all aspects of American Indian law, see Monroe E. Price, *Law and the American Indian: Readings, Notes and Cases* (Indianapolis: Bobbs-Merrill, 1973).

those lands from which aboriginal claim was explicitly withdrawn.

LEGAL PRECEDENTS

Though most Indian tribes had no prior concept absolutely parallel to the European idea of land title, they were quick to learn, and entered into hundreds of treaty negotiations (including some exclusively among themselves), ultimately ceding tenure to a large portion of their erstwhile lands. They did so for two major reasons: for one, their populations had been decimated by disease, and for another, the British (and to a lesser degree, the French) offered strong positive (and negative) inducements for cooperation. In exchange for their surplus hunting grounds, tribes were promised annuities in money and trade goods, health and education benefits, and, most important, the security of a permanently uncontested land base where they could live in peace and independence "as long as the waters flow and as long as the grasses grow." Such perpetuity clauses, unusual in international negotiations Europeans carried out among themselves, were routinely made part of promises made to Indians, possibly because European signatories did not expect the descendants of their native counterparts to survive long enough to reap the benefits.

In certain respects, what those first treaties actually stipulated—all were routinely violated by European nations—

matters less than the fact that they were made at all. The very act of treaty-making implied a European recognition of nationhood to the native party prior to its contact with Europe and, as a result, established a legal parity in sovereignty between aboriginal and European states.[13] This status, once in place, did not diminish when the relative power balance of the two sides shifted, nor did it erode with the passage of time. "Age has not invalidated the treaties any more than it has invalidated the Constitution which recognizes them as 'the supreme law of the land.' Nor does breach or violation of treaties nullify them any more than does the act of committing a crime nullify the law that forbids that crime."[14]

In spite of the repeated affirmations of native sovereignty by U.S. law, many Americans believe that land was "given" to Indians by the federal government. Just the opposite was the case: when internationally recognized tribal governments initially entered into treaties with the United States, they conferred *their* legitimacy to the fledgling nation.

The recognition of Indian tribes as sovereignties, albeit somewhat regulated in their external international affairs,

13. See, for instance, Imre Sutton, *Indian Land Tenure: Bibliographic Essays and a Guide to the Literature* (New York: Clearwater Publishing Co., 1975), pp. 23–44.
14. Institute for the Development of Indian Law, *Old Problems—Present Issues: Nine Essays on American Indian Law* (Washington, D.C.: Institute for the Development of Indian Law, 1979), p. 7.

persisted after the American Revolution. The Constitution itself makes particular note of the special relationship that existed between the new nation and Native American states. Article 1, Section 8, stipulates that "the Congress shall have power . . . to regulate commerce with foreign nations, among the several states, and with Indian tribes." Indian tribes are the only groups specifically so identified in the document. "Persons unfamiliar with Indian law mistake this distinction as one of a racial nature. Such is not the case. Indian tribes are distinct political entities—governments with executive, legislative and judicial powers."[15]

In 1790 the Congress further clarified its understanding of its interactive role toward native nations. The Trade and Intercourse Act of that year stated that only the federal government (by virtue of its sovereignty) and not states (because they were not sufficiently sovereign) may treat with Indian nations in the extinguishment of their aboriginal land claims. In other words, tribal lands may pass out of Indian hands only when the federal government, as an equivalent sovereign, is party to the transaction.

In the case of *Cherokee Nation* v. *Georgia* (1831), the Supreme Court added an opinion of its own. Chief Justice John Marshall wrote that the Cherokee reservation existed as a "domestic, dependent nation," having a special relationship to the United States. This ruling was made even more explicit in *Worcester* v. *Georgia* (1832), when Marshall

15. Ibid., p. 1.

termed the same reservation a "distinct, independent, political community." These definitions were by extension applicable to all other federally recognized reservations, and today remain among the fundamental principles guiding U.S. Indian law.

From the point of view of the tribes, their own legal and political situation was always perfectly clear. "Nationhood" may have initially been a foreign concept, but, from the first, tribes took seriously their compacts both with European powers and later with the American government. Without exception, they fulfilled to the letter all obligations incurred under these agreements, granting lands according to the terms of their respective treaties, and furthermore, they were well acquainted with the promised terms of payment.[16] Recent testimony shows that some tribes have maintained, through meticulous oral history, a complete inventory of these agreements, including the detailed accounts of all discussions surrounding their negotiations.[17] Tribes believe that they paid dearly in lands and opportunities to reserve for themselves and their descendants the rights of self-government, freedom of choice and expression within their own territories, plus any additionally noted compensations. Indian governments may have lacked, during the difficult period of the past 150 years,

16. Russell L. Barsh and James Y. Henderson, *The Road: Indian Tribes and Political Liberty* (Berkeley: University of California Press, 1980), p. 286.
17. For a detailed case study of oral historical testimony, see Roxanne Dunbar Ortiz (ed.), *The Great Sioux Nation: Sitting in Judgment on America* (Berkeley: Moon Books, 1977).

the military or political clout to protect their rights when
violated or ignored, but they never forgot what those rights
properly were.

MODERN CHALLENGES

By 1871, when the treaty-making process formally came
to an end,[18] virtually all tribes in the area that was to
become the forty-eight contiguous states had reached some
form of official accord with the American government, and
most were established on reservations. Almost immediately
thereafter—when Indians chose not to assimilate—people
or groups who called themselves "friends of the Indian"
began to interpret the status of Indian lands in a manner
antithetical to the law, treating reservations as if they were
intended as mere holding grounds where residents could be
controlled while subjected to the indoctrinations of missionaries and agents.[19] The Lake Mohonk Conference, held
in upstate New York by one such group, went so far as to
proclaim, "The organization of the Indian tribes is, and has
been, one of the most serious hindrances to the advancement of the Indian toward civilization, and . . . every effort

18. Congress, in an obscure rider to the Indian Appropriations Bill (U.S.
Statutes at Large. 16:566, March 3, 1871), outlawed further treaty-making
with Indian tribes. Thereafter, reservations were created by executive order;
see "Tribal Property Interests in Executive Order Reservations: A
Compensable Indian Right," *Yale Law Review* 69 (1960): 627–642.

19. See Robert A. Trennert, Jr., *Alternative to Extinction: Federal Indian
Policy and the Beginnings of the Reservation System, 1845–51* (Philadelphia:
Temple University Press, 1975).

should be made to secure the disintegration of all tribal organizations. . . . To accomplish this result the Government should . . . cease to recognize Indians as political bodies or organized tribes."[20]

Among the proponents for the abrogation of treaty promises was a writer who adopted a benevolent (if wrongheaded) interest in Indians in much the same manner that Harriet Beecher Stowe had used her writings to affect national opinion toward African Americans.

As she neared her fiftieth birthday, Helen Hunt Jackson was a well-established figure on the American literary scene. She was independent, somewhat overbearing, had a "distaste for associates in whom she was not interested," and was considered odd by her Colorado neighbors because she refused to attend church and would not sleep in a bed until the head was turned to the north.[21] She was professionally successful in an era when few women received income from their labors, and she was ambitious.

On a chilly November afternoon in 1879, Jackson visited Boston and happened to attend a presentation by Standing Bear, a sixty-one-year-old chief; Bright Eyes (Susette LaFlesche); and other Indians on tour with the tragic story of the Ponca tribe and its frustrating attempts

20. *Second Annual Address to the Public of the Lake Mohonk Conference* (Philadelphia: Indian Rights Association, 1884), pp. 6–7.
21. Quote is from Susan Coolidge's Introduction to *Ramona* (Boston: Little, Brown, 1900), pp. xix–xx.

to avoid deportation from its aboriginal territories in Nebraska to a reservation in Oklahoma. Theirs was an emotional program, full of wrenching speeches identifying outrageous injustice and overt racism, and Jackson was deeply moved. She became fueled with a consuming indignation that affected and directed the work she would do for the rest of her life. "I have now done, I believe," she wrote to a friend during this period, "the last of the things I have said I never would do. I have become what I have said a thousand times was the most odious thing in the world, 'a woman with a hobby.' But I cannot help it. I cannot think of anything else from night to morning and from morning to night."[22]

Jackson was an unlikely reformer. She had remained steadfastly uninterested in temperance and the idea of Negro equality with whites, and had no sympathy with the suffrage movement. In letters from her first trip to California, she had described Indians as "loathsome," "abject," and "hideous."[23] But in her empathy with the Ponca cause she apparently underwent a complete transformation. Within a month she was engaged in a heated public exchange with Secretary of the Interior Carl Schurz, a man she described as a "blockhead" because he opposed the collection of funds for a Ponca court defense. She

22. Ruth Odell, *Helen Hunt Jackson* (New York, 1939), p. 155.
23. Helen Jackson and Abbot Kinney, *Report on the Condition and Needs of the Mission Indians of California* (Washington: Government Printing Office, 1883), pp. 6–7.

became a one-person letter-writing campaign, taking on all comers, from the Denver *Rocky Mountain News* and *Harper's* to the *New York Times* and the *Christian Advocate*. She immersed herself in research during an intensive six-month period at the Astor Library in New York City, and amassed a selective record of government double dealings toward various tribes—Utes, Cheyennes, Nez Percés, Delawares, Cherokees, Sioux, as well as Poncas—which she collected and published as *A Century of Dishonor* (1881).

Though unimpressive either as history or as literature, the book was important in several respects. In the wake of the defeat and destruction of the 7th Cavalry by the Sioux and Cheyenne in 1876, national sentiment toward Indians was quite antagonistic; *A Century of Dishonor* offered a strikingly different perspective in which Native Americans were victims, not aggressors. Helen Hunt Jackson was popular, uncontroversial, and even beloved by many. Her name had not heretofore been connected with any political party or position, and that very fact gave her credibility. She was an educated woman of the mainstream, and when she was upset, readers noticed. Moreover, she had access to the national media in a way few other writers could command, and she wrote prose that was, in its context, gripping, emotional, and appealing. Most important, she was fiercely sincere in her beliefs, and sent at her own expense a copy of *A Century of Dishonor* to each member of Congress. In taking up the Indian cause, she preceded a growing number of 1880s' East Coast liberal reformers who lobbied throughout the decade for Indian policy reform, especially in respect to the issue of land ownership and to the advocacy for Indian citizenship.

Following publication of her book, Jackson went first to Europe for a rest and then to California to compose a series of sketches for *Century* magazine. She was especially interested in the conflict between Hispanic colonial society and the increasing flow of American immigrants to the area, but she also made attempts to stop at small Indian communities. In 1883 President Chester Arthur appointed her a commissioner of Indian Affairs, with the assignment of formally reporting on the conditions of California's Mission Indians. Traveling by a two-horse, double-seated carriage with her fellow commissioner, Abbot Kinney, she journeyed throughout the Santa Barbara–Los Angeles–San Diego corridor collecting information and occasionally intervening on behalf of an Indian whom she felt was being cheated of legitimate land rights.

At this time she was growing heavier (slightly over 150 pounds though under five feet, three inches tall) but seemed indefatigable. She must have made an impressive appearance, since she always wore a hat composed of the entire head of a large grey owl. This bird, which, unbeknownst to her, symbolized death to a number of tribes she visited, intimidated many of those with whom she wished to converse.

The results of Jackson and Kinney's investigations appeared as the *Report on the Condition and Needs of the*

Mission Indians of California (1883), issued by the Government Printing Office. The commissioners called for women teachers, itinerant physicians, free legal aid, and justice for Indians under the law. Their brief fourteen-page document, supplemented with an additional twenty pages of appendices, was more focused and fact-based than *A Century of Dishonor,* but no less strong an indictment of federal disregard.

> Our Government received by the treaty of Guadalupe Hidalgo a legacy of a singularly helpless race in a singularly anomalous position. It would have been very difficult, even at the outset, to devise practicable methods of dealing justly with these people, and preserving to them their rights. But with every year of our neglect the difficulties have increased and the wrongs have been multiplied, until now it is, humanly speaking, impossible to render to them full measure of justice. All that is left in our power is to make them some atonement. . . . That drunkenness, gambling, and other immoralities are sadly prevalent among them, cannot be denied; but the only wonder is that so many remain honest and virtuous under conditions which make practically null and void for them, most of the motives which keep white men honest and virtuous.[24]

24. Coolidge, Introduction to *Ramona,* pp. xx–xxi.

It did not take long for the federal government to respond. Sen. Henry Dawes, a former officer of the Indian Rights Association of Philadelphia, proposed legislation that would allot the reservations "in severalty," assigning to each male head of household, unmarried woman, and orphaned child a discrete plot of land to "prove" for a period of twenty years or more, after which they might petition to become U.S. citizens. Under the provisions of the General Allotment Act (also called the Dawes Act) of 1887, the president was empowered to unilaterally abrogate existing international agreements with Indian tribes.[25] Each Indian allottee was granted a share or a portion of a share, usually not exceeding 160 acres; according to this schedule, there was considerably more remaining Indian land than there were Indians to whom to distribute it (according to the preassigned average schedules). Thus, in one stroke of the pen, almost one-half of all the lands controlled by Indians in 1885 were declared "surplus" and passed out of native control.[26] Over the next forty-five years during which the act was in force, substantially more land was lost (ninety million acres, or two-thirds of the former land base, all together) because of theft, chicanery, sale, or fraud.

It is undoubtedly true that some of the people who spon-

25. D. S. Otis, *The Dawes Act and the Allotment of Indian Lands,* Francis Paul Prucha (ed.) (Norman, Okla.: University of Oklahoma Press, 1973), pp. 5–6.
26. Arrell Morgan Gibson, *The American Indian: Prehistory to the Present* (Lexington, Mass.: D.C. Heath and Co., 1980), pp. 500–503.

sored and supported the Dawes policy sincerely believed that they were acting in the best interests of Indians; however, the results were disastrous for the supposed beneficiaries. In 1928 the Institute for Government Research (Brookings Institution) published *The Problem of Indian Administration*—popularly known as the Meriam Report (after the project's director, Lewis Meriam)—detailing the economic and social conditions of the Indians as they were almost fifty years after the passage of the allotment act. The report found "deplorable" conditions prevalent in almost every Indian settlement in the country, and concluded that the federal government's "allotment in severalty" and "Americanization" programs were failures. It recommended, among other things, increased appropriations for Indian health and education, cessation of allotments, and more effective protection for Indians' property. In short, it discouraged forced assimilation as a policy, and urged that Indians be provided the wherewithal to exist in American society without being bludgeoned into it.

President Franklin Roosevelt's appointment of John Collier, a cultural anthropologist, to the position of commissioner of Indian Affairs furthered such impulses in the next decade. Collier's proposal for a sweeping set of reforms was embodied in the Indian Reorganization Act of 1934. This legislation recognized afresh the right of Indian tribes to remain distinct functioning political entities, and reaffirmed the special trust relationship between the American and tribal governments. Funds were allocated for Indians to repurchase some of the lands lost through allotment, and reservations were strongly urged to design and enact tribal constitutions based on the U.S. model. Though some religious and assimilationist groups opposed this "return to tribalism," the vast majority of Indians hailed aspects of the act as an overdue reinstitution of the legal relationship that had formerly existed between the United States and Indian tribes.[27]

This "New Deal for Indians" didn't last long. Within two decades, House Concurrent Resolution 108 (1953) proclaimed that it was the intent of the United States to abolish federal supervision over the tribes as soon as possible. With this resolution, the government began the process of "termination"—the cynical, unilateral cancellation of its treaty responsibilities.

The language of Resolution 108 was as euphemistic as had been that of the Allotment Act some sixty-six years before. It talked of giving Indians "equal rights" and of "freeing" them from "federal supervision and control and from all the disabilities and limitations specifically applicable to Indians"—as if no one realized that in equalizing rights, Indians were forfeiting those very advantages for which their ancestors had exchanged most of North

27. For a discussion of some of the problems of conception and implementation of the Indian Reorganization Act, see Angie Debo, *A History of the Indians of the United States* (Norman, Okla.: University of Oklahoma Press, 1970), pp. 339–342.

America. Native Americans would henceforth be subject to state taxes and to state fishing and hunting laws, and would lose federal protection over their lands and the right to self-governing status.

Passage of this resolution was quickly followed by the adoption of Public Law 280 (1953), which extended state jurisdiction over criminal offenses committed by or against Indians and over specified parts of "Indian Country." Obviously the Congress no longer construed reservations as Justice Marshall's "distinct, independent, political communities." In fact, the General Allotment Act, House Concurrent Resolution 108, and Public Law 280 had all passed by simple voice vote.

RECENT DEVELOPMENTS

The only good thing that can be said about the termination policy is that it proved to be socially and economically unfeasible faster than it could be implemented on a large scale, and therefore did not directly harm the vast majority of reservation people.[28] However, its attack on the precept of tribal sovereignty and integrity, coming so close on the heels of the resumption of that recognition in the Indian Reorganization Act, alerted tribes that they must act con-

28. Of the larger reservations, only the Menominee and the Klamath were actually terminated. For a discussion of the history of the policy in the former case, see Deborah Shames (ed.), *Freedom with Reservations* (Madison, Wisc.: National Committee to Save the Menominee People and Forests, 1972).

scientiously and cautiously if they were to protect their inherited constitutional rights.

Jurist Felix Cohen articulated the legal and political basis for tribal autonomy when he wrote:

> 1. An Indian tribe possesses, in the first instance, all the powers of any sovereign state.
>
> 2. Conquest renders the tribe subject to the legislative power of the United States, and in substance, terminated the external powers of sovereignty of the tribe . . . but does not by itself affect the internal sovereignty of the tribe. . . .
>
> 3. These powers are subject to qualification by treaties and by express legislation of Congress, but, save as thus expressly qualified, full powers of internal sovereignty are vested in the Indian tribes and in their duly constituted organs of government.[29]

Indian tribes have not carried on "external powers of sovereignty"—that is, conducted international relations except with the United States—since the War of 1812.[30] Although Congress asserts plenary (i.e., overriding) author-

29. Felix Cohen, *Handbook of Federal Indian Law* 1971 (Washington, D.C.: U.S. Government Printing Office, 1958), p. 123.

30. Some tribes or confederacies (e.g., Hopi and Iroquois) have on occasion demonstrated their conviction that they retain some of the prerogatives of external sovereignty through acts such as separate declaration of war on the Axis powers in 1941 and the issuance of tribal passports for certain types of international travel. The latter have, in recent years, been accepted by at least some European nations.

ity in dealing with Indian tribes, the tribes retain their authority unless legislation has expressly denied it. These as yet unrestrained powers constitute "residual authority."

Furthermore, the United States, by virtue of its suzerainty over tribes, is obliged to certain responsibilities. These obligations fall into three broad areas: (1) protection of Indian trust property; (2) protection of the Indian right to self-government; and (3) provision of social, medical, and educational services for survival and advancement of the Indian tribes.[31]

The Native American appointees on the American Indian Policy Review Commission stated unambiguously at the conclusion of their *Final Report* (1977) that "there are two elements essential to the ability of all Indian tribes to progress towards economic development and eventual self-sufficiency: self-government, i.e., sovereignty, and the trust relationship."[32]

Indeed, from the earliest formal compacts between the United States and Indian tribes, it's been clear that legally at least some of the prerogatives available exclusively to nations apply for Indians. The Cherokee treaty of Hopewell (1785), for instance, stipulated: "If any citizen of the United States, or other person not being an Indian, shall attempt to settle on any of the land . . . hereby allotted to the Indians . . . such person shall forfeit the protection of the

31. Institute for the Development of Indian Law, *Old Problems*, p. 3.
32. American Indian Policy Review Commission, *Final Report*, vol. 1 (Washington, D.C.: U.S. Government Printing Office, 1977), p. 622.

United States, and the Indians may punish him or not as they please."[33]

Furthermore, a variety of Supreme Court decisions, both early[34] and more recently,[35] have upheld the concept that tribal authority naturally prevails over that of surrounding or contiguous states.

To this day, Indian tribes have general powers to

1) make laws governing the conduct of persons, including non-Indians, in Indian country;

2) establish bodies such as tribal police and courts to enforce the law and administer justice;

3) exclude or remove nonmembers from the reservation for cause; and

4) regulate hunting and fishing, land use, and environmental protection.[36]

When Congress voted in 1924 to make all Indians citizens of the United States, it specifically noted that "the granting of such citizenship shall not in any manner impair or otherwise affect the right of any Indian to tribal or other property." But on a day-to-day basis, did Indians thereafter

33. Charles Kappler (ed.), "Treaty of Hopewell with the Cherokees, 1785," in *Indian Affairs: Laws and Treaties*, vol. 2, pp. 8–11. The treaty then goes on to limit that very authority: "If any Indian   or person residing among them, or who shall take refuge in their nation, shall commit a . . . capital crime . . . [the tribe] shall be bound to deliver him . . . up to be punished according to the ordinances of the United States."

34. *Cherokee Nation* v. *Georgia, Worcester* v. *Georgia, Holden* v. *Joy*.

35. *McClanahan* v. *Arizona Tax Commission, Fischee* v. *District Court*.

36. Institute for the Development of Indian Law, *Old Problems*, p. 5.

operate primarily under the laws of the United States or those of their home reservation?

As always in Indian law, one must search first for historic judicial decisions as precedents. *Talton* v. *Mayes* (1896) held that federal courts have no authority to review Indian court convictions by the writ of habeas corpus; in other words, the tribe's right to punish offenses is not limited by the Fifth Amendment, because the Bill of Rights applies only to federal government actions, and Indian tribes are not federal powers. *Native American Church* v. *Navajo Tribe* (1959) simply ruled that the First Amendment guarantee of free exercise of religion was not binding over the Navajo tribe, nor by analogy could it extend to any other functioning tribal government. The Fourteenth Amendment's due process provision is also nonapplicable, because Indian tribes are not states. They have a status higher than that of states.

In terms of the legislative branch, the Indian Civil Rights Act of 1968 imposes on tribal governments the guarantee of specific and slightly modified individual rights derived from the First, Fourth, Fifth, Sixth, Eighth, and Eleventh Amendments to the Constitution. The Indian Self-Determination Act of 1975 recognizes the right of Indians to "control their relationships both among themselves and with non-Indian governments, organizations and persons," and goes on to observe that "the prolonged Federal domination of Indian service programs has served to retard rather than enhance the progress of Indian people and their communities."

A 1978 Supreme Court decision, *Santa Clara Pueblo* v. *Martinez*, limits the circumstances in which an individual can bring suit against a tribal government, and affirms the sovereignty of such a government. In that ruling, it was stated that "in addition to the [Indian Civil Rights Act's] objective of strengthening the position of the individual tribal members vis-à-vis the tribe, Congress also intended to promote the well-established federal policy of furthering Indian self-government."

In *Oliphant* v. *Suquamish* (1978), the Supreme Court found that tribal courts have no criminal jurisdiction over non-Indians when they commit crimes on reservation lands, yet in a related decision in the same year, it ruled that "Indian tribes still possess those aspects of sovereignty not withdrawn by treaty or statute, or by implication as a necessary result of their dependent status."[37] Legal critics Russell Barsh and James Henderson point out that *Oliphant*'s theory of power reaches much higher. According to one federal district court, tribes now lack civil jurisdiction over non-Indians and non-Indian firms as well, frustrating zoning, environmental regulation, and the enforcement of public health and safety standards on reservations.[38] Without the power to protect reservation residents, tribes cannot maintain political legitimacy.

37. *U.S.* v. *Wheeler*, 98. S. Ct. 1079, 1086 (1978).
38. Russell Barsh and James Y. Henderson, "The Betrayal: *Oliphant* v. *Suquamish* Indian Tribe and the Hunting of the Snark," *Minnesota Law Review* 63 (4) (April 1979): 609–637.

CONTEMPORARY CIVIL RIGHTS

Where, then, do congressional and judicial decisions of the past twenty years, not to mention the previous two hundred, leave Indians? There are any number of ways to interpret the Indian Civil Rights Act (1968) as it is reflected in the major Supreme Court decisions of *Santa Clara Pueblo* and *Oliphant.* From a strictly assimilationist perspective, the act, together with the Major Crimes Act (1885), makes "drastic inroads on the judicial sovereignty of the tribes."[39] According to this line of thought, tribal courts are too expensive and—despite the historical rationale for special status—inequitable, in that they separate one ethnic population from the general court system of the United States.

A less radical view regards the Indian Civil Rights Act as limiting, rather than obliterating, tribal sovereignty. "The answer lies in tying tribal power to its purpose," this argument goes. "Thus limited, the exercise of tribal power would have no impact on non-members, yet such exercise would be unfettered by congressional supervision within its proper sphere."[40] It is proper, then, that tribes have jurisdiction over members (*Santa Clara Pueblo*) but not over nonmembers (*Oliphant*).

An even more liberal interpretation emphasizes the protectorate relationship, "whereby tribes retain their political

39. Samuel J. Brakel, *American Indian Tribal Courts: The Costs of Separate Justice* (Washington: American Bar Foundation, 1978), p. 8.

40. Frederick J. Martone, "Of Power and Purpose," *Notre Dame Lawyer* 54 (5) (June 1979): 831.

independence except as limited by express provisions in the federal statutes, treaties or by [inherent] restraints"[41] between the federal government and the tribes. Proponents believe that the rights specified in the Indian Civil Rights Act should be applied and interpreted in the same manner as those outlined in the Bill of Rights.[42] Any disputes between the two should be resolved by Congress or by flexible standards determined by the courts.

Finally, the Indian Civil Rights Act places limits on the power of Indian governments by guaranteeing certain individual rights to all persons within tribal jurisdiction. Nonetheless, the Supreme Court has asserted that these limitations were intended to strike a balance with, and not to override, the well-established federal policy of further Indian self-government.[43]

This leads to another, more positive interpretation of the act: in a perverse way, by limiting tribal sovereignty, Congress reaffirmed its existence.[44] Though nontribal members are excluded from jurisdiction by *Oliphant*, the residual authority of Indian courts to try civil actions exclusively within their domain persists, as upheld in

41. Robert G. McCoy, "The Doctrine of Tribal Sovereignty: Accommodating Tribal, State, and Federal Interests," *Harvard Civil Rights, Civil Liberties Law Review* 13 (2) (Spring 1978): 376.

42. Ivan B. Rubin, "Federal Indian Law: Criminal Jurisdiction in Indian Country," *Annual Survey of American Law* (New York University School of Law) 3 (1977): 517–533.

43. McCoy, "Doctrine of Tribal Sovereignty," p. 394.

44. Keith M. Werhan, "The Sovereignty of Indian Tribes: A Reclamation and Strengthening in the 1970's," *Notre Dame Lawyer* 54 (1) (October 1978): 5–26.

Santa Clara Pueblo. It would seem by this standard that a continuing refinement of the meaning of tribal sovereignty, and not a total usurpation of it, is under way. Alvin Ziontz, an attorney specializing in federal Indian law, observes:

> The Indian Civil Rights Act remains, of course, an imposition of values of the dominant American culture which sharply conflicts with the tradition of many tribes. But *Martinez* v. *Santa Clara Pueblo* allows the tribes to implement the Indian Civil Rights Act in a manner which preserves their ability to decide difficult questions in accordance with tribal values, and more importantly, in a manner consistent with tribal sovereignty.[45]

THE COURTS, INDIANS, AND OTHER AMERICANS

A greater degree of judicial activity regarding Indians has taken place within the past twenty years than in any previous equivalent period, and a good part of the reason for this explosion in litigation must be due to the greater awareness within the Indian community, not only of the rights that proceed from treaties and legal precedents, but of the means by which to articulate and assert claims and to protect rights in court. There has been a dramatic

45. Alvin J. Ziontz, "After Martinez: Civil Rights Under Tribal Government," *University of California at Davis Law Review* 12 (March 1979): 35.

increase in the number of Native American attorneys and of non-Indian lawyers specializing in Indian law. And national Indian legal and advocacy organizations, such as the Native American Rights Fund, the National Indian Youth Council, the Institute for the Development of Indian Law, and the Association of American Indian Affairs, have pressed cases and research of all types.

American Indians constitute under 1 percent of the American population, but when they challenge or are victorious in court over larger and more economically powerful groups, they soon cease to be regarded as emblems of nobility. Their erstwhile non-Indian sympathizers seem positively irate when they realize that Indians still expect treaties made long ago to apply, and are more chagrined still when the courts agree. Sam Deloria, director of the American Indian Law Center at the University of New Mexico, has noted that benevolent Indian policy runs in cycles, peaking when competition between Indians and other Americans is low and dipping when it is high.

During the 1960s, Indians in the abstract were regarded fondly by the general public. A spate of "plight" books, capped by Dee Brown's *Bury My Heart at Wounded Knee,* an appealing but somewhat simplistic and one-sided recounting of Indian history, had the country beating its collective breast for past sins toward the noble Red Man, and the quasi-mystical writings of Carlos Castaneda convinced sundry hippies and New Agers that Indians were fashionable. Bloomingdale's department store in New York City stocked and sold stylish clothing festooned with quantities of beads and feathers, and Native American was chic. The love-in ended abruptly, however, when it became clear that contemporary Indians were not content to play the role of designer label.

By the late 1960s, a new generation of young Indian people had grown up in cities, at the same time maintaining their ties to reservation communities. As they reached adulthood, they organized pan-Indian activist associations such as the Indians of All Tribes and the American Indian Movement. The former group occupied and demanded title to Alcatraz Island; the latter took possession first of the Bureau of Indian Affairs headquarters in Washington (which they termed the "Native American Embassy") and then the hamlet of Wounded Knee, South Dakota. Both actions, though symbolically powerful in and of themselves, were legally grounded in Indian interpretations of the provisions granted to tribes under existing treaties, and were carried out to call attention to the fact that the U.S. government was not living up to its part of these bargains.

At the same time, those same treaties were being tested and upheld in important court cases and congressional actions. Tracts of lands of various magnitudes, ranging from the relatively small Taos Blue Lake to the massive forty million acres of the Alaska Native Claims Settlement Act, were returned to native peoples on the basis of their treaty or aboriginal rights. The Menominee Reservation in Wisconsin, terminated in response to House Concurrent

Resolution 108, was restored. Other significant land claims cases were advanced, with varying degrees of success, in Maine, Massachusetts, New York, Rhode Island, Connecticut, and South Carolina.

In one of the most famous, controversial, and far-reaching decisions of the 1970s, *U.S.* v. *Washington* (1974), Judge Boldt of the 9th Circuit Federal Court affirmed the inherent superiority of treaty rights over the privileges of ordinary citizens, and maintained that the state could regulate treaty-protected fishing only if it could be shown that it could not obtain the desired ends of conservation by any other means.[46] In this historic case, later substantially upheld by the Supreme Court in *Washington* v. *Washington State Fishing Vessel Association,* the Court decided that treaties gave the tribes the right to take between 45 and 50 percent of the total amount of harvestable fish in the state.[47]

In the area of water rights, some fifty Indian suits have recently been filed in the West and Southwest.[48] These assert, largely on the basis of the *Winters* v. *U.S.* (1908) decision, that treaties guarantee the tribes as much water as it takes "to make their reservations flourish," and that

46. See American Friends Service Committee, *Uncommon Controversy: Fishing Rights of the Muckleshoot, Puyallup and Nisqually Indians* (Seattle: University of Washington Press, 1970).

47. "*Washington* v. *Washington State Commercial Passenger Fishing Vessel Association,*" *U.S. Law Week* 47 (50) (July 2, 1979).

48. For an excellent summary article on this issue of water rights, see M. C. Nelson, *The Winters Doctrine: 70 Years of Application of "Reserved" Water Rights to Indian Reservations,* Arid Lands Research Paper no. 9 (Tucson: University of Arizona Press, 1977), NTIS PB U.S. 564 (1908).

they have prior claim on the use of any waters that lay under, flow by, or pass through their territories. The so-called Winters Doctrine gives tribes "command of the lands and waters"—control of all their beneficial use whether kept for hunting, for grazing herds of stock, or turned to agriculture or other forms of development. In the system of Western water law, where first users have prior rights, Indian tribes, by virtue of their ownership of the lands from time immemorial or because the establishment of a reservation generally predated any contiguous permanent settlement, have a first use that makes their water rights paramount over those of all other users. In areas where tribes, such as the Pueblo, hold unextinguished aboriginal land title on lands where waters were used in precontact times to support agriculture (e.g., through irrigation), there are "concomitant appurtenant unextinguished aboriginal" water rights that supersede all others.

Needless to say, this list of successfully pursued claims has won Indians few friends among those non-Indian citizens most directly competitive with them on a local or regional level. Backlash movements have sprung up in a number of states, many of them part of an organization ironically titled the Interstate Congress for Equal Rights and Responsibilities. As in the past, equalization of Indian rights translates to mean reduction of Indian rights—that is, concession of those elements of special status that derive from agreements reached in the eighteenth- and nineteenth-century treaties between the tribes and the

United States. One widely circulated booklet, *Indian Treaties/American Nightmare* (1976), by C. Herb Williams and Walt Neubrech, regards residual treaty rights as a threat to civilization as we know it and calls for their speedy elimination, primarily because they interfere with current majority convenience or profit in some areas.

In 1978, a bill introduced in the 95th Congress by Rep. John Cunningham (D., Washington) called for the abrogation by the president of all treaties with Indian tribes entered into by the United States.[49] It was predictably titled the Native American Equal Opportunities Act, and it called for the unilateral termination of the trust relationship between the tribes and the federal government and the liquidation of all tribal lands and assets, which would be distributed to individual tribal members. This act received little support in Congress and was summarily defeated, but to many Indians it seemed to portend a rebirth of a terminationist philosophy. To demonstrate the depth of their opposition, native people from throughout the United States participated in a cross-country march on Washington to lobby in favor of the maintenance and further realization of treaty rights.

The insistence on the right to special status distinguishes Indian "activists" from those of virtually every other minority group, and it is often a bone of contention between Native Americans and their potential supporters. To some it

49. Larry Light, "Backlash in Congress Seen as Indians Push Claims," *Congressional Quarterly Weekly Report* (December 2, 1978), pp. 3385–3388; eleven bills, including HR 13329, were introduced in the 95th Congress to restrict Indian hunting, fishing, and land claims rights.

appears, in the words of the Supreme Court of the State of Washington, that "the law has . . . conferred upon tribal Indians and their descendants what amounts to titles of nobility, with all that entails."[50] From a legal point of view, however, Indian tribes ceded only certain of their sovereign rights to the United States, and thereby to a degree remain in control of everything not expressly granted.[51] Indians do not want "equality"; they feel they have paid well—and in advance—for the few special privileges remaining to them. In fact, the right to self-determination on the part of an Indian tribe is virtually the opposite of equal access.

Indians also contrast with other groups in terms of their legislative or judicial aspirations. Whereas most oppressed groups traditionally seek the overthrow of, radical change in, or major concessions from the government that has discriminated against them, Indians merely want actualized what they have been consistently promised on paper for one or two hundred years—agreements made by the United States when Indian power was relatively stronger. Consequently, tribes have often fared best in courts where conservative judges apply the letter of the law rather than reinterpret it.

50. See 73 Wash. 2d 677, 687, 440 P.2d. 442, 448 (1968), as quoted in Wilcomb E. Washburn, School of Law, Duke University, 40 (1) (Winter 1976).
51. Barsh and Henderson, in *The Road*, make an extremely interesting observation pertinent to the point of Indians granting rights to the United States: "The federal government did not, historically, create the sovereignty of tribes. Acts of Congress limited, modified, and channeled tribal powers, usually without tribal consent. The termination of what Congress created should therefore result in an increase in tribal self-governing powers. Instead, Congress has acted as if the termination of tribal dependency results in the dissolution rather than the emancipation of the tribes" (p. 285).

FUTURE PROSPECTS

At the end of the 1970s, American Indians seemed to be at a crossroads. Statistically they remained among the poorest economically, the least employed, the unhealthiest,[52] the lowest in education and income level,[53] and the worst-housed[54] ethnic group in America—though there are now signs of improvement in each area.

The remote areas of the American west where many large reservations were established turn out to be rich in minerals and oil. It is estimated that over fifty-three million

52. Lawrence Rosen, Foreword to *American Indians and the Law* (New Brunswick, N.J.: Transaction Pubs., 1976), p. 1. Thirty-eight percent of Indians identifying themselves in the 1970 census had incomes below the poverty line; in the poorest areas of Arizona and Utah this figure reaches upwards of 65 percent. Death from tuberculosis, dysentery, and accidents occurs four times more frequently among Indians than among the rest of the population. Unemployment for reservation men, averaging 18 percent nationally, climbed well above 30 percent in many areas.

53. Office of Special Concerns, Office of the Assistant Secretary for Planning and Evaluation, Department of Health, Education and Welfare, *A Study of Selected Socio-Economic Characteristics of Ethnic Minorities Based on the 1970 Census*, vol. 3: *American Indians*, HEW pub. no. (OS) 75-122, July 1974. In educational achievement, 34 percent of Indian males were high-school graduates (compared with 54 percent of all U.S. males); percentages were 1 point higher, respectively, for Indian females and all U.S. females. In income levels, 64 percent of rural Indian men earned less than $4,000 per year; 46 percent of urban Indian men earned less than $4,000 per year; only 31 percent of all U.S. men earned less than $4,000 per year.

54. Testimony of Margaret S. Treuer before the Subcommittee on Rural Housing and Development, Committee on Banking, Housing and Urban Affairs, U.S. Senate, April 1, 1980, p. 3. A 1970 Census Bureau report on housing characteristics indicated that 62.4 percent of the housing units on Indian reservations were substandard, compared with 12.9 percent in the United States as a whole. In March 1978 the General Accounting Office issued a report on Indian housing that estimated that fully 60 percent of all Indian families were living in substandard housing.

of the ninety million acres owned by Indian tribes on over two hundred reservations in twenty-six states contain raw materials this nation desperately needs.[55] Nearly two-thirds of all the low-sulphur coal reserves in the country are contained either on or near tribal land, and almost all of the potential uranium resources are found in Indian Country. Other tracts of reservation lands contain, or are adjacent to, deposits of copper reserves, have significant geothermal potential, or have the capacity for lucrative oil and gas production.

More specifically, the Southern Utes in Colorado, the Uinta-Ouray Utes in Utah, and the Blackfoots in Montana all have gas and oil reserves, as do the Shoshones and Arapahos in Wyoming. The Bannocks and Shoshones, whose reservations are located in Idaho, control one of the richest phosphate mines in the West. The Navajo and the Hopi reservations in the Southwest contain vast oil and gas fields, as well as stores of uranium reserves and so much coal that the former Navajo tribal chairman, Peter MacDonald, estimated the quantity to be half of all strippable coal in the United States.[56] To concentrate their clout, twenty-five Indian tribes formed the Council of Energy Resource Tribes (CERT) in 1975; the council's goals are the promotion of the well-being of member tribes

55. *Conference on Energy Resource Development and Indian Lands* (Washington: American Association for the Advancement of Science, 1978), p. 26.

56. Wallace Stegner, "Rocky Mountain Country: Arabs of the Plains," *Atlantic Monthly* (April 1978), p. 56.

through the protection, conservation, control, and prudent management of natural resources.

The major legal questions to be addressed by Indians and their representatives in the coming years will determine who will ultimately control these resources—who will decide if and when and where and how much to develop, and who will have the final say if a tribe and the federal, state, or adjacent city government disagree over priorities. Conceivably, Congress could assert plenary power, claim eminent domain, and unilaterally break its treaty promises by confiscating "in the national interest" the exhaustible mineral resources of Indian tribes. Or, the courts could further define the reserved rights of tribal sovereignty, protecting the trust relationship and underlining the self-determination ability of Indian nations.

Whichever course is followed—grasping self-interest or respect for the law—Indians will once again play the role of the miner's canary, testing the integrity of this nation's promises. There is little doubt that a few tribes will experience a degree of affluence in the coming few years, unparalleled since the European invasion. As they begin to achieve a degree of economic parity with other segments of the population, it is likely that some non-Indians will once again assume that all sovereignty and trust status should end. It is then that the real mettle of the American system will be tested. As the American Indian Policy Review Commission concluded in its *Final Report:*

The cornerstone of Federal Indian Policy can be stated simply and clearly. From the very beginning of this country, the law has recognized that the Native people in this country possess a right to exist as separate tribal groups with inherent authority to rule themselves and their territory. Although the United States necessarily exercises predominant power, it has time and again bound itself to respect this basic Indian right and has assumed the responsibility to protect the Indian people in the possession of their lands and in the exercise of their rights. Consequently, self-government (i.e., sovereignty) in conjunction with the trust relationship, is truly the inheritance of Indian people. Although times and conditions change, the United States' adherence to a policy of continuing to keep faith with the Indians on this fundamental level will always remain the foundation of Federal Indian Policy.[57]

Dædalus
Spring 1981

57. American Indian Policy Review Commission, *Final Report*, p. 622.

THE HUNDRED YEAR WAR
FOR WHITE EARTH

written with Louise Erdrich

A terrible irony underlies the beauty of the White Earth reservation in west-central Minnesota. Of the 762,000 acres promised to the original Chippewa settlers, only 53,100 acres—about 6 percent of those Indians' guaranteed domain—still remain in their possession.

For Chippewa, the nightmare has been ongoing for nearly a hundred years, since the Dawes Act of 1887, when one stroke of a Washington, D.C., pen virtually halved all remaining aboriginal holdings in the United States, subdividing reservations into 80- to 160-acre tracts, some parceled to Indian families so that they could "benefit" from the experience of private (versus communal) ownership. Twenty years later, the White Earth Band was singled out for a special variety of pseudolegal swindling, the scheme of lumber baron lawyer turned senator Moses A. Clapp.

Not content with Henry Dawes's provision that Indians had to wait twenty-five years before they could sell or lose their parcels, Clapp pushed through a rider to the Indian Appropriations Bill of 1906 that declared that mixed-blood adults on White Earth were "competent" to dispose of them immediately. What followed was a land grab orgy so outrageous that few to this day, regardless of ethnic heritage, speak of it without a sense of bewildered shame. Threatened, duped, or plied with drink, many Chippewa unused to the capitalist system and unfamiliar with the concept or implications of fee simple title signed away their deeds with an *X* or a thumbprint and received as payment tin money, ancient horses, harnesses and sleighs, used pianos, graphophones, and other worthless junk.

Indian homesteads were mortgaged and almost immediately repossessed; children were followed into government schoolrooms and tricked out of their inheritances. Later, Chippewa who disputed the sales were declared mixed-bloods via such anthropological quackeries as the test Dr. Ales Hrdlicka developed. This test, Hrdlicka wrote, "consisted of drawing with some force the nail of the forefinger over the chest. . . . In the full-bloods the reaction as a rule is quite slight to moderate [while] . . . in mixed-bloods, unless anaemic, it is more intense as well as lasting." It is not surprising that by such criteria only 104 out of 5,173 enrolled tribal members were judged to be "full-bloods," and over half the original acreage assignments soon passed from Indian control.

The effect on the Band was devastating. While lumber companies clearcut millions of dollars' worth of pine from forests located within White Earth, dispirited and broken Indian families clustered ten or more to single-room cabins on surviving allotments. Trachoma, scrofula, tuberculosis, and alcoholism became epidemic. The pattern of economic ruin, repeated over and over again on other reservations throughout the west, overtook the tribe that called itself "Anishinabe," the Original People.

In the ensuing sixty-two years, land within White Earth was bought, sold, and, a cynical method, often confiscated for lack of county tax funds. The legal boundaries did not cease to exist, however, either in the collective memory of the Chippewa—many of whom were not even allowed to vote in state or federal elections until the Citizenship Act of 1924—or ultimately in the opinion of federal courts.

In 1961 the auditor for Clearwater County, Minnesota, executed a tax certificate of forfeiture on allotment land owned by a tribal member named Zay Zah, or Charles Aubid, and a landmark case, decided in 1977, nullified the Clapp Act and affirmed the ongoing trust status of White Earth land. Title for all property lost under the discredited policy was suddenly open to litigation.

Several key rulings over the past two decades have upheld the limited sovereignty of federal Indian reservations, territories not so much bestowed on tribes by the United States as never ceded by tribes in the first place. This corroboration of the promises of longstanding Senate-ratified treaties is a victory for tribal governments, but for those non-Indian residents on reservations who find themselves without a franchise in local government because they are white, these rights are often perceived as threatening.

In 1985, bipartisan state, county, and tribal officials finally reached a compromise solution to the problem (the tribe later rescinded its endorsement). The solution presumed that the complaints of all actual and hypothetical heirs were legitimate and would prevail in court, and awarded each eligible individual compensation based upon value of land at the time it was inappropriately lost, plus 5 percent compound interest on that amount up to the present time. It further mandated that the Bureau of Indian Affairs locate all heirs and inform them of their benefits; ordered the U.S. Treasury to grant $6.6 million for the economic development of White Earth; and endorsed a state and county plan to return to the Band some ten thousand acres, selected by the tribal council from over one hundred thousand acres of designated land located within the reservation's borders (this territory would return to trust status and not, therefore, be taxable). Having done all that, the legislation, known as the White Earth Land Settlement Act (WELSA), supposedly quieted forever most clouded non-Indian land titles.

Any full or partial heir to an allotment who found these conditions unacceptable was enjoined to bring suit for the outright return of land within a six-month period. In so doing, however, he or she would concede all WELSA benefits, win or lose. After the termination of this statute of limitations, no further legal contests over disputed tracts would be heard. Thirty-nine Chippewa elected this option and sued; none has as yet prevailed. The act was voted by Congress in 1985 and has since become law, subject to an appeal now in progress.

We enter the reservation from the east, the same direction from which scattered bands of Mississippi, Pembina, Pillager, Lake Winibigoshish, and Lake Superior Chippewa arrived in the mid-nineteenth century, pushed to the far edge of Minnesota by the crush of European settlement. Our highway is lined by thick stands of birch, just beginning to leaf. Deer graze beside the road and are the only other traffic we encounter. Whole stretches of White Earth State Forest look uninhabited, much the same as they must have appeared a century ago to Native Americans who agreed to trade their vast aboriginal claims for this spot where Henry B. Whipple, then Episcopal bishop of Minnesota, foresaw "such a future as no Indian has ever had on this continent."

Unfortunately, this future turned out to be the same old story. White Earth in the 1980s has been a hotbed of controversy, acrimony, and discontent, the locus of a well-meaning land claims settlement that, on the surface, seems to have left everyone except its architects upset. The newspaper testimony of conflicting parties seems self-contradictory in that everyone sounds right, every position justifiable. So we've come, in person, to see if some clarity might emerge. This is not the first reservation where land and historic right is in dispute, and it surely will not be the last. Enormous cases loom in the near future involving the Oneida in New York State and the Lakota in South Dakota.

We stop for gas in Naytahwaush, one of few reservation communities where Chippewa form a majority. Like Ponsford and the town of White Earth, it is small, sleepy, peaceful looking. Trailers and old board cabins are set deep in tangled scrub oak and box elder trees. A general store sells wild rice and other necessities. On the perimeter, efficiently constructed and brightly painted prefab houses are wedged together as if enclosed by an invisible city. But only expanses of state-managed forests, water, and fertile dark soil tilled by non-Indian farmers fence these enclaves, constant reminders of loss, of a sad and appalling history, of a complex legal miasma that now divides the inhabitants of this place.

The contemporary reservation checkerboard is the unhappy result of the long-ago efforts of Dawes (the "reformer" from Massachusetts) and Senator Clapp, who put the interests of the lumber industry above any promises made to Indians. Bills that these two men and others pushed through Congress between 1887 and 1910 stripped the White Earth Chippewa of protections guaranteed them by an 1867 treaty and created an inevitable scenario by which Indians lost most of their territory. In the ensuing decades the process continued, and by the time the process was tested in court in 1977, the confusion over land ownership was immense. The struggle to clarify the situation and adequately compensate the heirs of those who were mistreated has dominated state Indian affairs for ten years, and is not over yet.

For local non-Indians like Jane and John Reisch, who moved to White Earth from the Twin Cities in 1975, the trouble commenced in 1980, when registered letters arrived from the U.S. Department of the Interior warning that title to their land was suspect. The twenty-seven-acre resort the family had purchased in good faith and made into both home and livelihood was suddenly in jeopardy, only instead of being forced from their land, the Reisches were stuck there. They could not sell, trade, or use it for collateral until the issue was settled in Washington, D.C.

We meet with several members of the United Township Association, a local group of non-Indian farmers and resorters, on a crisp April morning that happens to coincide with spring clean-up. In keeping with state beautification laws, the turn-off to the Jolly Fisherman, the Reisches' pride and joy, is marked only by a rectangular signpost. A long shady lane gives way to a clearing where teenagers are raking pine needles from the brown grass lawns, preparing cabins for the coming season. Jane Reisch, an energetic young woman with short brown hair, invites us into her kitchen, overlooking the waters of a dazzling lake, and the first order of business, as it would also be in any traditionally polite Indian home, is coffee.

We are surrounded by homemade crafts—quilts, pillows, embroidered samplers, stained glass. Bob Bruns, a quiet man with a level gaze and chiseled features, introduces himself as the owner of Whaley's Resort, listed with a realtor for the past twelve months.

"I'm selling because of frustration," says Mr. Bruns. "I worked day and night eighteen years to build a profitable business. Yet I'd sell it." He takes a sip of coffee, then looks around the table. "But you know, this time I'd check the title."

He is answered by rueful and knowing laughter. Jim Jirava, a third-generation Czech-American farmer, has taken a few hours from planting on the six thousand acres he tills with other members of his family (up from an original eighty-acre homestead gained by his grandfather in 1904) in order to join us. He points out that 70 percent of those who now live on the reservation are nontribal members. For him, as for Ann Schoenburn, an intense and impressively well-versed farmer who subscribes to the *American Indian Law Review*, the dealings with state and federal officials have been an exercise in disillusionment. Mrs. Schoenburn passionately opposed parts of what eventually became the White Earth Land Settlement Act because she felt it unfairly increased the jurisdictional and economic power of the White Earth Tribal Council over every non-Chippewa living within the reservation's borders. For her, as for many white residents, the issue has changed from fear of losing land to fear of losing authority over it.

"The power to control is the power to destroy," Mr.

Bruns asserts. Ann Schoenburn nods, concerned about local trespass ordinances. "We have a farm, partly in the woods," she explains. "I have to know who's going on my property, whether they're putting traps in my fields. Or someone's out there with a thirty-aught rifle and I've got my five children. I've got my cattle in my field. I have to know for safety's sake who's out there, who's on my land, and who's not. But if you have a tribal government that has control over the trespass, I've lost all that control."

These are reasonable, hard-working people, frightened and indignant. It is impossible not to sympathize with their dilemma, with their desire to defend their homes and, in some cases, legacies. Their ineffectuality in forestalling the act has caused them to question some basic principles of American government, to switch or abandon political parties. *We weren't told the land was on a reservation,* they repeat again and again. *We didn't understand all these implications when we paid our mortgages and our taxes. We are American citizens.*

But the situation is even more complicated. It turns out that, when questioned, nearly everyone in the room is related by blood, marriage, god-parentage, or long friendship to members of the White Earth Chippewa band. Despite everything, Jane Reisch says, their group will never "look at our neighbors and say 'you are the cause of my problems.'"

The cause is buried in history. When some non-Indians identify a focus for their apprehensions, Darrell "Chip"

Wadena, chairman of the band for twelve stormy years, is often cited. In the minds of some he's almost legendary in his power and despotism, yet when we arrive at his home in Naytahwaush, not half an hour from the Jolly Fisherman, we meet a pleasant man of medium build, curly hair, a moustache, and deep laugh lines. He waves to us from the door of a mobile home with brown siding and weathered steps. One of his grandchildren has been excavating near the foundation with a toy truck. We pull into the yard and park between Mr. Wadena's pink Cadillac and a large, white all-terrain vehicle that bears the new reservation-issued vanity license plate "Chip 1."

Inside, at the kitchen table, we sit beneath a reproduction of Leonardo da Vinci's "Last Supper" and other inspirational pictures affixed to varnished wood. Our conversation is punctuated by the static hiss of a CB radio hook-up. It is obvious, from the first word, that Mr. Wadena has a firm grasp of political strategy, and a mission. Among the nearly three thousand Chippewa on White Earth (another twelve thousand tribal members live off the reservation much of the year), unemployment is 73.5 percent, and the median income a few years ago was $2,523. Mr. Wadena's sworn job is to improve this.

The Zay Zah decision, a 1977 court ruling that retroactively undid more than fifty years of federal law regarding White Earth Chippewa land policy, was a wedge in the door, the first sign of hope. "We started a small project to investigate other cases where land title on the reservation might have some defect," says Mr. Wadena. "We were using hired college prelaw students. And we found it was a lot larger than we first thought. We then pulled back and contracted with the Bureau of Indian Affairs to continue the investigation."

This process soon led to the letters that non-Indian property owners received. "They were quite enraged and you couldn't blame them," notes Chip Wadena mildly. "Nobody had the answers. The BIA didn't have the answers. Our lawyers could only speculate. As a result, tempers flared, emotions ran amok."

Mr. Wadena, members of his council, and an ad hoc and outspoken group called Anishinabe Akeeng, "The People's Land," at first agreed in their opposition to a single legislative solution, believing that no one bill could fairly address all aspects of the complex situation. The initial proposal by local congressman Arland Stangland did not succeed, but as the land freeze dragged on, tensions mounted and one longtime advocate for Indian interests, Sen. Morris Udall of Arizona, advised Mr. Wadena, "If you don't come up with a consensus on what you want, Congress will make up your mind for you."

Now Mr. Wadena defends WELSA, which he eventually endorsed, against the strenuous objections of other elected tribal officials, as the best compromise available at the time, balancing a century of real estate chicanery and a present-day Office of Management and Budget obsessed with international deficits. "Acting Deputy for the BIA, John Fritz, said to me, 'Chip, the stagecoach is rolling, and the most you can do at this point is add baggage,'" Mr. Wadena explains with a sense of realpolitik. "My loyal opposition, AIM [American Indian Movement] people, Anishinabe Akeeng, took the all-or-nothing stance and I couldn't explain to them that what you'll get is nothing. And I'm not sure the White Earth people want nothing."

Less than an hour down the road, in a small yellow cement-block building on the dusty outskirts of White Earth village, the "loyal opposition" is photocopying the 1867 treaty. Anishinabe Akeeng—staffed by both young and veteran activists, funded in part by Christian churches, endorsed and broadly directed by a board of elders—officially rejects the settlement act.

Led by Marvin Manypenny, Winona LaDuke, John Morin, and Rich Bellecourt, this grassroots organization has from the outset acted as a kind of conscience for fair play, a constant reminder of the deprivations brought upon Indians through federal government mismanagement. Anishinabe Akeeng successfully raised the ante of settlement versions in the past as it stubbornly lobbied for the return to the Band of most of the land on the reservation as well as for a much larger damages payment. Recently, supporters have brought suits in Washington, D.C., and St. Paul challenging, respectively, the due process and class action viabilities of WELSA. "It's the non-Indians whose claim the feds should buy out," argues Ms. LaDuke, who was educated at Harvard and is expecting her first baby. "Not the Indians."

Both legal actions substantively failed in their first hearing, but each has been appealed, with the plaintiffs expressing a willingness to pursue their course all the way to the U.S. Supreme Court.

Kurt Bluedog, a former Native American Rights Fund lawyer and an enrolled Sisseton Sioux, is handling the Minnesota case. "We're basically outgunned here all the time," he says. "We're like one David up against six Goliaths. It's hard to explain this to my clients. If I were to paint a composite picture of them, it would be an older, conservative, more traditional person. They're quiet people, disinherited people."

John Morin, a slight, gentle-looking man whose long hair is held back in a tail, greets us at the door to the Anishinabe Akeeng office. He is a university-trained Lake Superior Chippewa who has become passionately involved in the struggle to reclaim White Earth land and who believes that Mr. Wadena's support of WELSA stems from "mental slavery caused by the system."

"Non-Indians on our reservation are afraid that if we get power, they'll be treated the way they treated Indians," Morin says. "But we could never turn around and do that to them." Mr. Morin's outlook is serene, earnest. "The issue here is not how much land we get back or they retain, but how we are going to coexist as human beings."

Marvin Manypenny came in third (behind, respectively, Mr. Wadena and Eugene "Bugger" McArthur) in an election for tribal chairman held this past June 14, and is a participant in both lawsuits. He is more aggressive, more self-consciously a leader than Chip Wadena, and calls WELSA "a non-Indian Relief Act," accusing U.S. officials of "dereliction in their trust responsibility. They screwed up and consequently our estate was stolen out from under our noses."

While continuing their efforts to block the implementation of the act, some members of Anishinabe Akeeng have also become pragmatists. Winona LaDuke proposes an ambitious, long-term land recovery project. Endorsed by Mr. Wadena, as well as by her own organization, the plan "places no burden on any non-Indian," but rather stipulates that interest money from the Indian Claims Commission or other land settlements be used to repurchase acreage that over the years has passed out of tribal control.

According to Ms. LaDuke, parcels owned by banks, the state of Minnesota, insurance companies, private corporations, or religious groups would be targeted first. "And then there's the Boy Scouts," she says enthusiastically. "They've got a camp on a lake shore that belonged to my great-great-grandmother. She took a $50 loan from a land dealer and later found out she'd sold."

For moral reasons, tax reasons, economic reasons, Ms. LaDuke speculates that non-Indians on the reservation might sell to the tribe. Certainly Bob Bruns, or the owners of Kruse's Hideaway, who long to retire but have found no buyer in the past five years, would agree. Whatever lands so recovered would return to the Chippewa domain, thus giving the Band a base for economic growth as well as for something less tangible—a form of hope, a validation, and something terribly rare in Indian country, a victory.

South of White Earth, we pass through the rich loam fields of central Minnesota prairie. Once on the interstate highway, it is only hours to the Twin Cities, where we have appointments with the state officials who, according to the United Township members, ignore their wishes, who infuriate Anishinabe Akeeng, who put psychological pressure on Chairman Wadena, whom everyone we've met seems to resent in one way or another. We are prepared to encounter villains, and instead, the next morning in the state capitol rooms of Minnesota governor Rudy Perpich, beneath the huge romantic oil painting by Jean-François Millet of Chief Little Crow signing the treaty of Travers de Sioux, we meet a group of public servants whose views on Indian sovereignty are light years ahead of their counterparts in most other states.

"Indian tribes are nations," says Governor Perpich, almost irritated that we raise a question concerning his perception of reservation political status, "and we deal with them as such."

Assistant Attorney General James Schoessler, on the way to his office, points out a name card on a hallway door: Clapp. "He's a descendant of the Moses Clapp that introduced the rider in 1906 [which Zay Zah overturned] and boy, do I give him grief!" Mr. Schoessler, a slim, precise Minnesotan with degrees from Harvard and Princeton, has taken lots of heat himself. He first became involved with the dispute on White Earth after the Bureau of Indian Affairs issued the ubiquitous clouded title letters and, as he says, "all heck broke loose."

"The problem cried out for a legislative solution," he explains. Along with Minnesota attorney general Hubert H. Humphrey III, Mr. Schoessler sincerely believed that, although the state was technically responsible only in a limited way, it owed a "philosophical and moral claim to the White Earth Chippewa as a people."

The conflicting claims were necessarily complex: up to 100,000 people, averaging out to about 150 disputants for every individual sixty-five-acre claim, could potentially bring suit. Furthermore, the legal waters were so murky that no one could firmly predict which side—current or former land owner—would ultimately prevail after years of what promised to be rancorous litigation and guaranteed to empty the pockets of Indians and non-Indians alike and to wreak havoc on an agricultural region already economically strapped. If even a fraction of these cases went to court, Mr. Schoessler was convinced that "at the bitter, and I do mean bitter, end," no real justice would be done. So, under Mr. Humphrey's direction, he attended over ninety meetings, shuttling back and forth from White Earth to St. Paul to Washington, D.C., to explain why WELSA's particular terms—the return of some land, no "cap" on the monetary allocation, the payment of compound interest to injured parties—were more equitable than those in almost all previous Indian land claims cases.

Such relative arguments offer little comfort to Seraphine Rock, Fred Weaver, and Margaret Norcross, Anishinabe Akeeng board members and plaintiffs in the St. Paul class action suit who insist they have a compelling entitlement to all the reservation land stolen from their ancestors. They insist upon a broad perspective: they have lived their whole lives on tiny lots in a village crowded into a corner of their own reservation and they have been denied the good life for which their ancestors peacefully bartered most of Michigan, Wisconsin, and Minnesota. Theirs is the argument of adamant Israelis or Palestinians—the insistence on an absolute, final right to a home.

The arguments continue—in Washington and St. Paul and Naytahwaush and in farmhouse kitchens—between unhappy antagonists often related by blood or history or geography or economics. As in a family, each position, though contradictory to all others, is persuasive, wrenching. There are no wild-eyed profiteers here, no evil geniuses; the authors of the turn-of-the-century deals that caused this mess are dead and mostly forgotten. None of the clichés seem to apply: the state is liberal, sensitive, the tribal government efficient, the protesters idealistic, the non-Indians salt-of-the-earth people whose complaint is with policy, not race. It's nothing personal, everyone seems to proclaim.

At the Jolly Fisherman, vacationers unsophisticated in the intricacies of Indian history rise early to drop lines for walleyes. Perhaps they've bought their bait from Theodore Hoagland, a plaintiff in the class action suit who hopes to regain some family land. For now he's selling minnows and leeches to make a living. Jim Jirava's new crop of soy beans, barley, and wheat bakes in a record drought. Anishinabe Akeeng prepares to attend a sit-in scheduled for the one locale on a nearby Cass Lake Reservation large enough to accommodate a crowd: the bingo palace. Filming has begun on a TV mini-series based on Will Weaver's 1986 novel, *Red Earth, White Earth.*

As Darrell Wadena prepares to take office for another term as chairman, White Earth Chippewa who live in the Twin Cities are generally upset. One spokesman, an employee of the city public school system who will give his name only as Mahneengun ("Wolf"), bitterly asserts, "We got five cents an acre for land in the millions now. It's hard to be nostalgic when they wave the flag." Michael Ratner of the Center for Constitutional Rights, in tandem with Steven Schwartz from the New York mega law firm of Weil, Gotshal and Manges, has filed briefs in Washington to have WELSA overturned. And thousands of men and women throughout America, many in 1988 as yet unaware that they are even eligible, will soon learn they are to receive a monetary award compensating them for the damages suffered by their White Earth ancestors.

In the end, of course, it all comes back to the land: black, sloping gently into wild rice marsh and lake, forested with deep pine and brilliant stands of birch, it exerts a hold on its inhabitants many times more binding than history or the arcane legislation that attempts to regulate the relationships of one group to another. Like the persistent calls of Minnesota lakebirds, the writings on the walls of neighbors and old friends who find themselves on opposite sides of a heart-rending issue speak to each other in our memory: "As you walk through this land, take time to appreciate the beauty of the flowers," exhorts a framed poster over Chip Wadena's window. "A woman is like a teabag," a calendar page stuck to Jane Reisch's refrigerator warns. "You don't know how strong she is until you put her in hot water."

The protagonists on and about the White Earth reservation see themselves as righteous and heroic, for all parties are archetypically in the position of defending what they believe to be their birthright either as Chippewa or as American citizens, a territory paid for by labor and affection and long residency, the immutable inheritance they had hoped to pass on to their children. "How firm we stand and plant our feet upon our land determines the strength of our children's heartbeat," proclaims a slogan above the copying machine at Anishinabe Akeeng's headquarters, a sentiment echoed eloquently by Jim Schoessler: "It's land," he says. "It touches the essence."

New York Times Sunday Magazine
September 4, 1988

LEARNING
FROM
MISTAKES

FOR INDIANS, NO THANKSGIVING

Maybe those Pilgrims and Wampanoags actually got together for a November picnic, maybe not. It matters only as an ironical footnote.

For the former group, it would have been a celebration of a precarious hurdle successfully crossed on the path to the political domination, first of a continent and eventually of a planet. For the latter, it would have been, at best, a naive extravaganza—the last meeting as equals with invaders who, within a few years, would win King Philip's War and decorate the entrances to their towns with rows of stakes, each topped with an Indian head.

The few aboriginal survivors of the ensuing violence were either sold into Caribbean slavery by their better-armed, erstwhile hosts or ruthlessly driven from their Cape Cod homes. Despite the symbolic idealism of the first potluck, New England—from the emerging European point of view— simply wasn't big enough for two sets of societies.

An enduring benefit of success, when one culture clashes with another, is that the victorious group controls the record. It owns not only the immediate spoils but also the power to edit, embellish, and concoct the facts of the original encounter for the generations to come. Events, once past, reside at the small end of the telescope, the vague and hazy antecedents to accepted reality.

Our collective modern fantasy of Thanksgiving is a case in point. It has evolved into a ritual pageant that almost every one of us, as children, either acted in or were forced to watch—a seventeenth-century vision that we can conjure whole in the blink of an eye.

The cast of stock characters is as recognizable as those in any Macy's parade: dour-faced Pilgrim men, right-to-bear-arms muskets at their sides, sitting around a rude outdoor table while their wives, dressed in long dresses, aprons, and linen caps, bustle about lifting the lids off steaming kettles—pater- and materfamilias of New World hospitality.

They dish out the turkey to a scattering of shirtless Indian invitees. But there is no ambiguity as to who is in charge of the occasion, who could be asked to leave, whose protocol prevails.

Only "good" Indians are admitted into this tableau, of course, as in those who accept the Manifest Destiny of a European presence and are prepared to adopt English dining customs and, by inference, English everything else.

These compliant Hollywood extras are, naturally enough, among the blessings the Pilgrims are thankful for—and why not? Holiday Indians are colorful, bring the food, and vanish after dessert. They are something exotic to write home about, like a visit to Frontierland. In the sound bite of national folklore, they have metamorphosed into totems of America as evocative, and ultimately as vapid, as a flag factory.

And members of this particular make-believe tribe did not all repair to the happy hunting grounds during the first Christmas rush. They lived on, smoking peace pipes and popping up at appropriate crowd-pleasing moments.

They lost mock battles from coast to coast in Wild West shows. In nineteenth-century art, they sat bareback on their horses and stoically watched a lot of sunsets. Entire professional sports teams of them take the home field every Sunday afternoon in Cleveland, Atlanta, or Washington, D.C.

They are the sources of merit badges for Boy Scouts and the emblem of purity for imitation butter. They are, and have been from the beginning, predictable, manageable, domesticated inventions without depth or reality apart from that bestowed by their creators.

These appreciative Indians, as opposed to the pesky flesh and blood native peoples on whom they are loosely modeled, did not question the enforced exchange of their territories for a piece of pie. They did not protest when they died by the millions from European diseases.

They did not resist—except for the "bad" ones, the renegades—when solemn pacts made with them were broken or when their religions and customs were declared illegal. They did not make a fuss in courts in defense of their sovereignty. They never expected all the fixings anyway.

As for Thanksgiving 1988, the descendants of those first

party-goers sit at increasingly distant tables, the pretense of equity all but abandoned. Against great odds, Native Americans have maintained political identity, but, in a country so insecure about heterogeneity that it votes its dominant language as "official," this refusal to melt into the pot has been an expensive choice.

A majority of reservation Indians reside in the most impoverished counties in the nation. They constitute the ethnic group at the wrong extreme of every scale: most undernourished, most short-lived, least educated, least healthy. For them, Thanksgiving was perhaps their last square meal.

New York Times
November 24, 1988

NATIVE AMERICAN LITERATURE IN AN ETHNOHISTORICAL CONTEXT

During the past several thousand years, Native American people have produced literatures rich in diversity and imagery, ancient in tradition, and universal in significance. On the other hand, there is no such thing as "Native American literature," though it may yet, someday, come into being.

The roots of this apparent paradox are not difficult to examine or comprehend. "National" literatures, be they French, Sanskrit, Japanese, or whatever, emanate from and are the expressions of coherent aggregations of people. They tend to reflect aspects of a shared consciousness, an inherently identifiable worldview, a collective understanding of custom, language, and tradition. The pool from which both artist and primary audience are culled is generally circumscribed by common linguistics. English literature is expected to be presented initially in English, and to be therefore accessible first and foremost to English-speaking readers.

If there had ever been a North American language called "Indian," the mode of communication within a society called "Indian," then there would undoubtedly be something appropriately labeled "Indian literature." But there was not, and is not. On the contrary, the pre-1492 Western Hemisphere was among the most linguistically and culturally plural areas the world has ever known. The estimated ten to twenty million people who lived in what is today the United States and Canada spoke languages derived from no less than seven different language families, each as distinct from the other as each was distinct from Indo-European. Within each of these families, there existed many separate and mutually unintelligible languages, and within each language, the potential for a variety of diverse regional dialects was high.

More than three hundred cultures, each differentiated to a greater or lesser degree by language, custom, history, and life way, were resident north of the Rio Grande in 1492. Moreover, the linguistic affinity groupings were rarely geographically clustered; for instance, languages belonging to the Athapaskan family were spoken in central Alaska (Ingalik), near Hudson Bay (Chipewyan), on the Plains (Sarsi and Kiowa Apache), in the Southwest (Navajo), and in California (Hupa). Interspersed between them were cultures using languages derived from the Algonquin, Peneutian, Uto-Aztecan, Hokan, Muskogean, and Eskimo-Aleut families.

Heterogeneity in all things was the norm, and each

group took pride in its own distinctive features, including its own oral (literary) traditions. And yet, apparently to early European interlopers, they all "looked alike." Just as inhabitants of Africa were once incorrectly lumped as "Ethiopes," so too was the indigenous North American misclassified. It seems simply to have been assumed that because (a) people lived in North America and (b) none of them was European, then therefore (c) they must all be the same. To carry this logic to its obvious conclusion: (d) because Europeans thought they were heading toward the Asian Indies when they collided with America, and (e) since Europeans were never wrong, then (f) these all-the-same people must of course be INDIANS! Thus was born in the myopic minds of a few culturally traumatized and geographically disoriented individuals a new ethnic group.

It remained only to convince the members of the several hundred cultures in North America that there were no differences among them and that henceforth they should identify themselves collectively by an appellation marginally appropriate only to a transpacific population they had never heard of. Though it frustrated and infuriated generations of European and American administrators, it should come as no surprise that Mohawks steadfastly remained Mohawks, that Aleuts did not become Chickasaws, that Hopis persisted as Hopis, and that all regarded the suggestion that they do otherwise as a lunacy to be politely ignored.

Sense and sensibility, however, often give way to the

dictates of power, and the cultural dominance Europeans and their descendants came to exert in North America assured the persistence of the misnomer and its erroneous implications. The question of why Native Americans lost political control of their homelands is a complex issue. By and large, American Indian societies had little precontact experience in the activity known in Europe as "war." The ideas of national conquest, total victory or defeat, and the development and evolution of a sophisticated military technology were conspicuously absent. This "liability," coupled with the lack of natural immunity most Native Americans displayed toward Old World diseases, preordained a swift and relatively facile European accession in North America. The very survival and recent resurgence of indigenous peoples and cultures, and not the ease of their historical conquest, is the significant and somewhat miraculous point.

Because the European perspective at least temporarily prevailed, it was entirely predictable that the dumping of all Native Americans into the mythological "Indian" category persisted in the evolving Euro-American consciousness. Used as an adjective, the know-nothing and misleading term *Indian* often preceded, but in no way illuminated, such classifications as "music," "art," "history," "language," "religion," "philosophy," and "literature." There is certainly nothing generic about any of these activities, though certainly each and every Native American culture included unique expressions of them.

Hence the concept of "American Indian literature" is largely ambiguous and begs more questions than it answers. Does it refer to the sum total of all oral literary traditions in each of more than three hundred mutually unintelligible languages? If so, does such a category make any scholarly or even common sense? Clearly it would be a far less reasonable concept than its oversimplified analogue, "European literature." Can such a genre, spuriously based on assumed, but nonexistent, inherent similarities, yield any meaningful depth or insight? Would such a category stimulate the study of a single Native American language or aesthetic? Is it a helpful academic tool or simply an excuse not to study, a rationale for dismissal on the grounds of overcomplexity or inaccessibility?

It may perhaps be argued that Native American literature, under this definition, is a reasonable idea in that a relatively small but growing fraction is becoming available via translation into English. However, while this may well be a positive and promising development, the question persists: is there any intellectually sound reason for examining arbitrarily anthologized particles of many separate traditions in connection with each other? On what grounds should or could one study under the same rubric a Shoshone (Uto-Aztecan family) song, a Navajo (Athapaskan) mountain chant, and a Cherokee (Hokan) quest tale? Why not also include a Tibetan hymn, a Latvian poem, or an Ashanti blessing? A course that attempts to unite "Native American literature's greatest hits" tends to become a vain search for commonalities that have no reason to be there. In the process, the beauties, insights, and styles of the particular literatures are ignored or become falsely homogenized, and the resulting amalgam is often a dreary and sparkless mediocrity.

Unquestionably, an understanding of any national literature depends very much on an awareness of the larger cultural context. Without some knowledge of language, of history, of inflection, of the position of the storyteller within the group, without a hint of the social roles played by males and females in the culture, without a sense of the society's humor or priorities—without such knowledge, how can we, as reader or listener, penetrate to the core of meaning in an expression of art?

The difficulty of gaining access to the literature of a different culture may be illustrated by an exemplary folktale (in translation) from the Tanaina (Athapaskan) culture of south-central Alaska. It might be titled "The Beaver and the Porcupine Woman" and would typically be told to a general audience within the society, including the full range of ages from early childhood to grandparent; it would be recounted with gesticulation and exaggeration by a performance specialist. It would be expected to have different meanings to the various categories of listeners—instructive, entertaining, reinforcing, or all three. But even with this foreknowledge, even admitting the obvious artificiality of reading versus hearing the story in a social and cultural context, and even allowing for the problems inherent in translating between languages and language families, can the story be understood without some interdisciplinary, ethnographic attempt to know something substantive about the culture that produced it? A brief version of the story, and a discussion of its meaning, follows.

Once upon a time there was a porcupine woman. She was extremely fat. One day she decided to do some hunting on the far side of the river, so she went to the bank, where she met a beaver.

"Hello," she said to him. "I need to do some hunting over there. Will you ride me across on your back?"

"I'd be glad to," replied the beaver. "Hop on."

So the porcupine woman climbed on his back, and he started swimming for the other side. When he had almost made it, the porcupine woman said, "Oh my! I've forgotten to bring my sack. I'll need to go back to the other bank and get it."

"All right," said the beaver, and swam back. He was panting while the porcupine woman went to get her sack. Her quills had become water-logged and she was even heavier than she looked.

"Okay," she said. "Let's go." So they started across again. The beaver was swimming much more slowly. When they had practically reached the other side, she said, "Oh my! I've forgotten to bring my needle. We'll have to go back and get it."

This time the beaver didn't say anything—he didn't have enough breath! But he turned around and pulled them back to the shore and nearly passed out while she got her needle.

"Hurry up, now," the porcupine woman said as she climbed back on his back. He could hardly keep his nose above water, she was so soaked and weighty, but he had almost made it to the far bank again when she said, "Oh my! I've forgotten my staff. We'll have to. . . ."

Before she had finished her sentence the beaver had flipped over in the water and dragged himself onto the bank, where he lay half dead. The porcupine woman managed to make the shore too, and climbed up onto a bear path. When she had caught her breath, she turned on the beaver and quilled him to death.*

In attempting to understand the sense of this superficially minor vignette (whose only English translation exists in a book intended for primary school children), let us commence with what it does not mean. Tanaina people do not literally believe that beavers and porcupines talk to each other, nor do they impart anthropomorphic qualities to animals, except as a stylistic convention.

---

* A similar story can be found in Bill Vaudrin's excellent collection, *Tanaina Tales from Alaska* (Norman, Okla.: University of Oklahoma Press, 1969).

To properly comprehend the story, it is necessary to know several facts. First of all, Tanainas live in an environment that could euphemistically be described as "difficult." Survival, especially in the wild, is always precarious. Further, they were, in the precontact period, a nonliterate people. Oral communication was therefore the method of cultural transmission, legal understanding, and meaningful communication. It is also necessary to know that a "staff," as mentioned in the story, functions as both a walking stick and a weapon, and that in the Tanaina symbol system, porcupines were supposed to be rather ponderous, dull-witted creatures, and beavers were thought to be energetic and industrious but overly spontaneous and erratic.

Armed with this data, the story becomes more accessible as a lesson in contract law, with several additional minor themes. A culturally attuned listener would notice, for instance, that when the porcupine woman proposed passage to the beaver, he agreed without any stipulations or clarifications of the terms. He should have said something to the effect that "I'll take you across one time, two at most," or, "I'm at your disposal for the next fifteen minutes, no more." But he gave a basically open-ended agreement—made a contract—and hence the porcupine woman was perfectly within her rights both in demanding that he return three times and in quilling him to death when he reneged.

The story is not, however, without its moral for the porcupine women of this world. Her stated aim is to go hunting, and yet she sets out without the three essentials of that endeavor: a sack in which to carry home her game, a needle with which to sew up the intestines, and, most important, an implement with which to hunt and defend herself. True, she had an open-ended contract, but where does she wind up at the conclusion of the story? Sitting, exhausted, quills used up, weaponless, and not only on the wrong side of the river from her home (having in effect "burned her bridges" in her righteous indignation) but on a bear path! The hunter is about to become the hunted, and all because of her own improvidence.

Told in the right context by the appropriate teller and to a cued audience, this little tale has great impact. It is at once serious and comic; it underlines the binding nature of verbal agreements—and hence the caution with which one must proceed in entering into one. It comments upon forethought and the consequences of insisting upon total, though technically "just," retribution for an offense. It is a transmission replete with cultural values, and it acts as a vehicle for their effortless communication from one generation to the next. In terms of the keys to its understanding, it has next to nothing in common with a Papago origin myth, a Chippewa haiku-style poem, or a capitulation oration attributed to Chief Joseph of the Nez Percé. But it is in just such company that it is likely to appear, if in fact it does appear at all, in a course titled "Native American Literature."

*   *   *

As if it weren't impossible enough to subsume the extra-ordinarily large and diverse corpora of traditional Native American oral literatures under the single rubric of "Indian literature," other types of writing as well are often included within the genre. By far the greatest volume of fiction pertaining to Native Americans has been written about them by non-Indians. Such works have enjoyed wide and consistent popularity among the Euro-American readership for at least the past three hundred years and have spawned such diverse offshoots as Wild West shows, cowboy and Indian movies, Boy Scout ceremonies, and cigar-advertising statues.

Disregarding the obvious propagandists for an exaggerated image of Native Americans (either savage or unearthly noble), many serious authors have attempted to cope literarily with the existence and complexity of the "Redman." Rousseau and Shakespeare (let us not forget Caliban), James Fenimore Cooper and Helen Hunt Jackson (her mournful *Ramona* has been translated into film more times than any other novel), Faulkner and Barth have all developed, marveled over, and almost always eventually killed off fictional Native American characters. Still other writers have virtually built their careers on books about "the Indian world" and how to understand it. Novels of continuing interest—such as Frank Waters's *The Man Who Killed the Deer* (1942), wherein Hopis often appear to be telepathic as well as paranoid regarding the outside world; Oliver La Farge's *Laughing Boy* (1929); Hal Borland's *When the Legends Die* (1963); and Edwin Corle's *Fig Tree*

John (1971)—give testimony to the abiding fascination Euro-Americans seem to have with "their" Indians. The basic plot line of these books and of their hundreds of less successful imitators is highly formalized.

Initially the natives of a small society are described as happy and mindless children. Garden of Eden imagery abounds and harmony reigns . . . until that fateful day when, through no fault of his or her own, a Child of the Forest is snatched from the nest and sent off into the Great White World to go to school, train for a job, join the army, or the like. Regardless of the task at hand, our hero fails and returns to his or her community in semidisgrace. The protagonist may have been corrupted to the point of prostitution (such as Slim Girl in *Laughing Boy*) or only made contemptuous of the native traditions (such as Martiniano, of *The Man Who Killed the Deer,* who insists on wearing shoes with heels). Eventually, usually after a long struggle (with periodic doses of supernatural intervention thrown in), the taint of the outside world is exorcized and the protagonists are brought back to the bosom of their tribes, either by ritual or through death. Slim Girl might well have paraphrased the famous nineteenth-century pronouncement in concluding that, for her, the only way to be a good Indian was to be a dead one.

Anglo writers almost invariably portray Native American cultures as fragile, regressive, deteriorating entities, teetering on the brink of extinction. These fictitious societies give no evidence of internal vitality, rarely betray any sense of humor (Clair Huffaker's *Nobody Loves a Drunken Indian* [1967], long a reservation best-seller, is a notable exception), and confirm to the non-Indian reader that contact with Euro-Americans was the most significant event in the forty-thousand-year history of native people on this continent—indeed, their citizens seem unable to think or talk of anything else. The novels that often surface in "American Indian Literature" courses are sociologically dubious and suggest at best an individual etic (outsider's) perspective—yet they are often treated with an obsequious reverence bordering on the unctuous. Whatever their intentions, these books are too often mistaken for ex cathedra pronouncements about "real" Indian life, and as such they reinforce stereotypes (e.g., other-worldly powers) and depict native societies where change is anathema. No wonder tourists visiting reservations, upon viewing a person clad in other than a blanket, riding in something other than a dog-pulled travois, often bemoan the "loss of culture"; somehow they seem oblivious to the fact that they themselves are not passing through on a covered wagon and wearing homespun dickeys.

An additional liability posed by these novels is in their perpetuation of the convention that Native Americans, even when conversing with each other in their own language, find it impossible to speak articulately and to the point. With only the evidence of these novels to go by, a reader might well conclude that metaphor formed the basis of every indigenous thought pattern. This ritualized form of language, the bastardized product of eighteenth- and nine-teenth-century clerical translators at treaty conferences, has become so associated with Native American utterance that today its usage in certain circles is practically manda-tory to ensure ethnic credibility.

A debate recently raged within a Northwest Coast tribal community regarding a collection of translated, traditional stories to be used in the classroom. The elder, non-English-speaking members of the community argued strongly for the inclusion of scatological and sexual allusions—main-taining that censorship had never been exercised toward children in the past. More "progressive" tribal members, concerned with public image, wanted the book to include only "proper" and unspicy language. They lost and the lit-erature won, but such victories are rare.

Insistence on a single "appropriate" manner of native self-presentation has had wide effect and certainly may be observed in the final genre to be discussed here: the writ-ings in English by native people and about "native" themes. Historically the earliest examples of this mode are largely confessional and coauthored (or dictated) autobi-ographies: *Black Elk Speaks* (Lakota), *Crashing Thunder* (Winnebago), *Two Leggings* (Crow), *Mountain Wolf Woman* (Winnebago), and the two Charles Eastman (Lakota) books, *Soul of the Indian* and *Old Indian Days*, all of which appeared in the first half of the twentieth century. These works differ from the traditional literatures of their authors' respective tribes in at least two overall respects: they were originally composed in a foreign language (English), and their intended audience is primarily Euro-American and not tribal. As such they are written to conform to the aesthetic of their day; their diction, organization, style, and points of emphasis give greater testimony to the popular fashion of American lettres than they do to the indigenous rules of expression of the "teller." The influence exerted by the nonnative transcriber—ranging from very great in the case of John Neihardt (*Black Elk Speaks*) to blessedly nonintrusive in Nancy Lurie's case (*Mountain Wolf Woman*)—cannot be discounted.

N. Scott Momaday, among the most celebrated contemporary Native American writers, was awarded a Pulitzer Prize for his novel *House Made of Dawn* (1967). The book deals creatively with a variety of "Native American" themes, both in a reservation community and in an urban/outside-world setting. Momaday is in a position to bring a bicultural perspective to his subject matter, for he writes of a context with which he is familiar and thereby lends credibility to the notion that this book is truly a personal "statement," though certainly not *the* Native American point of view.

However, *House Made of Dawn* is told not in the Kiowa (Momaday's tribe and the focus of his two more non-fiction works, *The Way to Rainy Mountain* [1969] and *The Names* [1976]) or "Pecos" (the protagonist's fictional tribe) tradition, but in highly formal, stylized, and conventionally laudable prose. As such, the book is accessible to a wide readership, most of which is totally unlearned about Native American lifestyles and presumed values, but less so to the majority of contemporary Native American people, most of whom know quite a bit about the parameters and stresses of their own existence but lack a fluent literacy in English. Momaday and a growing number of ethnically Native American writers in English (or Spanish), therefore, fulfill a rather nontraditional artistic role; rather than primarily interpreting or imagining a fresh vision of society for their context communities, they are interpolating and translating their communities for another culture.

Certainly this intermediary function did not originate with Momaday; he may, in *House Made of Dawn,* be best understood as a Native American Henry James, Ralph Ellison, or James Joyce. There is a danger, however, that the American reading audience may take Momaday's books as literal statements of fact rather than as the products of artistry and license. It can certainly be argued that this confusion of literature and sociology is more prevalent in cases where either the central themes and contexts are unfamiliar and somewhat exotic to the general reader or there exists a political state of dominance/subordination between the two "bridged" communities.

Momaday writes of an unglorious period in modern U.S. history known to Native Americans as the "relocation years." Abel, his protagonist, undergoes successive, externally conceived experiences of forced assimilation: the army and a move from his reservation to a city. He is not simply a rural person deprived of a familiar context, but an

Indian in a hostile, non-Indian America. Native American orientation is further highlighted in the novel by the presentation of the events not in a chronologically unfolding "progressive" sequence but bound within the limits of the book's almost identical opening and closing segments. Thus sandwiched, the bulk of the novel appears to exist within a cyclical context—certainly a common mode in many traditional Native American literatures. Finally, Momaday seems to soften the book's rather bleak realities by the occasional interjection of parts of a Navajo chant that promises recurrent, if not present, hope, beginning, potential: dawn.

House Made of Dawn is thus firmly rooted in an "Indian" context, but it translates and interprets that experience for a nonnative audience. Abel is not "everyindian" or maybe even "anyindian." He is not the product of his background (and therefore "representative"), but he rather moves through his life in his own unique way. Writers of many cultures—from Steinbeck to contemporary Chicano novelists—also have written of the California experience; large segments of Momaday's work should be viewed in that "immigration" context, and not as a set of norms to which all Indians are likely to conform.

However, it is virtually inevitable when writing about Native Americans in a contact situation and in English that certain stereotypes of language and cultural behavior will be reinforced, especially if the failure syndrome and supernatural sensitivities of previous "Indian" protagonists (Martiniano, Laughing Boy, Tom Black Bull [*When the*

Legends Die], Ramona, etc.) are echoed. Formulary roles, conclusions, and situations replace humanity and individual diversity. Indian characters are validated and made credible by acting in ritualized patterns, speaking in archaic slogans, and, above all, nobly not succeeding.

Euro-American interest in Native Americans, occasionally bordering on mania, is as old as contact history itself; and Native American authors are sufficiently rare that their works too often tend to be treated as revelation (the enduring campus popularity of *Black Elk Speaks,* with its obvious transcription complications, is a case in point). Native-created protagonists may fallaciously assume the proportions, for some readers, of prototype—underlining anew the old, hopeful dogma that "they" must really be all alike. Flesh and blood Native Americans at variance in dress, thought, or activity from this instant yet too familiar image are accused of abandoning their culture. Myth both becomes and predicts the acceptable ethnic reality, and the diversity, past and present, of Native America is once again ignored.

Clearly popular taste in Indian literature is directed by historical misinformation: Indians are most familiar and recognizable when ahorse and inarticulate. Indeed, according to the nineteenth-century literary convention (as exemplified by William Simms's *Yemassee,* for instance), tribal members could not even speak grammatically in their own "tongues"! The genre, then, can function as a kind of ethnohistorical frieze, leaving Native Americans bereft of and precluded from cultural dynamism and condemned to a static and zoo-like presentation.

Obviously the social history of Native American/Euro-American relations lends itself to exploration through literature; and it particularly challenges creative artists, such as Momaday, who are attempting to break new ground. His *Way to Rainy Mountain* is a classic of traditional Kiowa literature. Composed in English, it cannot be understood without major reference to its tribal symbol system. It may misleadingly appear, like much oral literature when written down, simple and straightforward and the non-Kiowa reader who approaches the work in isolation will likely miss much of its depth and hence most of its beauty and significance. Fortunately, ethnographic and historical materials, albeit of varying quality, exist for nearly every indigenous society, and increasingly they are being re-published by the tribes themselves.

This movement of tribes to take charge of their own public image is long overdue. There is a new and maturing generation of Native American people, both on reservations and in urban communities, who are by necessity culturally adaptive. Their primary language of expression is English, but an English accommodated to the special needs of their individual tribal histories and realities. In their literature, whether oral or written, this transformed English is adjusted to correspond to their unique ethnohistorical aesthetics.

The prose and poetry of such major writers as James Welch, Leslie Silko, and Simon Ortiz demonstrate the complexity and richness of this emerging category of Native American writing. Their perspectives fall squarely within the traditions of historical, ethnic communities and accordingly they tend to expand the scope of English language composition and criticism. Their creations exhibit qualities rarely found in fictional, English language Indians—humor, irony, intelligence, and stamina; the protagonists are good and bad in ordinary human ways, rather than spectacularly exotic, and share complicated and changing relationships with each other and with the world.

Welch in particular has evidenced an artistic vision spanning and uniting tribal and American literary traditions. His first novel, *Winter in the Blood* (1974), has been widely read and acclaimed by both native and nonnative readers. In this book, people who happen to be Indians abide on a reservation in Montana. While the lifestyle portrayed clearly has much in common with rural, white American society, it is also distinctly native. *Winter in the Blood* is a novel that deals with poverty but also with the survival, against great odds, of tradition and of culture. It may well be, together with such works as Leslie Silko's *Ceremony* (1977), among the first manifestations of a new era in Native American expression; at long last a pan-tribal tradition of true "Native American literature" may be happening.

As should by now be obvious, designing a curriculum in which to teach the literature of indigenous North America has inherent pitfalls. If the approach is too facile, too generalized, or too shallow, the effort itself may be counterproductive and may promote, rather than discourage, stereotyping and ethnocentrism. Native American societies and their respective literary traditions are not ornamental and historical artifacts of America's past, but are both ancient and ongoing—and as complicated as those of any other of the world's peoples. If not approached with this awareness, they may appear cute, childish, one-dimensional, and dull.

Diluting or oversimplifying any art, much less that of a politically oppressed and misunderstood group, serves little purpose, and a multiethnic course or unit that simply perpetuates the old Euro-American notion that everything not European must somehow be "the same" and a bit inferior (i.e., not worthy of serious scrutiny) is pointless. Such practice does a severe disservice to all concerned, for it deprives the student of the wealth of human experience, insight, and imagination bound up in each and every tradition, and it deprecates the brilliance and complexity of ancient and fascinating civilizations. Oral tradition is a cornerstone of every tribal society, the vehicle through which wisdom is passed and by which sense is made of a confusing world. It is responsible in large part for the education, entertainment, and inspiration of the community, and its study offers the opportunity to experience new and provocative visions of reality.

To adequately investigate any literature, the student must examine its evolution and development through time, must know something of the language—its rules, its implied worldview of its creation—must know something of the culture's history of being influenced by peoples other than itself, and must know something of its modern social setting. The study of Pueblo literature, for instance, must begin with an awareness of the dialect and philosophy of the creation stories. It is important to realize that a special archaic language exists within the culture exclusively used for rote-memorized, sacred "texts." One must then proceed through a reading of the myth cycles, the historical sagas, the riddles and songs and religious chants, the treaties and diaries and autobiographies, and then continue with the work of Simon Ortiz—*Going for the Rain* (1976)—and Silko. If the process appears easy, something is wrong—for it is truly difficult to cross the boundaries of culture and time and class and language in order to see the world through another's eyes.

The effort, however, is not without reward. Even today, the student reared and nurtured in the Euro-American tradition of expected homogeny is shocked and astounded to discover that cultural pluralism is real, that people can actually think, believe, and act differently and still be people. It is no small educational accomplishment to appreciate only that American Indian societies have depth and intellectual complexity.

Though the task is long and demanding, to uncover this fact about one tribe, one non-Western people—be they Pueblo or Lakota, Ashanti or Ainu, Eskimo or Malay—is to

understand and accept it by inference for all the rest. The
discovery of just one alternate way of being and becoming
human puts to rest forever, for that discoverer, the destructive myth that any single group holds a monopoly on civilization or imagination.

College English
October 1979

MR. REAGAN AND THE
INDIANS

When, in 1988, university students in Moscow asked Ronald Reagan to explain the disastrous economic and social conditions of this country's American Indian population, the president became reflective.

"We have provided millions of acres of land for what are called preservations—or the reservations, I should say. [The Indians], from the beginning, announced that they wanted to maintain their way of life, as they had always lived there in the desert and the plains and so forth. But," he mused, "maybe we made a mistake. Maybe we should not have humored them in that, wanting to stay in that kind of primitive lifestyle. Maybe we should have said, 'No, come join us. Be citizens along with the rest of us.'"

Not a very original idea, Mr. President. Five hundred years ago, people in what is now this country tried that plan. Rich and populous, they felt sorry for a few stragglers who washed up on their shores, bereft of food or shelter, in need of medicine and instruction, so they said to these lost vagabonds, "Come join us."

What happened next, as the president might describe it,

is show-biz history, reminiscent of that vintage comedy *The Man Who Came to Dinner.* Like Sheridan Whiteside, who exploits and abuses his horrified hosts, turning their once placid home into a nightmare, our garrulous leader's forebears repaid aboriginal hospitality with centuries of chicanery, bad contracts, broken promises, and outright lies.

And now, according to this president—under whose administration the quality of life for Native Americans has declined in every sphere more drastically and more rapidly than at any previous period since the Bureau of Indian Affairs was a subdivision of the Department of War—it's the Indians' fault.

Let's set the record straight on a few basic issues. As Suzann Harjo, executive director of the National Congress of American Indians, put it, Europeans "weren't dragging any land behind them when they came to this country." In 1492 the Western Hemisphere was thoroughly inhabited, supporting tens of millions of people—more than one hundred million, by one demographic calculation—living in a tremendous variety of cultures. During their millennia of residence, they had developed cities, commerce, agriculture, aesthetic traditions of art, philosophy, and religion. What they lacked, unfortunately, was a natural genetic immunity to Old World diseases.

It is estimated by some demographers at the University of Texas that roughly nineteen out of twenty Indians on this continent died from such maladies as smallpox, tuberculosis, measles, and influenza passed on, for the most part inadvertently, by European explorers and settlers. As a result of this decimation, huge tracts of cleared land, including the sites for many present-day American cities, became vacant.

In an attempt to salvage something for their descendants, Indian leaders made treaties with European powers and later with the U.S. government. The deals were simple: in exchange for the peaceful cession of most of North America, a few relatively small parcels would be retained in perpetuity by tribes as secure homelands. The sovereignty of these areas, which of course preceded that of the United States, was somewhat modified by these understandings, but it was never lost.

Even the U.S. Supreme Court, in nineteenth-century decisions that apply, defined Indian lands as "dependent, domestic nations," a fine point of law that the executive branch of the government, from Andrew Jackson to Ronald Reagan, has found difficult to comprehend or uphold.

Before his advisers could turn him off in Moscow, the commander-in-chief went on to prattle about that old saw— oil-rich Indians. Tell that to the people on the Pine Ridge or Crow Creek (Sioux) reservations, residents of Shannon and Buffalo counties, South Dakota, the poorest in the United States with per capita incomes of $2,637 and $2,642, respectively. Tell it to the 70 percent unemployed on Rosebud, to the Indian students without college money in Montana, to the Alaska Natives, who have to travel hundreds of miles to poorly equipped Indian Health Service clinics.

And what of the "primitive lifestyle" to which the president believes Indians are so attached? Is it the reservation system or is it broken treaties that are ultimately responsible for the nation's highest teenage suicide rate, soaring infant mortality, shortened life span (37 percent of all Indians die before the age of forty-five), poverty, and chronic alcoholism?

Has "humoring" Indians on those "reservations" (i.e., encouraging them to believe in the solemn agreements ratified by the Senate that made their survival a national trust) caused racism, cultural genocide, or environmental catastrophe?

Certainly, Ronald Reagan's administration has done its level best, through neglect or through direct assault, to overturn programs and policies that have historically protected Indians' rights. Reagan first vetoed major Indian health-care legislation, then reduced existing services by 13 percent. Even during years of economic growth, his appointees cut budget appropriations for education, housing, and legal aid.

Not even Indians' rights as U.S. citizens are respected. Reagan's Supreme Court nominees, led by Sandra Day O'Connor, this year ruled that an easement for a logging road in northern California took precedence over protecting lands sacred to the practice of a one-thousand-year-old Karok tribal religion.

For the one and a half million Indians of this country, including almost four hundred thousand full-time reservation residents, "primitive lifestyle" is as good a description as any for the deprivations suffered over the past eight years. There's nothing humorous about it.

And for the information of Mr. Reagan, Indians have been citizens of the United States since 1924. Some may have even voted for him. Once.

Los Angeles Times
June 12, 1988

DANCES WITH INDIANS

In *Dances with Wolves,* the Sioux and Lt. John Dunbar meet cute: he's naked, and that fact so throws a group of mounted warriors off their normal stride that the ingenuous young soldier lives to tell the tale, a sort of Boy Scout "Order of the Arrow" ritual carried to the *n*th power. The plot begins when Dunbar (Kevin Costner), a Civil War–era recruit, arrives at his western frontier post after it has been completely deserted. Alone, he is befriended first by the eponymous wolf. Then, taken in by local Indians and aptly renamed Dances with Wolves, he quickly earns merit badges in Pawnee bashing and animal telepathy. In short order, he marries Stands with a Fist (Mary McDonnell), a passionate young widow who just happens to herself be a white captive/campfire girl of impressive cross-cultural accomplishments. Eventually the "With" family strikes out on their own—the nucleus of a handsome new Anglo tribe—sadder, wiser, and certainly more sensitive as a result of their Native American immersion.

Kevin Costner's Dunbar follows in a long tradition of literary and cinematic heroes who have discovered Indians. Robinson Crusoe did it off the coast of Brazil, Natty Bumppo did it in New York State, and everyone from

Dustin Hoffman (*Little Big Man*, 1970) to Richard Harris (*A Man Called Horse*, 1970, and *Return of a Man Called Horse*, 1976) to Debra Paget (*Broken Arrow*, 1950), Natalie Wood (*The Searchers*, 1956), and Robert Redford (*Tell Them Willie Boy Is Here*, 1969) has done it in Hollywood.

The first time I saw a white guy get spiritually redeemed by life among the Indians was at a matinee in 1958, when I was in the sixth grade. Of course, when push came to shove at the end of *The Light in the Forest*, little James Mac-Arthur sold out his adopted people and went back to his own kind.

Usually these visits by outsiders do not bode well for the Indians involved—just ask the Mohicans! Appreciative white folks always seem to show up shortly before the cavalry (who are often searching for them) or Manifest Destiny, and record the final days of peace before the tribe is annihilated. Readers and viewers of such sagas are left with a predominant emotion of regret for a golden age now but a faint memory. In the imaginary mass media world of neat beginnings, middles, and ends, American Indian society, whatever its virtues and fascinations as an arena for Euro-American consciousness raising, is definitely past tense.

Thematically, virtually all such films share a subtle (or not so subtle) message: Indians may be poor, they may at first seem strange or forbidding or primitive, but, by golly, once you get to know them they have a thing or two to teach us about The Meaning of Life.

The tradition goes back a long way. Europeans like

French philosopher Jean-Jacques Rousseau and turn-of-this-century novelist Karl May (whose many books, a mixture of Louis L'Amour and the Hardy Boys, have been a rite of passage for generations of German youth) laid out a single range for Indians to inhabit: savage-savage to noble-savage. Indians embody the concept of "the other"—a foreign, exotic panorama against which "modern" (i.e., white) men can measure and test themselves, and eventually, having proved their mettle in battle, be anointed as natural leaders by their hosts.

Placed within the genre, *Dances with Wolves* shows some signs of evolution. Director/star Kevin Costner obviously worked hard and spared no expense in order to achieve a sense of authenticity in his production. He filmed on the Pine Ridge reservation in South Dakota and defied conventional Hollywood wisdom to assemble a large and talented Native American supporting cast. Great attention was clearly paid to dressing the actors in ethnographically correct costumes, and if the streets in the native camp seem a tad too spotless to be believed, at least the tipis are museum-quality.

Impressively, large segments of the film are spoken in Lakota, the language of the western Sioux, and though the subtitles are stilted (Indians in the movies seem incapable of using verbal contractions and are overly fond of explaining the minute details of their motivation), they at least convey the impression that Native Americans carried on an intellectual life among themselves.

When I saw *Dances with Wolves* at an advance screening, I predicted to a friend that it would be less than a box-office smash. Though spectacular to look at, it struck me as too long, too predictable, too didactic to attract a large audience. One hundred million dollars in revenues and twelve Academy Award nominations later, was I ever wrong. In fact, it's possible that the movie sells tickets precisely because it delivers the old-fashioned Indians whom the ticket-buying audience expects to find. Kevin Costner is our national myth's everyman—blandly handsome, Robert Bly–sensitive, flexible, politically correct. He passes the test of the frontier, out-Indians the Indians, achieves a pure soul by encountering and surmounting the wilderness.

Yet, if *Dances with Wolves* had been about people who happen to be Indians, rather than about INDIANS (uniformly stoic, brave, nasty to their enemies, nice to their friends), it might have stood a better chance of forming a bridge between societies that for too long have woodenly characterized each other. The film's tremendous popularity is sure to generate a bubble of sympathy for the Sioux, but hard questions remain: will this sentiment be practical, translating into public support for Native American legal cases before the U.S. Supreme Court, for restoration of Lakota sacred lands (the Black Hills) or water rights, for tribal sovereignty, for providing the funding desperately needed by reservation health-care clinics? Pine Ridge is today, according to the U.S. Census Bureau, the most economically impoverished corner of America, but will its modern Indian advocates in business suits, men and women equipped with laptop computers and articulate English, be the recipients of a tidal wave of popcorn-fed good will?

Or will it turn out, once again, that the only good Indians, the only Indians whose causes and needs this country can embrace, are lodged safely in the past, wrapped neatly in the blankets of history, comfortable magnets for our sympathy because they require nothing of us but tears in a dark theater?

New York Times
February 1991

OPENED
DOORS

BEATING THE SYSTEM

When I was a little boy we lived in a neighborhood too small for a bookstore—not a major problem because we didn't have enough money to buy books anyway, and a branch library, constructed of yellow bricks, was located nearby. The building consisted of one large room, neatly bisected by the reference/checkout desk. To the right were encyclopedias, atlases, telephone books, and The Illustrated Bible in twenty-two volumes. There were shelves of children's books, reading tables, and self-help magazines. All available to the holder of my "young person's" library card.

To the left was everything I really wanted to read—the adults-only stuff. I don't know who made the designation— that Sinclair Lewis and Twain (the real thing) and Flaubert in translation were safe only to those old enough to be drafted. But I do know it was not Evelyn Westlock, the librarian, because she was one of my two coconspirators.

The other was my very literate Aunt Marion, who had been pushed into the labor force at the age of fourteen by the Great Depression but spent the next forty years of evenings reading. Ever the free thinker, she didn't subscribe to ageism or bureaucratic rules, and so gave me a note, a kind of literary passport: "Please permit Michael to check out books for me," she had written, then signed her name—pointedly not specifying which or how many books she meant.

It was a bald ruse, a fragile causeway over the gulf from right wing to left. And Evelyn Westlock didn't fall for it one bit. The first time, at age eleven, I presented her with a stack of adult books—Marx, I know, was tucked among them, unobtrusively I hoped—my palms were sweaty. My heart beat faster than usual. This was my bibliophile's version of presenting a false ID at a package store.

Evelyn Westlock scowled at the note, frowned at me, spread the books before her (Marx!—and this was, after all, during the McCarthy era) and slowly, silently read the titles. When she had finished she fixed me with such a fierce stare that I couldn't drop my eyes. And so I heard, rather than saw, her conclusion.

Stamp. A book slammed. Stamp. The next. She gave me three weeks to poison my mind, and pushed the pile back to me with what I'm sure was a wink. I was so relieved, so thrilled, that I didn't wait to go home. There, on the library steps, in the early evening twilight, I began Main Street, its cover poorly concealed by an opened Popular Mechanics. I was Carol, trapped and misunderstood in a small town—we suffered as one.

I was hooked.

Booklist
January 1, 1990

TRUSTING THE WORDS

On the Banks of Plum Creek was the first brand-new hard-back book I ever bought for myself. It was not a casual or impulse purchase—such a luxury was beyond a family of our economic level—but a considered acquisition. Two summers before, during my daily browse in the small neighborhood library a short walk from where I lived, I had stumbled upon the shelf of Laura Ingalls Wilder novels. With their pastel covers, gentle illustrations, large type, and homey titles, they were appealing, inviting, but which one to try first? In the manner of Goldilocks, I decided that *Farmer Boy* looked too long, *Little House in the Big Woods* too short. *Plum Creek*, though, was just right. More than just right: by an amazing coincidence I had just an hour before consumed a plum for lunch!

Naturally, like thousands of other readers over the past fifty years, I was captured from page one. The snug little dwelling dug into the side of a creek bank was as irresistible to me at age eight as Bilbo Baggins's similar den proved to be some ten years later. The ever-mobile Ingalls family—adaptable, affectionate Pa; conventional, resourceful Ma; pretty, good-girl Mary; baby Carrie—were the Swiss Family Robinson next door, the us-against-the-world American ideal of underdogs who, through grit and wit and optimism, prevailed over every natural disaster and took advantage of every available resource in their inexorable path toward increased creature comforts and status. As linchpin and leading protagonist, second child Laura was full-swing into the adventure of growing up, and as such she was not just like me, but like me the way I aspired to be: plucky and brave, composed of equal parts good will and self-interest. Her life was a constantly unfolding tapestry, its events intricately connected and stitched with affectionate detail. The cast of human and animal players auxiliary to the central family was limited and manageable enough for a reader to grasp as distinct individuals, and within the balanced, safe context of ultimate parental protection, even a week-long blizzard was the occasion for a chapter titled "A Day of Games."

I doubt if any of today's powerful publishing marketing committees would project the young me as a likely target audience for the Wilder books. Superficially, Laura and I had so little in common, so few intersections of experience with which I should logically have been able to identify. Those experts would probably conclude that I—as a mixed-blood, male, only child of a single-parent, mostly urban, fixed-income family—would prefer novels more reflective of myself. True, I wasn't immune to "boy books." I dutifully followed every scrape that Frank and Joe Hardy fell into, worked my way through James Fenimore Cooper, Charles Dickens, and Alexandre Dumas, and had a stack of *D.C. Comics* in which both Superman and Batman figured prominently. But when the time came to buy a real book, to receive the first volume in what has become an extensive personal collection of literature, I didn't hesitate: *On the Banks of Plum Creek* was an old friend I was sure I'd want to read many more times in the years to come, as indeed I have.

The nine Little House books—*Little House in the Big Woods, Little House on the Prairie, On the Banks of Plum Creek, By the Shores of Silver Lake, The Long Winter, Farmer Boy, Little Town on the Prairie, These Happy Golden Years,* and *The First Four Years*—together with two subsequent collections of Laura Ingalls Wilder's diary entries (*On the Way Home*) and letters (*West from Home*), supplemented by related songbooks and cookbooks, chronicle and particularize like no other source the mythic American frontier journey from precarious adversity into middle-class security. If, as it appears from *The Ghost in the Little House,* William Holtz's new and convincing life of Rose Wilder Lane (Laura's only child, who grew up to be a thoroughly modern woman and one of the most far-flung and daring journalists of the 1920s and 1930s), the novels are more collaborative biography than homespun autobiography, their power is in no way diminished. That the characters are crafted verisimilitudes rather than drawn word-for-word upon fact only contributes to the readability of the series. The belated discovery that the generous, self-taught, talented, and complicated daughter shaped the rough yet keenly precise recollections of her farmer mother into art is an intriguing surprise—but certainly does not undermine either the historical or the humanistic value of a saga that at its heart depicts the universal struggle of a child growing to adulthood and independence.

Far more problematic, at least for me, were the issues raised when, with the enthusiasm of a father who had long looked forward to sharing a favorite tale, I set down last year to begin reading the books to my two daughters, ages seven and eight. Not one page into *Little House in the Big Woods*, I heard my own voice saying, "As far as a man could go to the north in a day, or a week, or a whole month, there was nothing but woods. There were no houses. There were no roads. There were no people. There were only trees and the wild animals who had their homes among them."

Say what? Excuse me, but weren't we forgetting the Chippewa branch of my daughters' immediate ancestry, not to mention the thousands of resident Menominees, Potawatomis, Sauks, Foxes, Winnebagos, and Ottawas who inhabited mid-nineteenth-century Wisconsin, as they had for many hundreds of years? Exactly upon whose indigenous land was Grandma and Grandpa's cozy house constructed? Had they paid for the bountiful property, teeming with wild game and fish? This fun-filled world of extended Ingallses was curiously empty, a pristine wilderness in which only white folks toiled and cavorted, ate and harvested, celebrated and were kind to each other.

My dilemma, as raconteur, was clear. My little girls

looked up to me with trusting eyes, eager to hear me continue with the first of these books I had promised with such anticipation. I had made "an event" out of their reading, an intergenerational gift, and now in the cold light of an adult perspective I realized that I was, in my reluctance to dilute the pleasure of a good story with the sober stuff of history, in the process of perpetuating a Eurocentric attitude that was still very much alive. One had only to peruse newspaper accounts of contemporary Wisconsin controversies over tribal fishing rights, bingo emporia, and legal and tax jurisdiction to realize that many of Grandpa and Grandma's descendants remained determined that there could be "no people" except those who were just like them.

Okay, I admit it. I closed the book rather than be politically correct at 8 P.M. in my daughters' bedroom. I'd save the cold water of reality for the light of day, and anyway, I seemed to remember that once Ma and Pa pushed west they had encountered native people.

"Let's start instead tomorrow with *Little House on the Prairie*," I suggested. This idea went over well, since it evoked in my girls the visual image of the pretty, if often saccharine, TV series of the same name.

Fast forward to the next evening, paragraph two: *"They were going to the Indian country."*

Good sign! The packing up and the journey west were lovingly and minutely related. The sense of space and sky found on the plains was gloriously rendered. The pages turned, my daughters' eyes stayed bright long past their usual bedtime, the book was everything I remembered—realistic, lyrical, exciting in all the right ways. And then, page 46.

Laura chewed and swallowed, and she said, "I want to see a papoose."

"Mercy on us!" Ma said. "Whatever makes you want to see Indians? We will see enough of them. More than we want to, I wouldn't wonder."

"They wouldn't hurt us, would they?" Mary asked. Mary was always good; she never spoke with her mouth full.

"No!" Ma said. "Don't get such an idea into your head."

"Why don't you like Indians, Ma?" Laura asked, and she caught a drip of molasses with her tongue.

"I just don't like them, and don't lick your fingers, Laura," said Ma.

"This is Indian country, isn't it?" Laura said. "What did we come to their country for, if you don't like them?"

Ma said she didn't know whether this was Indian country or not. She didn't know where the Kansas line was. But whether or no, the Indians would not be here long. Pa had word from a man in Washington that the Indian Territory would be open to settlement soon.

What was a responsible father to do? Stop the narrative, explain that Ma was a know-nothing racist? Describe the bitter injustice of unilateral treaty abridgment? Break into a chorus of "Oklahoma!" and then point out how American popular culture has long covered up the shame of the Dawes Act by glossing it over with Sooner folklore?

This time, I simply invented an extra line of dialogue.

"That's awful, Ma," I had Laura say. "I'm ashamed to hear such a thing."

But the fantasy of the 1990s-enlightened Laura evaporated not ten pages later.

> That night by the fire Laura asked again when she would see a papoose, but Pa didn't know. He said you never saw Indians unless they wanted you to see them. He had seen Indians when he was a boy in New York State, but Laura never had. She knew they were wild men with red skins, and their hatchets were called tomahawks.
>
> Pa knew all about wild animals, so he must know about wild men, too. Laura thought he would show her a papoose some day, just as he had shown her fawns, and little bears, and wolves.

That part, I confess, I simply skipped, edited right out, blipped. In no time flat Pa was back to his fiddle, Ma was doing something deft and culinary with cornmeal. Nature was nature.

Only the wind rustled in the prairie grasses. The big, yellow moon was sailing high overhead. The sky was so full of light that not one star twinkled in it, and all the prairie was a shadowy mellowness.

And there were no Indians, no cholera-ridden, starving reservations, no prohibitions to the practice of native religion, no Wounded Knee a few hundred miles to the north, no Sand Creek an equal distance to the west. Manifest Destiny protected its own, and family values prevailed, staunchly Calvinist and oblivious to any ethical messiness that might interfere with the romance.

The next chapter, "Moving In," was heralded by a drawing of tipis. I closed the book and kissed the girls goodnight, then retreated to my office to preview on my own. For a while, beyond Ma's offhand disparaging comments about not wanting to "live like Indians," the Ingalls family contented itself with building a house and fending off a wolf pack. Good clean fun, character-building hard work, the grist that made this country great.

Until . . .

suddenly [Jack, the bulldog] stood up and growled a fierce, deep growl. The hair on his neck stood straight up and his eyes glared red.

Laura was frightened. Jack had never growled at her before. Then she looked over her shoulder where Jack was looking, and she saw two naked wild men coming, one behind the other, on the Indian trail.

"Mary! Look!" she cried. Mary looked and saw them, too.

They were tall, thin, fierce-looking men. Their skin was brownish-red. Their head seemed to go up to a peak, and the peak was a tuft of hair that stood straight up and ended in feathers. Their eyes were black and still and glittering, like snake's eyes.

The Indians went into the new house and Laura worried for the safety of Ma and baby Carrie. "I'm going to let Jack loose," Laura whispered, hoarsely. "Jack will kill them."

But no, the Indians only wanted some of Ma's cornbread and Pa's tobacco. They were wearing skunk skins, which didn't smell good, and their eyes glittered some more, but otherwise they were perfectly benign. When Pa came home he at first dealt with news of the visit with laudable equanimity, but then went on, before stopping himself, to add, "The main thing is to be on good terms with the Indians. We don't want to wake up some night with a band of the screeching dev—."

The concluding chapters of *Little House on the Prairie* are full of Indians—some threatening, some noble. The settlers worry over the possibility of being attacked and driven out, but it doesn't transpire. Instead, inevitably, the Indians are forced to evacuate in an endless line that trails past the family home. Pa takes this banishment as a given.

> "When white settlers come into a country, the Indians have to move on. The government is going to move these Indians farther west, any time now. That's why we're here, Laura. White people are going to settle all this country, and we get the best land because we get here first and take our pick. Now do you understand?"
>
> "Yes, Pa," Laura said. "But, Pa, I thought this was Indian Territory. Won't it make the Indians mad to have to—"
>
> "No more questions, Laura," Pa said firmly. "Go to sleep."

Pa never felt as guilty as I would have liked him to, though he did disagree with his friend Mr. Scott who maintained that "the only good Indian is a dead Indian." Ma, on the other hand, remained an unreconstructed bigot—as late as *The Long Winter*, three novels and many years later, the very mention of even friendly, helpful Indians set her off.

> "What Indian?" Ma asked [Pa]. She looked as if she were smelling the smell of an Indian whenever she said the word. Ma despised Indians. She was afraid of them, too.
>
> For her part, Laura seemed typically open

minded, wanting at one point to adopt an Indian baby.

"Its eyes are so black," Laura sobbed. She could not say what she meant.

At last, the Ingalls family, emblematic of all those like them who went west with the blithe assumption that resident tribes had no title rights to the country they had occupied from time immemorial, witnessed the realization of their dream: a vanishing native population. Surprisingly, it was not a jubilant moment.

It was dinner-time, and no one thought of dinner. Indian ponies were still going by, carrying bunches of skins and tent-poles and dangling baskets and cooking pots. There were a few more women and a few more naked Indian children and Laura and Mary still stayed in the doorway, looking, till that long line of Indians slowly pulled itself over the western edge of the world. And nothing was left but silence and emptiness. All the world seemed very quiet and lonely.

As it turned out, I didn't read aloud the Little House books to my daughters because, quite frankly, I realized I couldn't have kept my mouth shut at the objectionable parts. I would have felt compelled to interrupt the story constantly with editorial asides, history lessons, thought questions, critiques of the racism or sexism embedded in the text. I would have studiously purified those novels, treated them as sociology or fixed them up to suit a contemporary and, I firmly believe, more enlightened sensibility.

Certainly they could be used that way, but, I wonder, would my daughters then grow up with the selective fond memories of each volume that I myself carried? Or would they learn from me that every page of a book had to pass a test in order for the whole to entertain? Would reading with me become a chore, a "learning experience," a tension, and not the pleasure I wished it?

Laura Ingalls Wilder and her daughter, Rose Wilder Lane, created a series peopled by characters who were, for better or worse, true to the prevailing attitudes of their day. Resisting the temptation to stereotype or sensationalize beyond the often ill-informed opinions of both adults and children, the actual incidents that involve Indians are portrayed as invariably anticlimactic—more ordinary and less dramatic than anyone, even Pa, expects them to be. Distilled from the aura of mystery and danger, the Indians on the periphery of the Ingalls family's vision are thin, unfortunate, and determinedly honest. Their journey is the sad underside of the bright pioneer coin, and their defeat and expulsion brings no one any glory. Ma and Pa's self-serving lack of compassion was probably no worse than most and much better than that of those who filed claims west of the Mississippi 150 years ago, and to create them otherwise and still present them as "typical" would be wishful thinking.

Ruminating on my own various interactions with the Little House books, I remembered that I had never much cared for Ma—even when I was a young boy she had struck me as prudish and cautious and uptight, with untested prejudices and unexamined rules that fairly cried out for rebellion. I remembered that I had Ma to thank, possibly more than anyone else in real life or in literature, for my first startling awareness that an adult authority figure could actually be dense and narrow minded. I remembered that those nagging, unanswered questions about what *did* happen to Indians in the nineteenth century (and why) had engendered an indignant pride in the Modoc part of my ethnic heritage. They had sent me to elderly relatives and to the history section of the library and that in turn had led to school research projects and maps, activism in the 1960s, and support of the American Indian Movement and, ultimately, no doubt, contributed heavily to my founding of the Native American Studies Program at Dartmouth College in 1972 and teaching there for the next fifteen years. Take that, Ma!

Books, important as they can and should be, are after all but a part of the much larger context that informs them. They illuminate our experience but at the same time our experience sheds light back upon their ideas and theories. A book converts less than it nudges us toward what we otherwise already think. The existence of characters who are distasteful or complicated merely reflects the world as it is.

I placed the Little House novels on the top shelf of the bookcase and told my daughters I thought it would be better if they read them, when and if they wanted to, to themselves. I trust that they will not be corrupted into Indianophobes even as they thrill to description of a runaway buggy or warm to the first blush of young love when Laura and Almanzo go courting. I trust that they will be able to differentiate courage from pettiness, justice from exploitation. I'll bide my time, and when, eventually, each of my girls bursts through a door, eyes ablaze with outrage, waving a book in her hand, furious . . . then we'll talk about it.

Booklist
June 15, 1993

SUMMER READING

When I was fourteen, I earned money in the summer by mowing lawns, and within a few weeks I had built up a regular clientele. I got to know people by the flowers they planted that I had to remember not to cut down, by the things they lost in the grass or stuck in the ground on purpose. I reached the point with most of them when I knew in advance what complaint was about to be spoken, which particular request was most important. And I learned something about the measure of my neighbors by their preferred method of payment: by the job, by the month—or not at all.

Mr. Ballou fell into the last category, and he always had a reason why. On one day he had no change for a fifty, on another he was flat out of checks, on another, he was simply out when I knocked on his door. Still, except for the money part, he was a nice enough old guy, always waving or tipping his hat when he'd see me from a distance. I figured him for a thin retirement check, maybe a work-related injury that kept him from doing his own yard work. Sure, I kept a running total, but I didn't worry about the amount too much. Grass was grass, and the little that Mr. Ballou's property comprised didn't take long to trim.

Then, one late afternoon in mid-July, the hottest time of the year, I was walking by his house and he opened the door, motioned me to come inside. The hall was cool, shaded, and it took my eyes a minute to adjust to the muted light.

"I owe you," Mr. Ballou began, "but . . . "

I thought I'd save him the trouble of thinking up a new excuse. "No problem. Don't worry about it."

"The bank made a mistake in my account," he continued, ignoring my words. "It will be cleared up in a day or two. But in the meantime I thought perhaps you could choose one or two volumes for a down payment."

He gestured toward the walls and I saw that books were stacked everywhere. It was like a library, except with no order to the arrangement.

"Take your time," Mr. Ballou encouraged. "Read, borrow, keep. Find something you like. What do you read?"

"I don't know." And I didn't. I generally read what was in front of me, what I could snag from the paperback rack at the drugstore, what I found at the library, magazines, the back of cerial boxes, comics. The idea of consciously seeking out a special title was new to me, but, I realized, not without appeal—so I browsed through the piles of books.

"You actually read all of these?"

"This isn't much," Mr. Ballou said. "This is nothing, just what I've kept, the ones worth looking at a second time."

"Pick for me, then."

He raised his eyebrows, cocked his head, regarded me

appraisingly as though measuring me for a suit. After a moment, he nodded, searched through a stack, and handed me a dark red hard-bound book, fairly thick.

"*The Last of the Just,*" I read. "By André Schwarz-Bart. What's it about?"

"You tell me," he said. "Next week."

I started after supper, sitting outdoors on an uncomfortable kitchen chair. Within a few pages, the yard, the summer, disappeared, the bright oblivion of adolescence temporarily lifted, and I was plunged into the aching tragedy of the Holocaust, the extraordinary clash of good, represented by one decent man, and evil. Translated from French, the language was elegant, simple, overwhelming. When the evening light finally failed I moved inside, read all through the night.

To this day, thirty years later, I vividly remember the experience. It was my first voluntary encounter with world literature, and I was stunned by the undiluted power a novel could contain. I lacked the vocabulary, however, to translate my feelings into words, so the next week, when Mr. Ballou asked, "Well?" I only replied, "It was good."

"Keep it, then," he said. "Shall I suggest another?"

I nodded, and was presented with the paperback edition of Margaret Mead's *Coming of Age in Samoa.*

To make two long stories short, Mr. Ballou never paid me a dime for cutting his grass that year or the next, but for fifteen years I taught anthropology at Dartmouth College. Summer reading was not the innocent pastime I had assumed it to be, not a breezy, instantly forgettable escape in a hammock (though I've since enjoyed many of those, too). A book, if it arrives before you at the right moment, in the proper season, at a point of intermission in the daily business of things, will change the course of all that follows.

Detroit News
May 1991

REMEMBERING A BOOK OF REMEMBERING

In the traditional Navajo belief system, as well as in those of many other native peoples, harmony is regarded as the key to perfection. Illness, personal or group disaster, every manner of evil, comes into being because some disparate element within the universe has gone out of kilter. Health is restored only after the natural order of things is put back into synch by some established ceremony or sacrifice, only after the scales of every interaction are once again in balance.

An analogous legend in Jewish apocrypha concerns the required presence in the world of the *Lamed-Vov* ("Just Men"), "the hearts of the world multiplied, . . . into [whom], as into one receptacle, pour all our griefs." As described in *The Last of the Just* (1959), this cadre of otherwise ordinary individuals collectively acts as a kind of sponge for misery,

absorbing pain and cruelty before it spills out and over-
comes everything. "If just one of [the Just Men] were lacking," we are told, "the suffering of mankind would poison
even the souls of the newborn, and humanity would suffo-
cate with a single cry."

French author André Schwarz-Bart focuses on the lineage of the Levys, a Diaspora family renowned through the
ages for their gentleness and intelligence, but even more
because one son in each generation inherits the mantle of
being a *Lamed-Vov*. The nature and cosmic purpose of this
burden is not easy to explain, or to understand.

"If a man suffers all alone," Mordecai asks of
his beloved and adoring grandson, Ernie, "it is
clear his suffering remains within him. Right?"

"Right," Ernie said.

"But if another looks at him and says to him,
'You're in trouble, my Jewish brother,' what happens then?"

". . . I understand that too," [Ernie] said
politely. "He takes the suffering of his friend into
his own eyes."

Mordecai sighed, smiled, sighed again. "And if
he is blind, do you think he can take it in?"

"Of course, through his ears!"

"And if he is deaf?"

"Then through his hands," Ernie said gravely.

"And if the other is far away, if he can neither

hear him nor see him and not even touch him—do you believe then that he can take in his pain?"

"Maybe he could guess at it," Ernie said with a cautious expression.

Mordecai went into ecstasies. "You've said it, my love—that is exactly what the Just Man does! He senses all the evil rampant on earth, and he takes it into his heart."

A finger against the corner of his mouth, Ernie followed the course of a thought. He exhaled sadly, "But what good does it do to sense it if nothing is changed?"

"It changes for God, don't you see?"

The Last of the Just is about the nature of empathy, about why an old man must prepare a child for life with such a sad and bleak lesson, and more generally, it is a book that places the Holocaust within a wider frame in order to demonstrate that the Final Solution was but the culmination of a thousand years of religious persecution. Beginning with the Maccabean-like suicide of Rabbi Yom Tov Levi in York in 1185, Schwarz-Bart provides in rapid succession vignettes describing the martyrdom of each Just Man ancestor before focusing on a particular clan of modern Levys dwelling in the Polish town of Zemyock just before the turn of this century. For all their illustrious legacy of persecution, these characters initially seem more the stuff of folklore or domestic comedy than epic. Fathers

and sons dispute questions of religious practice, mothers-
in-law and daughters-in-law are at odds over child-rearing
issues, children struggle to grow up, and young people
stumble into unlikely and complicated romantic entangle-
ments.

And yet these simple, well-intentioned men and women
live in a time of gathering insanity. Ordinary events—a
confrontation with a schoolyard bully, a walk down the
street to a place of worship, the purchase of bread—are
laced with grave danger. The Levys have no choice but to
become reluctant heroes, tough and resilient, and for a
while their innocence, their love for each other, their large
and small acts of courage constitute the only evidence of
humane behavior, the earthen dam battered by a relentless
grind. But finally, inevitably, they are swept away along
with six million others—including André Schwarz-Bart's
own parents.

The bulk of the novel is set in Germany—where the
Levys migrated after a pogrom by White Russians—and
later in France—where they fled after the advent of National
Socialism. Much of the action is seen through the at first precocious and then prematurely old eyes of Ernie Levy, born
around 1920, as he comes of age in a world that seems bent
upon his obliteration. We watch him recoil from one disappointment, one injury after another, and yet he is not altogether beaten. There's a flame within him that yearns toward
goodness, that insists upon a modicum of peace, and through
his spiritual journey we contemplate the unthinkable, search

for meaning and sense where there seems to be only madness.

The sole survivor of his line, Ernie for a time shuns his heritage, becomes agnostic, passes for a Gentile, crosses safely into unoccupied territory, but he cannot sustain his escape and goes back into the maelstrom. "He had no intention of . . . separating himself from the humble procession of the Jewish people," and ultimately assumes the responsibility of a *Lamed-Vov*, perishing in an Auschwitz gas chamber while consoling a terrified flock of orphaned children. Throughout the novel, Ernie has functioned as a living embodiment of hope. When he dies without descendants, the world is forever a Just Man short.

The Last of the Just is very much a work of the postwar period, when the shock of the Holocaust was still immediate and raw—and as such it is a necessary and important book. The passage of time undoubtedly obscures the context, dulls our connection with victims who, in the words of one elderly patriarch, were "so permanently afraid." *The Last of the Just* brings them vividly and poignantly to life.

All the same, the attitudes with which the novel's characters regard events and social conventions are occasionally radically at odds with contemporary sensibilities. While graphically demonstrating the brutishness and awful consequences of intolerance, for example, Schwarz-Bart occasionally lapses into the language of condescending sexism. Of Ernie's mother we are told that "all women are little girls getting on in years, each endowed with a body greater and more important than her mind, and all of whom adore surrounding themselves with meaningless mysteries." Such instances of gender chauvinism—invisible, in all probability, to many readers thirty years ago—provide telling evidence that insidious cultural biases come in all shapes and sizes.

Equally arresting is the book's philosophical rationalization for passive submission. Those few characters who attempt to take up arms in self-defense are presented as relatively short-sighted, naive in their belief that destiny can be averted. "Occasionally," after virtually all of his family is shipped off to a concentration camp, "Ernie thought he should go downstairs and join one of the movements now forming in the ghetto and outside. There had been stories about the high deeds of certain young Jewish heroes. But all the Germans on earth could not pay for one innocent head, and then, he told himself, for him it would be a luxurious death." In the end, he not only refuses to fight, but literally presents himself at the gate of a camp, imploring the guards to take him in, to do their worst, and of course they oblige.

Today such head-bowed acquiescence seems an almost incomprehensible response. Using the lessons of genocide as their justification, many Israelis hold the position that the only alternative to being helpless is to be stronger, more aggressive than any opponent, to inspire fear rather than be fearful. This attitude is the antithesis, the repudiation, of Ernie Levy's route to blessedness.

Yet whatever one's politics, *The Last of the Just* remains a powerful argument. Every page demands to know: *Why? How could this abomination have happened?* Whether Jewish or Gentile, we are reminded how easily torn is the precious fabric of civilization, and how destructive are the consequences of dumb hatred—whether a society's henchmen are permitted to beat an Ernie Levy because he's Jewish, black, gay, Bosnian, or homeless. The novel endures precisely because it forces us to identify, and thus to remember.

And what of the most basic, most terrifying question: Was the anonymous death of the last Just Man meaningless?

When the mature Ernie Levy spiritually evolves to embody his grandfather's initial parable—when at last he sees, hears, feels, and even dares to imagine the grief that surrounds him—he in some small but significant way transcends suffering, transforms it into grace by imposing upon it his own forgiving interpretation. It changes for God.

Los Angeles Times
September 1991

SURVIVING

Sometimes, very rarely, a book is more than a book. Vital experience is captured on the printed page—condensed, searing, important to know—and the sum of words becomes an indelible part of the reader's imagination. Certain books are a shared dream, and others, like *Surviving the Holocaust: The Kovno Ghetto Diary*, are a collective nightmare.

Avraham Golub (now Tory) was born in 1909 in the Lithuanian village of Lazdijai, the son of a yeshiva-trained father and a mother whose parents were land-owning farmers. He had a promising future. The youngest of six children, he was active from an early age in the Zionist Youth Movement, and eventually studied law at the University of Kovno (Kaunas) and, as an exchange student, at the University of Pittsburgh, where he remained for almost two years. Before the war he traveled to Palestine as the captain of a Maccabi sports team and, on the same trip, represented Lithuanian Jewish students at an international conference in Jerusalem.

In 1933, the year Hitler came to power in Germany, Tory became a practitioner-clerk to a civil court judge, but continued his political activity. Six years later, while he was attending the twenty-first Zionist Congress in Geneva, Poland was invaded. Tory faced a crucial decision: to seek sanctuary in neutral Switzerland or to return home to what would soon be hell. He went back.

Jews had lived in Kovno since 1410, and over the succeeding five hundred years, the city had become a thriving intellectual and religious center. Four daily newspapers— three Zionist, one Bundist—operated during the brief period of Lithuanian independence between the wars. There was a Ministry of Jewish Affairs and a Jewish National Council, and in 1941 Kovno had more than thirty-five thousand Jewish residents, 40 percent of the total civic population. By the end of 1942, more than half of them had been systematically murdered—ten thousand people on one day alone: October 28, 1941. By 1944, all the rest were dead or deported.

Avraham Tory, as the embattled secretary of the Ghetto Council during this period, maintained a meticulous log of events, large and small. Against all odds he managed to preserve a file of the bureaucratic Nazi orders, a heartless trail of red tape that documents the incremental steps that led toward utter dehumanization. In addition, Tory kept a daily journal, a personal commentary on incidents as they transpired, and with the help of friends who risked their lives to do so, these hundreds of pages were hidden in the foundation of a building to be recovered when the horror had ended. That in and of itself was an act of faith, given the circumstances.

From the first entry, Tory is conscious of his role as eye and ear, as the final voice of thousands denied their chance to speak. A gifted writer with a flare for poetry, he strives to be accurate, precise, to include the telling detail. Time and again he records a snippet of conversation overheard on the street, a vignette of ordinary existence in a universe gone mad.

It is these "little" braveries, the everyday choices of life over death, that remain with the reader. Juxtaposed against the coldness of the endless official decrees and requisitions, they constitute a kind of transcendent affirmation, a refusal to surrender inner dignity even when all hope of rescue is lost.

The men, women, and children who populate *Surviving the Holocaust* are complex and unstereotypic, ordinary people in a situation without boundaries. They strive for normalcy, for a foothold, for some reminder of civilization. In the midst of chaos, they share a will to neither forget nor be forgotten.

And as their scribe, their microphone, Avraham Tory has given them a posthumous Pyrrhic victory. *Surviving the Holocaust* is unlike any book I have ever read. Eloquent, rough, particular, yet sweeping in scope, it does not shy from the awfulness of which human beings are capable, but it locates within the worst of that territory individual beacons whose lights are bright enough to cast long shadows.

Newsday
April 1990

ORDINARY MEN

Fifty years ago five hundred men in Hamburg were recruited by the German government to be reserve military policemen. For the most part, they were not members of the Nazi party or the SS, but were working-class citizens who,

{ 2 9 4 }

after leaving *Volksschule* ("terminal secondary school") at age fourteen or fifteen, had been employed in peacetime at regular jobs. By their own subsequent testimony, they weren't especially anti-Semitic, and had been raised in traditional households as Roman Catholics or Protestants. With the exception of a single World War I veteran, they had never been in armed combat, never seen a fellow soldier killed in battle, never been done personal physical harm by a foreign enemy.

Nevertheless, over a period of some sixteen months— from July 1942 through November 1943—these men slaughtered in cold blood some 38,000 defenseless, mostly Jewish, men, women, and children in Poland, and participated in the deportation to death camps of 45,200 others.

Ordinary Men, Christopher Browning's documentary study of the wartime and postwar records of Police Battalion 101, is a clear and dispassionate record of the process of dehumanization, a chronicle of progressive emotional emptiness. No fictionalizer of the macabre, no Stephen King or Dean R. Koontz or Thomas Harris could, in his wildest imagination, approach the cold evil that possessed this company of average men transformed into killing machines. Efficiently, occasionally righteously and piously, sometimes with relish though rarely, according to their recollections, with rage or hatred, 90 percent of them "followed orders"— even when offered the option to decline—and became murderers.

As Browning points out, "in mid-March 1942 some 75 to

80 percent of all victims of the Holocaust were still alive, while 20 to 25 percent had perished. A mere eleven months later, in mid-February 1943, the percentages were exactly the reverse." Those who died were, for the most part, confused peasants, with a smaller number of deported, terrified middle-class German Jews. Regarded in another way, they were all simply human beings.

The landscape of their terror is the Poland so eloquently described in Louis Begley's wrenching, unforgettable 1991 novel, *Wartime Lies*, and the list of towns "cleared"— Józefów, Łomazy, Międzyrzec, Kock, Parczew, Lublin, Majdanek, Poniatowa—is short. The 101 was responsible for a relatively minor operation, a hands-on microcosm, compared with the assembly-line volume of the large concentration camps. Of the six million Jews killed by the Nazis and those who collaborated with them in the Final Solution, the Reserve Police Battalion was physically responsible for the deaths of .006 percent. They merely shot the equivalent of a single small city—equal to the population of only a Danville, Illinois, a Burlington, Vermont, or a Vancouver, Washington.

However, this fraction, coupled with the particularity and brutality of the deaths documented, makes *Ordinary Men* a staggering book, a book that manages without polemic to communicate at least an intimation of the unthinkable.

Certainly, a contemporary reader will recoil at every page as the atrocities accumulate, losing, in their ceaseless repetition, their initial ability to shock, just as these acts apparently did for the men who committed them. "As the story of Reserve Police Battalion 101 demonstrates, mass execution and routine had become one. Normality itself had become exceedingly abnormal."

But do we not have a responsibility to reject the safety— afforded by the brief passage of time and by our geographic distance from the arena—of finding the awful statistics overwhelming, of allowing them to blur the faces of both the individuals who suffered and those who perpetrated the suffering? This happened, we must remind ourselves. This was carried out not by a legion of Jeffrey Dahmers or by nameless Hillside Stranglers. The ranks of the 101 were composed of people not so easy to spot or judge or dismiss. There's no obvious way for us to distance ourselves from them, as they were before the war or as they are now. If we encountered them on the street in 1992, we would find respected retirees who never served a day of their lives in prison, men who, in the sworn statements many made to investigators twenty years after the end of World War II, admitted neither remorse for nor incredulity at their actions. And why should they? Of the 210 members of the battalion brought to trial between 1962 and 1967 for their crimes, only 3 received light sentences. The rest went free.

No doubt judges found the explanations of the exoner- ated to be persuasive, within the amoral context of the *Judenfrei* mania. Contemplate, for instance, the thirty-five- year-old policeman—formerly a metal worker—who specialized in shooting Jewish children in the back of their heads. He rationalized in his testimony that he did his victims a favor: their mothers were doomed, after all, and had they lived they would surely have been neglected.

Another officer, Captain Wohlauf—young, handsome, ambitious—brought his new bride from the Fatherland to witness the round-up and slaughter of people whose only crime was that they belonged to the wrong ethnic group. And she watched without protest, that blushing bride; she was reportedly diverted, interested. It had nothing to do with her. It was nothing personal. When she wrote to friends and family in Hamburg of her honeymoon, what did she say?

Indeed, enthusiasm for murder seemed contagious. The night before the massacre of the Luków ghetto, an entertainment unit of the Berlin police, consisting of musicians and performers, mounted a show for the Germans. According to the memory of one policeman, "they asked, . . . even emphatically begged, to be allowed to participate in the execution of the Jews. This request was granted."

And what of those men who routinely volunteered for "Jew Hunts," who scoured frozen forests, tapped at suspicious walls, in pursuit of escapees? What of the group who demanded that an elderly Polish peasant in Kock surrender his daughter, accused of offering shelter to Jews in the cellar, and then killed her in his sight?

Our minds rebel, dismiss the possibility that "ordinary" men and women are capable of such dissociation. It could never happen to us, we say. We would have been the exception, the rare dissenter who said "no" even though in so doing we might be berated by a superior and lose face with our comrades—the worst consequence for a member of Police Battalion 101 for refusing to participate. (Incredibly, according to Browning, "in the past forty-five years no defense attorney or defendant in any of the hundreds of postwar trials has been able to document a single case in which refusal to obey an order to kill unarmed civilians resulted in . . . dire punishment." That was "them," we protest, and anyway, we know this already anyway. Why should we read this depressing book?

The answer is simple. Because if we weren't there we don't know, and if we were there, unless we are a Primo Levi, we can't convey the magnitude of the experience to others. Because, as we skim over the increasingly abundant morning newspaper reports of "hate" crimes committed against the helpless in our own society, as we walk by the homeless on our streets, as we blame AIDS victims for their illness, as we turn Haitian refugees from our shores and vote for David Duke, we, too, are in danger.

Christopher Browning's meticulous research in German archives, his examination and rejection of the various facile theories of temporary national psychoses that are often cited to "explain" the Holocaust, his unflinching juxtaposition of the deeds carried out by the 101, with their first-person self-justifying remembrances of those events, leads inevitably to one overriding conclusion: it is possible for a privileged and powerful group of people to forget or defer their sense of connection to others. And when that happens, when we lose our capacity for empathy and sympathy, when the outer boundary of our identity is defined by race or religion or nationality rather than by shared humanity, civilization evaporates.

If this concept is hard to grasp, simply look at the 1942 photograph from the Luków ghetto on the cover of *Ordinary Men*. Look at the smiles of the men who carry the guns. Look at the eyes of those who do not.

Look at their eyes.

Chicago Tribune
April 1992

WORD FROM THE FRONT

A harried man interrupted a meeting I attended at UNESCO in New York last week. He had opened the door to the wrong conference room, stumbled into a conversation about the crisis of African illiteracy instead of joining the discussion of European civil strife where he was scheduled to speak. For a few moments he failed to realize his mistake—after all, we were just another assemblage of dark suits around an oval table, our faces made serious by defeating statistics, our yellow legal pads covered with the usual question marks—and so he launched into his impromptu report.

"I'm just back from Sarajevo," the official announced in a vaguely British accent. "Haven't slept much. We were driving supply trucks for four days. Never saw anything like it. Every street we stopped became a target. Mortars coming out of nowhere. Could have been either side shooting. Both. Anything that moves is the enemy. Anything that stands still."

He glanced at a map on the wall, registered that it was Mali and not Bosnia, closed his eyes briefly and made to leave.

"Wait," asked the chair of our committee. "What's it like over there? What can you tell us?"

We put down our pencils, focused hard, waited while the man made three false starts, breaking off each time as he tried to find a beginning to the story.

"The thing is," he said finally, "you can't tell them apart. They're all Slavs. Same faces, same build. Divided by accidents of history, by whose ancestors got invaded by Austrians, whose by Turks. By whose mother gave her son a cross to wear around his neck, whose mother gave a crescent moon."

The man's eyes were bright with the exhaustion that comes from seeing too much, from absorbing without the temperance of words more than the human brain can process and organize. How could he explain to us a situation he didn't himself fathom, how could he unleash into the civility of a quiet room a storm of hatred that from the outside seems so clearly senseless and from within drowns out the voice of every rational thought? How to describe the force of a nightmare to men and women fortunate enough, at least for now, to be awake? How to persuade, without the promise of some clever, quick solution, that concern without the follow-through of succor is no concern at all? How to convince us to get up and join him behind the wheel?

Los Angeles Times
November 1992

HOUSE OF STONE

During one of the famines that raked the Horn of Africa in the past ten years, there was a community in which starving human beings and starving baboons were reduced to competing directly against each other for food. Baboons are wily, agile, and hard to discourage; but, desperate, the people devised a plan. A lone female baboon was ambushed, brought back to the village, and skinned alive. Her screams echoed into the hills and soon a ring of alarmed baboons approached the periphery of the invisible line that traditionally divided the territory of men and women from that of animals. The tortured baboon was untied and, blind with pain, she ran frantically in the direction of her home.

The sight, they say, terrible for a person to see, was even worse for another baboon. Unrecognizable, the victim was the embodiment of horror: the familiar inverted to nightmare. Some baboons ran, others attacked with teeth and claws until, finally, the thing was still. But from that day forward, villagers had no rivals in their quest for the few remaining fruits and roots and grains that survived in the region. The baboons had gone away.

*   *   *

Americans like me are always "discovering" grand-scale poverty, and being famously shocked by the magnitude of it. Most of the time, we flirt with awareness, gulp it from handsome network anchors or register it from newspaper photographs staged to produce a maximum impact. We shudder, we recoil, we maybe even write off the occasional check or buy an overpriced ticket to a benefit, thus entertaining ourselves and doing good simultaneously. But in general, distant disasters are treated like rumors, lacking the immediacy of fear, the focus of personal danger or entanglement. They're our problem only when we allow them time to capture our imaginations, and then, with the zeal of converts who've just received Revelation, we often become boorish and righteous. We accost our friends with dire statistics, censure their ignorance, demand their involvement. True, a few persist to make a real dent in the wall of tragedy by repeatedly crashing against it, but for the rest of us, burnout, disappointment, and frustration are merely a matter of when. We expect results, a bang for our bucks, a return on our emotional and financial investment. If we have the option of looking the other way, usually, eventually, we exercise it.

I tried to explain this—and the related big business of charity appeals—to Mark Nyahada, a local Save the Children deputy administrator, when I visited Zimbabwe last July. We sat with a small, tired group at the table of a guest house deep within a government-run oasis—an agricultural station with working wells and sprinklers, a dot of verdant green upon the red and tan lower veldt near the Mozambican border. A few miles to the north on an arid plateau was the starving community of Muusha and a few miles to the southwest was the sprawling refugee camp of Tongogara, where forty-two thousand people but not a single physician are encircled by a steel fence.

"I don't understand it," Mark said, frowning. "We don't need so much, but what we need, we need. Where is the help?"

I reached for the ubiquitous jar of coffee "substitute," sucrose and artificial creamer already mixed in, that, together with Coca-Cola and orange squashes, seems to be the beverage of choice in rural Zimbabwe.

"Imagine receiving your mail in the morning," I interrupt. "One or two personal letters, a few bills, and then a bunch of envelopes with return addresses of famous people—movie stars, ex-presidents. Inside each one is a professionally produced solicitation that tries to get you interested in a particular agenda: right to life, freedom of choice, American Indians, the election of a candidate who promises to make the country better, cancer research, kidneys, the protection of the environment. The texts are engineered by marketing experts—advertising executives with degrees in psychology—trained to grab you with an opening sentence and wring a few dollars from your conscience. Half the time you don't even open them up, just toss them in the trash so you don't have to think about everything you can't change."

"How do these people know your address?"

"Maybe a year ago you read an article about . . . AIDS," I answered. "Or you knew someone who's sick and looked for a way to show your sympathy, so you sent a contribution to support a hospice. The hospice needs money so it sold its mailing list of donors to another charity, and they did the same thing. Soon you're on everybody's computer as being good for $50 or $100, and the machines take over. There's only one of you and a thousand deserving causes. You can drown in them. They become all the same, all wanting your attention and your spare change, like a street lined with beggars, and most people shut their eyes, close their ears, speed up, run."

The next day I drive with Mark to Tongogara, where he is supposed to supervise a newly inaugurated program, operated cooperatively by Save the Children, the Zimbabwe government, and a U.S. team of psychologists and social workers from Duke University, aimed at both reuniting separated family members and caring for the youngest witnesses to unspeakable violence.

"Some of these children," he tells me in his very British accent, "have seen terrible things. They've been forced to kill their parents. Made to carry ammunition across enemy lines. Seen people locked inside houses that were then set on fire."

In the late morning torpor of the reception area, where the only sounds are the buzz of flies, the low conversation of soldiers assigned to guard duty, it's hard to imagine such atrocities—until I see the eyes of one little boy, who looks to be about ten years old. His expression is exhausted, devoid of curiosity, matching the listlessness of the elderly woman beside him.

Mark notices the direction of my gaze. "That's his grandmother," he tells me. "His mother is still somewhere in Mozambique. They hoped the father would be here, but so far we haven't been able to locate him."

Mark beckons, and the boy comes over, joins us, and in the custom of men conversing, we squat face-to-face. Unmoving, the grandmother stares through us as if watching another place and time. There are stretched holes in the lobes of her ears where jewelry once dangled. Mark estimates that she's no more than fifty, and yet she appears to me much older.

There's nothing childlike about this boy, nothing playful or energetic. Like so many people I will meet in these camps he has about him an air of distilled dignity, as if, stripped of every other possession, he has quietly retained possession of himself.

Mark speaks Shona and translates the story the boy elects to tell us, which is, within this inhumane context, undramatic, even typical. Yes, he's gone days without eating. Yes, he and his grandmother have walked shoeless from a long distance. Yes, he's hoping to find his father, who ran away from their village some time ago to avoid execution for being the in-law of the wrong person. The boy is neither rushed nor especially interested, just tired. He's never been to school but clearly he's intelligent, a survivor. If it weren't for his size, for the absence of lines on his face, I'd think I was in the presence of a resigned, mature man.

Mark promises that he'll circulate the boy's photograph throughout the several refugee centers scattered along the frontier; he'll even send it along to his counterpart in Malawi, where more than one million Mozambicans have fled. Perhaps the lost father will see it and contact authorities. Perhaps the story will have a resolution.

The boy nods, agrees, then rejoins his grandmother. Mark and I stand, brush off our knees, and walk toward our Toyota. We're running behind schedule, late for a meeting. Before I get into the car, however, I turn back for one last look. The boy is in the cradle of his grandmother's thin arms. His mouth is at her empty breast.

There are dozens of good reasons for us not to donate these days. "The economy," we complain, without being very specific. "And besides, I gave last year to (fill in the blank) and look, nothing has changed." We forgive ourselves with predictable scandals: the inflated salaries drawn by certain CEOs of philanthropic organizations, the percentage of every dollar that goes for vague "overhead," the imminence of closer catastrophes where our gift might have a more direct and monitorable impact. And then, of course, there's the suspicion that conditions are exaggerated by those who seek to tap our sympathy. We want proof—death counts, weight loss graphs, raw film footage—before we react. If we give at all, it must be to the best place, the neediest victim, the furthest gone.

Most new arrivals at Tongogara this season have been rerouted to Chambuta, a new camp Mark and I visit just beyond the dry bed of what, in a normal year, is the wide Runde River. It's on the other side of Gonarezhou National Park, where the United States is about to spend a million Zimbabwe dollars to implement an elephant preservation program, a scheme that involves the digging of bore hole wells exclusively for the watering of animals.

Now full beyond capacity at twenty thousand people—up from six thousand in January—Chambuta is divided into thirteen "villages," though two of them so far lack the most rudimentary shelter. The Zimbabwean government, reeling under its own drought deprivations, has provided sufficient water and food rations, but there is no disguising the utter bleakness of the place, the stark, thorny desert, the barrenness. It is, quite literally, the end of the road.

Most of the seven hundred people who arrive daily, the director, Israel Chokowenga, reports, are without clothing, confused, disoriented, sick, and always thirsty. Drought, not war, is their "presenting problem." Everywhere there is manifest evidence of calamity. An undersized boy, hot with the fever of measles, lies on the ground, his head propped against a canvas pack. A tiny girl, one leg stiff and too short, lugs a can for water toward an open spigot; as she hobbles, she leaves odd footprints—the left is as it should be, the right is only flexed toes. There are flies and more flies, ever seeking the moisture that resides at the corner of a person's eyes or mouth. Many at Chambuta seem to lack the energy or the will to blink. No one even begs.

Surprisingly though, life asserts itself in this desolate place. Waiting by the administration building, next to unused parking spaces demarcated in the dirt by carefully placed rocks, is an unofficial greeter. He's dressed in a knitted ski cap and a tattered Hard Rock Café T-shirt, has advanced glaucoma in both eyes, and bears the unreadable expression of a man in the midst of a long interior monologue. Yet, equipped with a branch stretched bent by a piece of wire, a hollow gourd for resonance, and a twig as a dancing hammer, he's making music.

Every day I spend in southeastern Zimbabwe pushes back the boundary of deprivation I believed human beings could endure. There is an unrelieved sense of waiting in the camps, but it's a waiting bereft of expectation, a queue so stalled that no one remembers what was supposed to be at the end. It's a waiting for the fickleness of weather, the eventuality of death, the unlikely news of civil peace, the abrupt interruption of food or drink. It hums with a passive inertia, a kind of dull concession that no individual act or thought can affect the outcome.

Bad luck has created this congestion, bad luck and the incessant meddling of foreign governments—who've lost interest in Southern Africa now that the Cold War is history.

At one end of the looping line is pain and at the other is carefree joy. At the far extreme stands that prematurely old little boy of Tongogara; a million options and possibilities away, are we, am I. Thrown together by arbitrary chance— at the coincident moment of time we found ourselves occupying the same place—we beheld each other, registered our similarities. For every child like him there are one hundred thousand more I don't happen to encounter, and for every man like me, there are millions he can't imagine, yet we stare across the chasm, try to fathom the other's life.

No greater distance separates us than this: he stays, I leave. But not entirely alone. Before I embarked on this trip, my daughter Persia, a shining girl about his age, emptied her bulldog bank and sent along her birthday money for me to give away. To her, on some unspoiled level, she and the boy I've just met have the obvious connection of brother and sister or potential playmates. She has not yet learned to tolerate injustice as inevitable, to become defeated in advance by the enormous odds against reaching out. For her, what's directly before her eyes is still visible, and the situation is a quite simple equation. They need. I have. Therefore, I give, in order to reestablish a fair balance.

Of the recent atrocities reported from the Mozambican front, one story stands out: A group of boys armed with automatic weapons appeared in a neighboring community. Swiftly they surrounded a group of local children no older than themselves, and shot them. When asked why, one fourteen-year-old explained that the children of that village had been kindly treated by adults, rarely beaten, and fed daily. The attacking boys were indignant, jealous, so they evened the score. In their experience of the world, a lack of suffering was a sufficient reason to be killed.

As Mark and I drive north on a two-lane road, past thatched-roof villages and straggling goats that seem more bone than flesh, the faces of two children—who will never meet—superimpose and fix permanently in my imagination.

Muusha, a name given to the cluster of buildings that functions as the principal town for two precincts with a combined population of twelve thousand farmers, is in the midst of its seventh and most severe winter of drought. The effect is brutal, dusty, too dry even for the waste of tears. If meteorological forecasts hold true, it won't rain again for another four months, and the first crop of maize won't be ready before May at the earliest.

All told, it's been a hard year in this Mutema region. The weather prohibited any harvesting whatsoever this season; only five rapidly depreciating wells remain to meet the water needs; economics eliminated the grade school children's lunch program, and as a result there are daily faintings and steep declines in attendance. The World Bank, anxious that the last vestiges of Zimbabwe's former inclination toward socialism be abandoned, urged the imposition of a token tuition charge for all grade levels. Equivalent to one U.S. dollar per year per child, this fee constitutes a burden to the poorest families, who have responded by sending only boys to classes. Too many of the girls, I was told, resorted to prostitution in order to eat.

On the flight back to the United States, my mind races, searching for some action, some call to arms, some original and efficacious idea in response to what I've seen. I tilt between the equally useless poles of helplessness and arrogance, of throwing up my hands and changing my life. What is the appropriate path between wanting to help, on the one hand, and having no idea how, on the other?

The answer, I realize, begins with empathy based at the most individual level. It's too easy to forget the picture of a crowd, no matter how miserable. We don't think of our parents, of our children, as a group, but as specific people, each with his or her own personality, perspective, and face. We must see through the burning, thirsty forest and find a tree to nurture, to water during the dry season so that it will provide shade in a later year. We must give as if to ourselves—automatically and practically, without the demand of gratitude or closure.

To be fortunate is, in a deep moral sense, to be obliged. Confusion is no excuse; doing something, even if mistakes are made, will help, especially in the early stages of trouble. And even from far away, our contributions can be specifically designated, if we make the effort to inform ourselves. In Zimbabwe, for instance, a dollar will send a little girl to school; $140 will buy a week's worth of lunches for four hundred students; $600 invested now will deepen an existing well, thus sustaining a whole community until the rains return, permitting people to stay independent rather than swelling the rolls of those forced to become internal refugees.

My final stop in Zimbabwe was the tiny settlement of Mola, far to the north, where food is very much on the mind of the village secretary for an emergency relief operation that provides a daily bowl of corn mush to children under five, as well as to pregnant and lactating mothers. A woman with strong arms and a sleeping toddler secured on her back, she spoke Tonga in a low voice and was all business in her translated negotiations with Ruben McKenzie, the local Save the Children administrator, who translated the proceedings for my benefit.

Her first proposal: a number of village women participate in this program on a rotating basis, measuring out grain or weighing children for government records; they, too, should be afforded the luxury of an occasional meal since lately some of them have passed out from hunger. Ruben should be clear, she added, that this provision will not extend to her or to members of her governing committee who, to avoid any suspicion of profiteering, have made themselves permanently ineligible for a ration.

Ruben, a handsome young man born and raised nearby, gravely explained that there was only a finite amount of food available; if more people partook, the portions would necessarily be smaller. The decision, however, was up to the woman and her colleagues.

She nodded, one item on her agenda ticked off, and moved on. What about the agency's pull-cart, she wanted to know. When it wasn't in use for this program, might she have permission to designate it for other purposes, such as transporting the sick to the airstrip? Otherwise, it would simply sit idle.

Once again Ruben confirmed her authority and once again the woman was satisfied, as was the audience of recipients who watch this drama for entertainment. There remained one final issue to be settled: would Ruben please find out and report on his next visit what would happen to the fifty-gallon tin drum, now loaned to store water, when the rains come back? The request was made casually, off-hand, but no one present believed for a instant that there wasn't already a specific task envisioned for this rusty object of foreign manufacture, a task that will, if humanly possible, be accomplished.

Where does your water come from now? I asked the woman, and was led nearly a mile down a path to the chalky expanse of what normally would have been a river bottom. Into a small hole, a scrape in the dirt, there seeped a puddle of brown water. We stood around the perimeter in silence, for the shallowness, the precariousness, was self-evident, and eventually I looked up at the secretary's face. She was frowning, thinking hard, absolutely determined to figure something out.

Mother Jones
October 1992

LITTLE FEARS

It all comes back to the illusion of permanent possession. If we have sight, we fear its loss. If we can hear, we dread silence. We worry at the thought of not tasting the flavor of life, of sensory deprivation, of consciousness shutdown. Imprisoned in a mortal body, the desperate phantom of self runs from window to window, calling, listening, craving contact, and through contact, reassurance, validation.

"You're there" is another way of saying "I'm here."

The more we doubt it, the louder we shout it, marking our territory with the impressions of our presence: voice, detritus, style, edifice. We compete to be the solo amid the chorus, the name over the title, our initials carved in stone.

Only the very young or the very old are without internal fear. The former, not differentiating themselves from the universe, can't imagine limitation, and the latter, if they have gained wisdom, know the futility and waste of protest. In between, we experience a parabola of dread, peaking just beyond midlife—the point currently approached by the bulge of the current American population whose baby boom demographics have managed to make their generation's attitude the defining style for each of the past four decades.

Now we who demanded change, abjure it. The dynamic we once viewed as the natural ascent to gain has become a slippery slope of loss. Instead of struggling forward we try to hold on, and when experience and the observation of those just preceding us reaffirms the ultimate triumph of gravity, a barely repressed vertigo dominates our every move. We attend to sentries, heedful for the whiff of pertinent bad news.

Most of us dwell within the confining perspective of a particular class, a specific geography, a floating but circumscribed temporality. In middle age, our measurements are usually close at hand, and the limits of our possibility are, save for the most incomprehensible extremes, narrow. They don't much tax our imaginations, for they involve more or less familiar currency, supporting a conservatism that ultimately reflects guarded privilege, walls erected around threatened treasure, badly locked doors.

In a broader context, our aspecific angst is a luxury, a form of metaphysical hypochondria, its cultivation and polish promoted by a surfeit of leisure. Unlike those in the world, past and present, who ordinarily have the opportunity for generalized worry only in the very late night or early morning—or in dreams—we pursue it at all hours and through multimedia, intentionally scaring ourselves with gory books and films as if by oversaturation and hyperbole we can dilute the reality of those fears for which we are truly culpable and accountable, those fears that don't disappear when the power button is punched off, those fears that, if deferred, are willfully bequeathed to our children.

Hungry Mind Review
Fall 1992

GOING
PLACES

AMERICANS ALL

I recognize them instantly abroad: on the street, in crowded rooms, on airplanes, at restaurants—but how? It's emphatically not skin color, not clothing, not little red-white-and-blues stitched to their breast pockets. They don't have to say anything, to show a passport, or to sing the "Star Spangled Banner" (god forbid!), but nevertheless they're unmistakable in any foreign setting.

Americans. We come in all varieties of size, age, and style. We travel singly and in groups. We're alternately loud and disapproving or humble and apologetic. We seek each other out or self-consciously avoid each other's company. We pack our gear in Gucci bags or stuff it into Patagonia backpacks, travel first class or on Eurorail passes, stay in youth hostels or in luxury hotels, but none of that matters. It's as though we're individually implanted with some invisible beeper, some national homing device, that's activated by the proximity of similar equipment.

This common denominator is manifest in shared knowledge (we all know who Mary Tyler Moore is), topics of mutual interest or dispute (guns, the environment, choice), and popular culture (do we or do we not deserve a thousand-calorie break today?). In other words, we take the same things seriously or not seriously, are capable of speaking, when we choose to, not merely a common language but a common idiom, and know the melodies, if not all the words, to many of the same songs.

Why, then, doesn't any of this count when we're not overseas? Why, at home, do we seem so different from each other, so mutually incompatible, so strange and forbidding? Do we have to recognize each other in Tokyo or Cairo in order to see through the distinctions and into the commonalities? How does that "we," so obvious anywhere else in the world, get split into "us" and "them" when we're stuck within our own borders?

The answer is clear: to be Americans means to be not the clone of the people next door. I fly back from any homogeneous country, from a place where every person I see is blond, or black, or belongs to only one religion, and then disembark at JFK. I revel in the cadence of many accents, catch a ride to the city with a Nigerian-American or Russian-American cab driver. Eat Thai food at a Greek restaurant next to a table of Chinese-American conventioneers from Alabama. Get directions from an Iranian-American cop and drink a cup of Turkish coffee served by a Navajo student at Fordham who's majoring in Japanese literature. Argue with everybody about everything. I'm home.

Newsday
October 1992

MARTYRS

I lived to die. At any moment, the Red Chinese might sweep across the Pacific, through California, ravaging the continent until they reached Kentucky and surrounded Holy Spirit Church while terrified, hymn-singing parishioners cowered bravely within.

I was well aware of the communists' ultimate goal: the ciborium, full of spare Eucharists, locked behind the carved golden door in the alcove at the center of the altar. Host-defilement was known to be a major motivator for nonbelievers of all stripes, and it had to be anticipated as adjunct to any invasion. The protection of sacred wafers, however, presented a problem for Defenders of the Faith because it entailed a tricky stipulation: with the exception of priests, consecrated hosts could be manipulated or touched only by the tongues of post–First Holy Communion persons (in the state of grace, naturally) and, to complicate matters even further, but one tiny disk could be consumed per capita per day.

What was a Catholic boy to do when at last the polished mahogany doors were battered down and enemy soldiers charged past the imported Italian marble holy water fonts and up the center aisle? I projected the ensuing scene as a vision reminiscent of Donald Duck's avaricious uncle cavorting with wild abandon in his money vault, except in this instance Scrooge was a Peking Duck and each silver dollar was transformed into a miniature Body of Christ.

How to forestall this abomination without, in the process, committing a mortal sin by swallowing multiple wafers? Did the end justify the means? Could omnipotent God make a rock so big He couldn't lift? In 1950s Irish-American Catholicism, paradox abounded.

We debated such philosophical topics in grade school, pausing even in the cafeteria over our sloppy joes and Jell-O. Timing, it seemed, played a key role—always implicated by a delicate system of checks and balances. Even when the intention was good, if the act were bad it was still a sin, whether one realized it or not. There were fine-print rules governing almost everything: the recitation of the names (in proper sequence) "Jesus, Mary, and Joseph" was good for a three-hundred-day commutation of one's eventual purgatory sentence, but only if they were vocalized. Simply thinking a rote litany gained one no time at all (unless communists were listening and would torture your parents if they overheard the magic words; under such circumstances, it was provisionally okay to simply mouth an invocation of the Holy Family without sound—unless there was a deaf communist present who could lip read, in which case . . . and so on and so forth).

You could sin by omission and commission, by desiring to do something bad you didn't actually do, or by begrudging something good you did. The Ten Commandments, in their various interpretations and subclauses, pretty much excluded all but a tightrope of permitted behavior toward your family, teachers, associates, and self, and God never, ever blinked or looked away in indulgent amusement. When I was nine—two years into the age of reason and therefore eternally, cumulatively responsible for every transgression—confessing my sins and doing penance twice weekly hardly seemed often enough, the list of slips and slides was that long.

There was, joyfully, one surefire escape hatch, one soul-bleaching rinse that erased even the most persistent stains. All was absolutely forgiven and forgotten in the event that—even if positively stuffed with unleavened bread, even having at one time or another given scandal to a Protestant by making a joke about a nun, even with a record as a prideful, self-abusing, Friday hamburger user—I managed to be persecuted for my faith and perish in the process. Martyrdom, that just-like-new Baptism of Blood, automatically canceled all debits.

Treasure Chest magazine and the *Junior Catholic Messenger* offered a weekly parade of historical and practically contemporary child saints who earned their wings through suffering. Maria Goretti succumbed intact to a pornography-crazed handyman. St. Martin was roasted on a spit rather than worship false gods. Father Brebeouf watched benignly while Iroquois tormentors ate his heart. St. Peter, even after thrice denying that he so much as knew the Lord ("Jesus who?"), ascended to heaven without detour after having been crucified upside down. Beheaded saints-to-be politely carried their own skulls to the graveyard, blessed their executioners with their final breaths, eschewed every "This is your last chance to dance naked before a golden calf statue" offer of reprieve. The message was clear: the road to heaven is filled with bamboo spikes, and the fastest route is to run barefoot.

Okay: I believed. I was ready. Test me. I wore a scratchy scapular against my bare skin and caused a rash on my chest. I did without—you name it: chocolate, pie, "I Love Lucy"—during Lent. I self-castigated, I regretted. I unfavorably compared my innate miserableness with that of every anti-Catholic reprobate from Attila the Hun to Henry VIII. I knelt on pebbles, gladly. Along with the rest of my family, I boycotted "Your Hit Parade" on television when one of its stars, the famously Catholic Giselle McKenzie, got a divorce. A year or so later, we collectively stopped speaking to an old friend when she paid admission to see the "condemned" film, *The Moon Is Blue.* I put up with, accepted, denied, prepared myself for the day the communists underestimated my resolve. I was so ready I became impatient, then disappointed, then bored. The moment of truth passed and I was left unscathed, yet I yearned to be scathed! It was like training and stretching before a race, then never hearing the gun go off.

In spite of my ambitions, unlike Dominic Savio, the preteen role-model saint who uttered the fateful phrase "Death rather than sin" and then conveniently died, I lived into the complexity of adulthood. The innocent right-and-wrong view of the world I had been offered by Sister Stanilaus Kostka shaded into layered ambiguity. Once I was removed from the regimen of Catholic-approved textbooks, issues that had seemed simply religious blurred into politics, psychology (as in paranoia), and ethnocentric or misogynist bias. Like Adam and Eve, who after eating of the Tree of Knowledge lost their comfortable digs in paradise, I found myself awash in a permanent state of unsureness—an emotion for which I had no preparation.

It was hard to imagine emulating the popular survivor saints in my grade school pantheon. St. Francis of Assisi talked to animals—and they answered! St. Teresa didn't eat anything but a daily host. St. Ann, an aged *prima para,* produced the Mother of God, while in the next generation St. Joseph remained on the sidelines while his wife, ever a virgin, gave birth to God Himself.

Without the drama of martyrdom, normal longevity—unless one possessed magic powers—seemed positively dull, an endless succession of Canaan conferences, compromise, toil without glory, and predictable imperfection. Real life didn't hold a candle to old-fashioned Catholic boyhood, which for me had a swashbuckling kick, a dizzy aura of danger and flamboyance and possibility—provided that it didn't last too long.

Catholic Girlhood and Boyhood
Forthcoming 1994

PEN PALS

"Dear Mohammed," I began my letter. "I'm very sorry but I am not able to send you a Kodak camera. However, I would still like to be your pen pal. How are things in Sierra Leone? Things here are fine."

Mohammed was the most persistently demanding of the five correspondents I maintained, at my peak, in Africa. The others—Margot (the youngest daughter of a Viennese Jewish family who had fled to Kampala, Uganda, just before the outbreak of World War II), Derek (an English-speaking white South African who lived in Pietermaritzburg on the Indian Ocean), Ali (a boy in Cairo who wanted to become an architect), and Anna (a high school student with perfect penmanship in Ibadan, Nigeria) were content to exchange occasional postcards, family photos, and canceled stamps.

We met each other through the services of the International Friendship League, an organization in Boston that, for a small fee, matched would-be letter writers from around the world.* I had heard of the league's existence on a radio program when I was twelve, and sent in my money and a request for a pen pal in Europe who shared my inter-

* The league, run by Margaret MacDonough, still operates.

ests in reading, history, and folk music. At the time, there was nobody nearby who seemed to care about any of those things, and I felt lonely and hopelessly weird. *Unpopular* is too kind a word to describe my status. I was the kind of kid who wore glasses from the second grade on and never took them off, the kind who got his homework in on the day it was due (sometimes typed), the kind who could not catch a ball even when it fell into his baseball glove. Everyone I knew seemed to be part of groups whose doors were closed to me, so I had plenty of time to daydream, to imagine traveling to far-off places, meeting interesting, exotic people, being appreciated for the fascinating individual I was sure I was.

The International Friendship League was my passport out of the town where I lived, my ticket to anywhere. Together with my first address—of a boy my age, also named Michael, who lived in London—I received a map of the world and a long scroll on which I could locate and list all contacts I made. There were fifty spaces for names, and, as I tacked the papers to the wall above my bed, I calculated that I had at least forty-nine friends to go. Before sleep I would browse the map and select the country from which I would seek my next pen pal. All I needed was a week's allowance, an airmail stamp, and the cooperation of the people in Boston, who never let me down.

Michael from England turned out to like mystery books, and sent one of his favorites along with his third letter. He was full of questions about America, about places and practices I took for granted, and answering him made me look at familiar things with a fresh perspective. My second pen pal, Ingrid, was from Sweden, and passionate about politics. She disapproved of some of the positions of the Social Democrats, the party in power in Stockholm, and through her vivid descriptions I grew to anticipate the next round of Scandinavian elections more eagerly than I did those in the United States. Ingrid demanded to know what progress was being made with the civil rights movement in this country and what I was doing about equal justice for the reservation. And her idealism was infectious.

The list on my wall began to fill; whenever I earned some extra money I went on a continental binge. One spring I splurged on South America, gaining as correspondents a soccer player in São Paulo, Brazil, a set of identical twins in Medellín, Colombia, and an aspiring radio announcer in Lima, Peru. Though they were friendly, their attitudes toward the United States, and toward me as a North American, were surprisingly cynical. I was forced to consider that in the eyes of our Southern Hemisphere neighbors, "we" were not always regarded favorably.

Tucked into each letter I received from Reiko in Tokyo was an origami figure, an intricately folded piece of paper fashioned to resemble a tiny animal. Masoud, in Tehran, supported the reform policies of the shah, and Jens, in Jakarta, was determined that I would at least learn to write a grammatical sentence in his language. Helen Scott from Melbourne wanted to be a nurse and move to Canada, and

Veronica Nops from Auckland opposed atomic power. She invited me to visit her in New Zealand, and twenty years after our initial exchange of letters, I did.

During the seventh and eighth grades and throughout high school I became "known" at our local post office. When mail from Ireland appeared, regular and without fail, on the first and fifteenth of every month, Grace George, my postmistress, would ask after the health of Eileen's blind mother. When the first letter arrived from a new place, Grace would weigh the envelope in her hand before giving it to me. "India has a lot to say," she might comment on one day, and on the next, "Those Portuguese sure like to spend their money on stamps."

After a few years, the map above my bed was festooned with colored pins—orange for males, green for females. At its maximum extent, there were thirty-two names on my "active" list. My room was decorated with snapshots and postcards, with wall chimes from Finland and tapa cloth from Fiji, with a miniature Italian flag, and with a pebble collected on my Turkish pen pal's school trip to the archaeological site of Troy. I had more friends than anyone I knew, and was secure in their affections. I watched the international news on television with a proprietary eye—I was acquainted with people who would be affected by what happened in foreign lands—and I paid close attention to every important story on events in this country because I knew that within a week or so I would be called upon to explain, defend, or condemn it in twenty different letters.

My pen pals and I seemed to share the adventure of being young on the same planet, of conspiring together across the distances of geography and culture, of consoling our failures and believing in the infinite promise of our adult lives. We were a kind of International Friendship League without boundary, without flag. Through an exchange of addresses my pals began to correspond with each other, and, in the ensuing years, some of us have met, directly or indirectly. Helen, now a nurse in Hope, British Columbia, visited me in New York. My aunt went to Dublin and stopped in to see Eileen and her mother. Ingrid adopted a child from Ecuador and, during a layover, showed him off to Rudolfo, now a TV newsman in Lima.

Over time, some pen pals became so involved in their own lives that they gradually stopped writing, and others were silenced by more troubling circumstances. After the Islamic revolution in Iran I never heard again from Masoud, and Derek, from South Africa, has not answered my Christmas cards for years. The world turned out to be neither as simple nor as small as we once believed it to be. But even now, years after the intensity of our associations, I can't look at a globe without populating it, not with faceless mobs of people, but with those to whom I was once so tenuously connected, those whom in some small respect I came to know.

Seventeen
August 1987

THE FORGOTTEN
ALGEBRA TEST
NIGHTMARE

It's 6 A.M. I sit up in my bed, desperate and in a panic. How could I have failed to prepare? How could I have forgotten that today was the day of the midterm? How could it have slipped my mind until this minute that I was enrolled in Intermediate Algebra? I have lost totally the ability to use my slide ruler. I have blanked on the meaning of "function," much less of a log or a sine. I am forty-three years old and obviously neurotic.

I was the first one in my fourth-grade class to learn the multiplication tables up through the twelves. I know a decimal point from a period. I can figure my agent's percentage. I could balance a check book if I wanted to. But say "set" to me, and suddenly it's the garlic festival in Transylvania.

You're hearing from a person for whom the quantitative section of the SATs was one mad, luck-filled dance through a mine field, who chose which university to attend on the basis of the fact that as a Georgetown freshman one could study ancient Greek instead of calculus, who to this day approaches Tuesdays, when the "Science" section of the *New York Times* appears, with a feeling of low self-esteem. You are dealing with a man married to a writer whose freshman computer science professor promised her a C in the course on the condition that she promise never, ever again to mess with artificial intelligence.

There is a moment I recall, from the fall of my junior year in high school. Algebra, my teacher announced, was not for everyone. Many would never grasp it. The next thing I knew, we were in the land of overlapped vocabulary, a place where a function was not a function, a root was not a something buried in the earth, a square was more concept than shape. Within days this joker wanted me to tell him who *x* was, and soon thereafter, *y!* Me, for whom the only "prime" was the TV viewing hours from 8 to 10, for whom "cosine" was what my uncle did, grudgingly, when my cousin got a bank loan for his mortgage.

I have a mind that gets trapped in trick questions. Show me a series of gears and pulleys, ask me to visualize what comes next, and my eyes begin to spin like the windows of slot machines. Inquire of me how many pieces of firewood six men can transport in four days if each one carries one and a half on Sundays and four on weekdays, and I say to you, Have none of these idiots ever heard of electric heat? Show me a sequence—1-3-7-17—and my response is: Yes, but will it win the lottery?

Do math teachers realize the power they wield? They have only to say, "Put away all notes and open your blue books," and they reduce otherwise confident professionals to sniveling whimperers. They know something the rest of us don't but believe we should, and it has something to do with No. 2 pencils. They have the real brains, the ones that send people to the moon and bring them home again, the ones that can decipher languages punctuated with equals signs and ending in Q.E.D., the ones that require chalk to express themselves. We verbal types are at their mercy, unable to so much as build a radio out of the odds and ends people like them find in their average wastebaskets and then bend to their will. We are the ones on whom 75 percent of the buttons on any hand-held calculator are wasted and dangerous, the ones who think formulas are baby food, whose vision of pie is cherry or pecan.

Let me tell you about the tenth grade. I took a course that can only be adequately described as Catholic Geometry (the precursor to Catholic Algebra and Catholic Biology). The class began with the recitation of the rosary—take that, Galileo!—an event that contained what statisticians might call a random factor in the person of the guy who sat immediately in front of me in the bolted-down row of desks. He was Vartan Stakiew, recently immigrated from Ukraine: affable, eager to be popular, and infinitely trusting. To his bad luck, he also happened to be the eleventh student in sequence, meaning it always fell to him to announce a Mystery. Now, depending on the day of the week, Mysteries normally fall into three categories: joyful, sorrowful, and glorious. But under the tutelage of those ribald wits who surrounded him, Vartan's Mysteries were never less than bizarre.

As the Hail Marys inched toward him, a look of concern would cross Vartan's face. He had forgotten again, and the whispered prompts began. "The Drinking of the Wine." "The Washing of the Feet with the Hair." "The Raising of the Dead." Or the perennial favorite, "The Taking Off of the Clothes."

Our teacher, Brother Columbo, must now be in heaven, having endured his hell on earth. He was not a young man, could have profited from a hearing aid, but was diligent in his determination to instill in his students the concept of the tangent. Oh yes, and beneath his long black gabardine cassock, he wore an old-fashioned wooden leg. For fifty minutes he patrolled the aisles, shooting questions about angles and circumferences willy-nilly. If you answered wrong he would encourage you to think more clearly by hitting you on the head with the textbook. To this day I duck at the sight of a rhombus.

We budding Euclids were equipped with the tools of our trade: protractors, those translucent pale green plastic half-circles, embossed with calibrated numbers. Graph paper. And sharp metal compasses, the implements of our sophomore rite of passage. As Brother Columbo ambled ominously among us, each student was required by long tradition to wing, once during the school year, his compass into the passing wooden left leg, then retrieve it on the next circuit without being detected.

Surely Columbo must have known. Surely, even if the daily thud of impact didn't alert him to the game, the nightly appearance of a new tiny puncture would have had to be explained. Probably he considered our daring counting of coups to be cultural, ingrained in our genes, a liability of missionaryhood, a relatively harmless concession to group pacification, and he therefore feigned to ignore it.

Until, late in the year, it was finally Vartan's turn at bat.

Of course, he pinned the wrong leg. *Sorrowful* doesn't begin to describe what happened next.

Tell me about math anxiety.

American Association of Science Teachers
1992

LIFE STORIES

In most cultures, adulthood is equated with self-reliance and responsibility, yet often Americans do not achieve this status until we are in our late twenties or early thirties— virtually the entire average lifespan of a person in a traditional non-Western society. We tend to treat prolonged adolescence as a warm-up for real life, as a wobbly ladder between childhood and legal maturity. Whereas a nineteenth-century Cheyenne or Lakota teenager was expected to alter self-conception in a split-second vision, we often meander through an analogous rite of passage for more than a decade—through high school, college, graduate school.

Though he had never before traveled alone outside his village, the Plains Indian male was expected at puberty to venture solo into the wilderness. There he had to fend for and sustain himself while avoiding the menace of unknown dangers, and there he had absolutely to remain until something happened that would transform him. Every human being, these tribes believed, was entitled to at least one moment of personal, enabling insight.

Anthropology proposes feasible psychological explanations for why this flash was eventually triggered: fear, fatigue, reliance on strange foods, the anguish of loneliness, stress, and the expectation of ultimate success all contributed to a state of receptivity. Every sense was quickened, alerted to perceive deep meaning, until at last the interpretation of an unusual event—a dream, a chance encounter, or an unexpected vista—reverberated with significance. Through this unique prism, abstractly preserved in a vivid memory or song, a boy caught foresight of both his adult persona and his vocation, the two inextricably entwined.

The best approximations that many of us get to such a heady sense of eventuality come in the performance of the jobs we hold during summer vacation. Summers are intermissions, and once we hit our teens it is during these breaks in our structured regimen that we initially taste the satisfaction of remuneration that is earned, not merely doled. Tasks defined as work are not graded, they are compensated; they have a worth that is inarguable because it translates into hard currency. Wage labor—and in the beginning, this generally means a confining, repetitive chore for which we are quickly overqualified—paradoxically brings a sense of blooming freedom. At the outset, the complaint to a peer that business supersedes fun is oddly liberating—no matter what drudgery requires your attention, it is by its very required nature serious and adult.

At least that's how it seemed to me. I come from a line of people hard hit by the Great Depression. My mother and her sisters went to work early in their teens—my mother operated a kind of calculator known as a comptometer while her sisters spent their days, respectively, at a peanut factory and at Western Union. My grandmother did piece-work sewing. Their efforts, and the Democratic Party, saw them through, and to this day they never look back without appreciation for their later solvency. They take nothing for granted. Accomplishments are celebrated, possessions are valuable, in direct proportion to the labor entailed to acquire them; anything easily won or bought on credit is suspect. When I was growing up we were far from wealthy, but what money we had was correlated to the hours one of us had logged. My eagerness to contribute to, or at least not diminish, the coffer was countered by the arguments of those whose salaries kept me in school: my higher educa-tion was a sound group investment. The whole family was adamant that I have the opportunities they had missed and, no matter how much I objected, they stinted themselves to provide for me.

Summer jobs were therefore a relief, an opportunity to pull a share of the load. As soon as the days turned warm I began to peruse the classifieds, and when the spring semester was done, I was ready to punch a clock. It even felt right. Work in June, July, and August had an almost biblical aspect: in the hot, canicular weather your brow sweats, just as God had ordained. Moreover, summer jobs had the luxury of being temporary. No matter how onerous, how off my supposed track, employment terminated with the falling leaves and I was back to real life. So, during each annual three-month leave from secondary school and later from the university, I compiled an eclectic resumé: lawn cutter, hair sweeper in a barber shop, lifeguard, delivery boy, mail carrier, file clerk, youth program coordinator on my Montana reservation, ballroom dance instructor, theater party promoter, night-shift hospital records keeper, human adding machine in a Paris bank, encyclopedia salesman, newspaper stringer, recreation bus manager, salmon fisherman.

The summer I was eighteen a possibility arose for a rotation at the post office, and I grabbed it. There was something casually sophisticated about work that required a uniform, about having a federal ranking, even if it was GS-1 (Temp/Sub), and it was flattering to be entrusted with a leather bag containing who knew what important correspondence. Every day I was assigned a new beat, usually in a rough neighborhood avoided whenever possible by regular carriers, and I proved quite capable of complicating what would normally be fairly routine missions. The low point came on the first of August when I diligently delivered four blocks' worth of welfare checks to the right numbers on the wrong streets. It is no fun to snatch unexpected wealth from the hands of those who have but moments previously opened their mailboxes and received a bonus.

After my first year of college, I lived with relatives on an Indian reservation in eastern Montana and filled the only post available: Coordinator of Youth Programs. I was seduced by the language of the announcement into assuming that there existed Youth Programs to be coordinated. In fact, the Youth consisted of a dozen bored, disgruntled kids—most of them my cousins—who had nothing better to do each day than to show up at what was euphemistically called "the gym" and hate whatever Program I had planned for them. The Youth ranged in age from fifteen to five and seemed to have as their sole common ambition the determination to smoke cigarettes. This put them at immediate and ongoing odds with the Coordinator, who on his first day naively encouraged them to sing the "Doe, a deer, a female deer" song from *The Sound of Music*. They looked at me, that bleak morning, and I looked at them, each boy and girl equipped with a Pall Mall behind an ear, and we all knew we faced a long, struggle-charged battle. It was to be a contest of wills, the hearty and wholesome versus prohibited vice. I stood for dodge ball, for collecting bugs in glass jars, for arts and crafts; they had pledged a preternatural allegiance to sloth. The odds were not in my favor and each waking dawn I experienced the lightheadedness of anticipated exhaustion, that thrill of giddy dissociation in which nothing seems real or of great significance. Finally, I went with the flow and learned to inhale.

The next summer, I decided to find work in an urban setting for a change, and was hired as a general office assistant in the Elsa Hoppenfeld Theatre Party Agency, located above Sardi's restaurant in New York City. The agency consisted of Elsa Hoppenfeld herself, Rita Frank, her regular deputy, and me. Elsa was a gregarious Viennese woman who established contacts through honesty, hard work, and personal charm, and she spent much of the time away from the building courting trade. Rita was therefore both my immediate supervisor and constant companion; she had the most incredible fingernails I had ever seen— long, carefully shaped pegs lacquered in cruel primary colors and hard as stone—and an attitude about her that could only be described as zeal.

The goal of a theater party agent is to sell blocks of tickets to imminent Broadway productions, and the likely buyers are charities, B'nai B'riths, Hadassahs, and assorted other fundraising organizations. We received commissions on volume, and so it was necessary to convince a prospect that a play— preferably an expensive musical—for which we had reserved the rights to seats would be a boffo smash hit.

The object of our greatest expectation that season was an extravaganza called *Chu Chem,* a saga that aspired to ride the coattails of *Fiddler on the Roof* into entertainment history. It starred the estimable Molly Picon and told the story of a family who had centuries ago gone from Israel to China during the Diaspora, yet had, despite isolation in an alien environment, retained orthodox culture and habits. The crux of the plot revolved around a man with several marriageable daughters and nary a kosher suitor within five thousand miles. For three months Rita and I waxed eloquent in singing the show's praises. We sat in our little office, behind facing desks, and every noon while she redid her nails I ordered out from a deli that offered such exotic (to me) delicacies as fried egg sandwiches, lox and cream cheese, pastrami, tongue. I developed of necessity and habit a telephone voice laced with a distinctly Yiddish accent. It could have been a great career. However, come November, *Chu Chem* bombed. Its closing was such a financial catastrophe for all concerned that when the following January one Monsieur Dupont advertised on the placement board at my college, I decided to put an ocean between me and my former trusting clientele.

M. Dupont came to campus with the stated purpose of interviewing candidates for teller positions in a French bank. Successful applicants, required to be fluent *en français*, would be rewarded with three well-paid months and a rent-free apartment in Paris. On my way to the language lab, I registered for an appointment.

The only French in the interview was *Bonjour, ça va?*, after which M. Dupont switched into English and described the wonderful deal on charter air flights that would be available to those who got the nod. Round-trip to Amsterdam, via Reykjavík, leaving the day after exams and returning in mid-September, no changes or substitutions. I signed up on the spot. I was to be a *banquier*, with a *pied-à-terre* in Montparnasse!

Unfortunately, when I arrived with only $50 in traveler's checks in my pocket—the flight had cleaned me out, but who needed money since my paycheck started right away—no one in Paris had ever heard of M. Dupont. *Alors.*

I stood in the Gare du Nord and considered my options. There weren't any. I scanned a listing of Paris hotels and headed for the cheapest one: the Hotel Villedo, $10 a night. The place had an ambiance that I persuaded myself was antique, despite the red light above the sign. The only accommodation available was "the bridal suite," a steal at $20. The glass door to my room didn't lock and in the adjacent room there was a rather continual floor show, but at some point I must have dozed off. When I awoke the church bells were ringing, the sky was pink, and I felt renewed. No little setback was going to spoil my adventure. I stretched, then walked to a mirror that hung above the sink next to the bed. I leaned forward to punctuate my resolve with a confident look in the eye.

The sink disengaged and fell to the floor. Water gushed. In panic I rummaged through my open suitcase, stuffed two pairs of underpants into the pipe to quell the flow, and before the dam broke, I was out the door. I barreled through the lobby of the first bank I passed, asked to see the director, and told the startled man my sad story. For some reason, whether from shock or pity, he hired me at $1.27 an hour to be a cross-checker of foreign currency transactions, and with two phone calls found me lodgings at a commercial school's dormitory.

From 8 to 5 each weekday my duty was to sit in a windowless room with six impeccably dressed people, all of whom were totaling identical additions and subtractions. We were highly dignified with each other, very professional, no *tutoyer*ing. Monsieur Saint presided, but the formidable Mademoiselle was the true power; she oversaw each of our columns and shook her head sadly at my American-shaped numbers.

My legacy from that summer, however, was more than an enduring penchant for crossed 7s. After I had worked for six weeks, M. Saint asked me during a coffee break why I didn't follow the example of other foreign students he had known and depart the office at noon in order to spend the afternoon touring the sights of Paris with the Alliance Française.

"Because," I replied in my halting French, "that costs money. I depend upon my full salary the same as any of you." M. Saint nodded gravely and said no more, but then on the next Friday he presented me with a white envelope along with my check.

"Do not open this until you have left the Société Général," he said ominously. I thought I was fired for the time I had mixed up kroner and guilders, and, once on the sidewalk, I steeled myself to read the worst. I felt the quiet panic of blankness.

"Dear Sir," I translated the perfectly formed script. "You are a person of value. It is not correct that you should be in our beautiful city and not see it. Therefore we have amassed a modest sum to pay the tuition for a two-week afternoon program for you at the Alliance Française. Your wages will not suffer, for it is your assignment to appear each morning in this bureau and reacquaint us with the places you have visited. We shall see them afresh through your eyes." The letter had thirty signatures, from the director to the janitor, and stuffed inside the envelope was a sheaf of franc notes in various denominations.

I rushed back to the tiny office. M. Saint and Mademoiselle had waited, and accepted my gratitude with their usual controlled smiles and precise handshakes. But they had blown their Gallic cover, and for the next ten days and then through all the weeks until I went home in September, our branch was awash with sightseeing paraphernalia. Everyone had advice, favorite haunts, criticisms of the Alliance's choices or explanations. Paris passed through the bank's granite walls as sweetly as a June breeze through a window screen, and ever afterward the lilt of overheard French, a photograph of Sacre-Coeur or the Louvre, even a monthly bank statement, recalls to me that best of all summers.

I didn't wind up in an occupation with any obvious connection to the careers I sampled during my school breaks, but I never altogether abandoned those brief professions either. They were jobs not so much to be held as to be weighed, absorbed, and incorporated, and, collectively, they carried me forward into adult life like an escalator, unfolding a particular pattern at once amazing and inevitable.

Antæus
1989

HOME

THE CHERRY TREE

Home is an ongoing character in our lives. It serves as elder, as friend, as reference, as point of both origin and return, as haven. We absorb its solace even though we pass through it ultimately as anonymously as those who preceded us. We leave behind no bronze statues, no markers, only the scars we've made, only the trees we've planted. Three years ago, my grandmother Federal Expressed from Washington State a branch from her oldest cherry tree, according to her my father's favorite source for pies as a child. The severed end came swathed in still-damp paper towels encased in a plastic bag tied with a rubber band. We carefully unwrapped it. Louise stripped an inch or two of bark and I gently pushed in soil, tamping it down around the bare claw, fast and firm, so there would remain no air to dry out the fine siphons that would sprout for water, reaching into the ground, digging deep.

Three Penny Review
June 1993

THREE YARDS

When I was five years old we moved to an old house in the Crescent Hill section of Louisville. The property was oddly shaped for an urban lot, and the backyard measured almost one-third of an acre. It seemed to me then—and still does, in memory—a vast, lumpy expanse, a veldt big enough to plant trees or till a garden or run in a straight line long enough to be winded. The story went that a century earlier, this property had been the city dump, and indeed a bit of digging was always rewarded. Over time I collected worn sherds of blue glass, broken tools, bits and pieces of detritus that, in its bounty if not its perfection, struck me as treasure worth preserving.

The backyard was a place of record, from the spreading oak against whose trunk I stood each birthday for a measuring snapshot, to the clovery dell where I retreated to write in my diary. The geography was generous and precise: a fire pit for burning trash and autumn leaves, a plain on which neighbor children and I staged theatrical performances (our parents assembled on the bleachers of the porch steps), a tangle of my grandmother's roses, a different variety planted every Mother's Day.

Our house wasn't rich, our neighborhood was unremarkable, but I was wealthy with privacy, affluent with quietude. By merely walking out the door I could reach a green island where the sounds of traffic were muted and, when I lay flat upon the earth, clouds were all there was to see.

Much later, in my twenties, I lived alone in a small cabin perched on a bluff overlooking Cook Inlet. I was in Alaska to conduct my first stint of anthropological fieldwork, observing the changes wrought in an Athapaskan native community by the discovery of offshore oil deposits. Doubly isolated by remote location and by my inability to speak the language, I spent many hours each day sitting at my table, staring through my one glass window at the greyblue waters. As the seasons altered, the light changed from day to night and the surface from rough-waved to an opaque frozen marsh that reached all the way east to Kenai.

The ocean is a taciturn companion, giving up less than it takes. At first its sweep drained rather than replenished my enthusiasm: it seemed simply too big, too alien, too much beyond calculation. In contrast to the benign, mowed lawn of my childhood lot, this crooked finger of the Pacific was a wall that seemed to separate me from everywhere I wanted to be—until one sunrise when the tide was turning. From that bright, sparkling-smooth mirror shone a single piercing idea: to do something about my loneliness, to initiate a process that eventually resulted in the adoption of my eldest son. Contemplation of the depths had, without my realizing it, reached bottom and become buoyant. Ever after in that spot, whether on cloudy days or sunny, the sea looked familiar as tomorrow, and now, when I cast my thoughts back a quarter-century, its face is the one I most clearly recall.

For seventeen years I've lived as an adult with my family in a rambling New England farmhouse fronted by a dirt road that carries little traffic. Our six children have played among the stone fences that transect the property, dodging the thorns of raspberry bushes and hiding from each other behind the weave of grape vines that drape the giant elm. The land, in its known history, has been put to many uses—fed sheep and cows, nourished crops, gone to seed. My wife and I are the latest to be married within its boundaries, in a grove of slender willows.

Our farm's former tenants would be surprised and pleased at our improvements: a new pond fed by underwater streams, concrete laid upon the dirt of their basement floor, a second well. But these are superficial changes, scratches on the surface. The smell of alfalfa in August is the same as it was. The wind through the pines sounds just as clean. The rocks still rise through the soil and must be harvested every spring before the furrows are dug.

Wherever we go from here, a part of us will stay rooted in this patch of earth, buried like a cache, ready to be redeemed by memory or by return. Domestication is a product of habit, a series of adjacent yards whose only fences are the limits of imagination, the length and circumference described by a line of sight in any direction.

Heaven Is Under Our Feet
1991

REAL AND TRUE ESTATE

I remember the moment in 1974 when I fell in love. I had been living with my oldest son, then five years old, in a tiny rented cabin on the shores of Mascoma Lake, near Enfield, New Hampshire. It was a compact house, very woody, with an "efficiency" kitchen in which every appliance was an extension of the same basic unit. Without changing my stance I could freeze, boil, and wash—though in severely limited quantities. In the winter, heat came from a fireplace or, more dramatically, from an oil-burning heater that sat in the living room and was activated by dropping into its gaping mouth an ignited wad of toilet paper. When the weather got cold enough, the danger inherent in this method was forgotten. If one heard the "thump" of internal combustion, one had survived.

There came a day in March, however, when the bottom fell out of things, literally. A tide of molten lava rolled from the corroded bottom of my "unit" and licked at the fake maple paneling. I had kept an extinguisher handy for just such an emergency—and it worked—but before Krakatoa erupted again I was determined to be far away.

House hunting was not easy, even in those glory days of

relatively low real estate prices in New England. I had exactly $645 in my savings account and a college teaching job that paid $11,000 a year. I should have been thinking mobile home or handyman's special, but I wanted the Yankee dream house. I grew up in the South and the West, geographies with their own allures but where the closest thing to Currier and Ives was a box of Christmas cards. If I was going to buy a house in Robert Frost territory, I wanted atmosphere, roads less traveled, Whittier's *Snow-Bound*.

Given my limited price range, I was shown a number of "interesting" properties: dwellings that had been constructed a room at a time, seemingly by demented carpenters who, following do-it-yourself plans, had managed to get the pages out of order. One so-called cape boasted a porch bigger than its interior. A saltbox was located next door to a rural used car dealership. I turned out to be hard to please.

Then late on a July afternoon my son and I were driving a back road in Cornish, looking for the turn-off where we were supposed to meet yet another realtor. I happened to glance to my left, and put on the brakes. There it was, a huge red barn of a place with a granite foundation, fruit trees in the yard, a circle driveway, two chimneys. This was the house against which I had unconsciously measured everything I'd seen, my heart's desire.

A woman was weeding in the flowerbed and, in a wistful impulse I stuck my head out the window and called to her.

"If you ever decide to sell . . ." I sighed.

She looked up, frowned.

"Just a minute," she said, and went into the house. Thirty seconds later she reappeared.

"Okay."

"Okay?" I was stunned, taken off guard, mortified. Who was I to propose such a thing?

"I probably can't afford it," I backpedaled. "It's beautiful, but it's so big."

"Look," the woman said. "My husband was just transferred this morning. We have to move immediately, next week. We'll take what you've got."

And they did. I bought the place, eleven acres with a pond, a house built before the Revolutionary War, for $500 cash and two thirty-year mortgages. The former owners left a lot of their furniture behind, which was fortunate since I didn't have any. Inside, the wide pine board floors had for some mysterious reason been painted dark green and the walls were covered with maroon paper, but I figured that was easy enough to fix. For the next fifteen years my family grew to inhabit all the rooms, to scrape and spackle and shore up. For a long time it seemed that no matter how much we did, how perfectly we realized our short-term decorating ambitions, visitors would enter, knit their brows, and pronounce that there were "great possibilities" here.

There were. There are. You don't get to be a New Englander in one generation, or maybe even two, but we've made a start, we've sunk roots. Our land became a country marked with memory: the final resting ground of pets who died from old age, the spots where our children learned how to balance a bicycle and pick their first raspberry, the shady clearing beneath the weeping willows where Louise and I were married.

Last year our neighbor, Bob LeClair, found at the Cornish Historical Society an old photograph of our house, taken in the 1880s. There are the windows of our parlor, the stone stoop. Two women and a man stand in our yard, posed and dressed formally as if for a special occasion. We don't know their names, but they are ancestors of a sort, people who inhabited and, we're sure, drew strength from the same plot of earth. Now we tend the trees they planted, wipe clean the watery panes of glass, grateful to have at least once turned the right corner and come home.

New Hampshire Profiles
January 1991

MAINTAINING A HOME

In contemporary America, where we come from is rarely our ultimate destination. We accept as natural the notion that the future follows from and is supposed to improve upon the past in a neverending trajectory. "What do you call home?" is a question for which we may provide many different answers in the course of our lifetimes; in some cases we've relocated so frequently and so dramatically in ambition for betterment that the only possible response is: "Nowhere." "New" is the adjective usually slapped on brand-name products that need a pick-me-up in sales, and "old" is what gets traded in the moment we can afford to do so.

This attitude, pervasive and, some would argue, necessary to an industrialized society, is in fact a particularly Western fad. Among our not so distant ancestors and in much of the world today, the connection between a person and a specific place has traditionally been intimate and consistent over time—in many respects one of the primary characteristics of both individual identity and group definition. In such contexts, the significant and enduring social truths are considered to have been discovered and tested long ago. Remembered history is both instructor and revered guide, and common practice, that overarching product of repeated trial and error, is the benchmark against which every novel idea must be measured.

Naturally enough, the arbiters of these systems are generally those who have functioned within them the longest. The presence in daily intercourse of elders—keepers of the hearth fire—protects stability, continuity, perspective, all highly valued. Men and women who have been through the seasons of life are honored as the segment of a population who can, by reference to their own experience and longevity, simultaneously take pleasure in the exuberance of a child, remember the confusion of an adolescent, empathize with the adult emotions of love and jealousy, grief and disappointment, anger and passion. Out of the fray, they alone can ideally attain the serenity of calm vision, offer advice without the suspicion of personal profit. They are, in a literal and figurative sense, "grounded."

Ambiguity about "home" simply does not arise for members of many cultures, because their locus is inflexible, often coterminous with family membership. In a matrilocal kinship system, a woman remains a resident in the household of her birth, and passes on the privilege to her own daughters and granddaughters. (A man does the same in a patrilocal schema.) To be apart from extended family is an almost incomprehensible hardship, a deprivation so ego-diminishing that it is avoided even in death: the ghosts of ancestors and the proximity of their remains persist in exerting influence within the limits of their former abodes. They must daily be recalled, invoked, and consulted. Belongingness is a continuum, a process stretching backward and forward in time, a landscape whose contours are framed in stone, bounded by rivers too wide to contemplate crossing. Entitlement is inseparable from birthright, and only tangentially—through marriage or formal adoption—do outsiders gain lateral access to the sanctum.

Casual mobility changes all guidelines, producing that incredible oxymoron: a new home. When approved custom dictates that a young person "leave the nest," never to return as a full-fledged inhabitant, the creation of a place of one's own immediately becomes both a goal and a directive. But of what qualities should this domicile consist? Is it realistically attainable? Will it satisfy? Nurture? Fulfill expectations? Upon whose criteria is it based? And, perhaps most pertinent of all, is it portable? Does it travel with its creator or must it be reestablished afresh with each transfer?

Most of these questions are not explicitly addressed in the heat of pursuit. Rather, in taking for granted the normalcy of change, though we generally hope for the best, we are not surprised at disappointment, at falling short of perfection. We harbor in our mythology a vague notion of an ideal ambiance even if we've never directly experienced it. We know or think we know how the sense of rightness would feel, believe we'll recognize and cherish it when we find ourselves within its embrace, judge all else against its hypothetical standard, presume that more fortunate or astute adults possess the secret of harmonious settlement, and castigate the universe, the economy, the perversity of others or even ourselves for our failure to achieve tranquillity.

The sad truth is that when home is deemed synonymous with permanence it is always illusionary. The pictures whose match we seek—the Norman Rockwell *Saturday Evening Post* cover of several generations gathered around a Thanksgiving table, the "family values" neighborhood of our second-grade reading book, the two-dimensional simplicity of the euphemistic good old days—have more to do with cherished fictions than with actual historical realities. Human life is, by its very nature, complex and dynamic. It requires frequent readjustment, compromise, and ingenuity. Moments, friezes, occur when empirical experience and fantasy align, but they are transitory, appreciated more often in anticipation or retrospect than in process.

Identifying home is then in essence an act of ongoing imagination. The trick lies in our own willingness to bestow recognition, to caption an agreeable situation with an affirming ascription. Home is not necessarily—though it surely could be—on the range or where the heart is, but it clearly is a mental state that bespeaks relative contentment. When we're home we don't pine to be anywhere else, we don't feel out of place or a stranger. We not only know the rules of conduct, we subscribe to them. There's no frustrating separation between desire and fulfillment, no chasm of distance or years dividing nostalgia and satisfaction.

But to settle, to be of one spot, means to release the promise of all other possibilities. Home entails commitment, the arguably irrational allegiance to a condition *known* over all other potentialities. Like every other self-imposed absolute, it works only by foregoing hypothetical alternatives.

I've lived in and cared deeply for many disparate settings. As the child of a single parent with a small income, I was often a guest in the house of a more established blood relation. While growing up, I had, variously, a room with my grandmother in Tacoma, a couch at my uncle's in Miami, a bed in the basement of a government duplex on an Indian reservation in eastern Montana, an alcove, kept private by quilts hung from clotheslines, in my other grandmother's house in Louisville. I was, it seemed to me at the time, perpetually the new kid in school, the outsider looking in, the embarrassed, untested last pick in a choose-up-sides ball game. The sole offspring of an ethnically mixed marriage, I was either the wrong color or the wrong attitude, the wrong accent or the wrong religion, wherever I happened to land.

What attachments beyond my family I formed were to books—library books to be precise—that described faraway locales. Being from no town or state in particular, I was free to imagine myself a citizen of any land, and before sleep each night I took to reciting a shifting litany: Egypt, Java, Greece, Afghanistan, New Mexico.

I went away to college at seventeen, away from there to graduate school four years later, and three years after that to a small Athapaskan-speaking fishing village in Alaska to do fieldwork in anthropology. Chance and a teaching job brought me to northern New England in 1971, and while it was "like" at first sight, I had no notion that, as things turned out, I at last had found my way home.

Primary home, to me, is where the formative adventures of my life have taken place, and, to my great surprise, that happened for twenty years to be in New Hampshire. There exist eleven acres in the town of Cornish where every worn outcrop of granite, every tree and stump, every structure, every pattern of weather or light resonates with association. There, beneath two old willows, my wife and I married each other. There, one son tipped over his bicycle without getting hurt. There, three daughters spent their initial nights on earth, their breath quick and marvelous against my chest, their weight light as a summer blanket. There, in one chilly corner of a very old house, I wrote the first and last lines of the books that changed the direction of my life. There, I often exulted in pleasure and there, superimposed on that happy image, I occasionally dragged through grief.

I know that oddly shaped plot of land as I know nowhere else, and with the knowledge comes the pleasure of ease, the gratitude for bounty. I've dug its soil, reaped its harvest. I've sunk into the quiet, almost undecipherable rhythm of accumulating snow, shifting leaves, renewing

grass, the smell of July sunlight on the tangle of wild raspberry with which I annually compete for space in the back
yard. Its limited vistas are imprinted upon my brain, reassuring as family portraits in an album. It's the territory for
which the only map I require is internal, a map whose
roads and pathways lead through time and space, all ultimately rejoining into interlinking circles. It's the place I
leave with the surety of return, the destination that does not
preclude an expanded itinerary, the safe box where I store
memory. It's the part of the earth that I miss constantly
when I'm not there, the topography I can least do without.
It informs my perception of anywhere else because it's
beyond my capacity to forget. Cornish doesn't compete for
my affection, for it abides in its own unassailable category.
As long as that small, rocky terrain is in the world, wherever I go a part of me is securely at home

To the objective eye there are sceneries more beautiful,
houses far more grand, arrangements more convenient,
neighbors more conventionally congenial. To a real estate
developer the property falls within that standard early-
nineteenth-century classification: too big for a modern family, too hard to heat, too small to make a profit as a working
farm. It lacks town plumbing or an artesian well; instead it
receives all water from an underground stream, part of
which, after a disproportionate amount of rain, temporarily
flows through a worn channel in the earthen cellar. Three
times in two decades, usually at the worst possible moment
of late summer, the spring has run dry for weeks at a time,

causing, shall we say, a lover's quarrel between the land and me: threats of divorce, of the importation of outside intervention, accusations of betrayal. But always before an enduring rupture has occurred the spring refinds itself, returns fresh and fragrant. Recriminations are put aside, appeased if not completely forgotten.

There are cracks in the house's foundation so old that they've been naturally refilled with packed dust, and the attic ceiling is insulated against the winter sky not with blown chemical foam but with layers of hundred-year-old weeklies; the paper has turned yellow but the type is still readable and the events of the town—the pattern of births and of accidents, the doings of the church, the visitations of strayed sons and daughters, the marvel at the extremities and fickleness of weather—were much the same then as they are today.

The floors of the downstairs are laid with hand-hewn white pine planks, wider than any contemporary tree could yield, thick enough to sustain countless resandings. They fit together poorly, those boards, their seams as ambling as the rivulets of a downpour upon a dirt incline, and a round object placed at the eastern quadrant of any room will slowly, with gathering momentum, find its way west.

The exterior landscape abounds with projects begun by one owner and abandoned by the next: barbecue pits of stacked fieldstone, unpruned apple orchards, tough gooseberry bushes, hand-dug wells dry eleven months of the year. Far from the gravel road that bisects the property can be found the wreck of a 1944 Ford, the doors still wedged open, the trunk stuck shut and secret. White stone posts mark the boundaries of fields no longer subdivided, and a small pond, once carefully tended, has become shallow with silt, the dark green amphitheater of frogs and crickets, an environment ideal for dragonflies and children.

We have never yet systematically researched the human history of our land, but in conversation with town clerks and road agents, with the dispensers of baked beans at town hall suppers, with John McCauley, the man who has delivered mail to the house for thirty years, we learn the odd fact or rumor. A suicide. A wedding predating our own by almost a hundred years to the day. An eccentric recluse.

Our place was at one time or another a turkey farm, the regional poor house, the residence of the minister. It gave long shelter to three siblings, two sisters and a brother, who never married and rarely socialized. There has been a peculiar pattern of proprietorship: every other deed for the past six has belonged to a different family named Smith. Indeed, in 1972 I bought from a Smith. To be consistent, we should someday sell to one as well.

But not soon. Not before we fulfill our store of legend to the place. To the normal run of marriages, births, deaths, we've added the creation of books. Louise finished her first volume of poetry, *Jacklight*, in the parlor one late spring afternoon. It was a decent hideaway for writing because it was the room least inhabited. I recall standing in the doorway, the breeze through the propped-open windows disturbing the precious, reworked pages, the look of fear and amazement on her face that at last this task was done. By the time she wrote her novel, *Love Medicine,* we had cleared the summer kitchen, and day after day she sat in solitude, perched on a green painted bar stool—found at a yard sale—before a door laid horizontal and used as a table. I read parts of the manuscript in a hammock strung between two trees in the side yard and I can hear the bang of the door as I rushed inside to sing praises of the words, to make my little suggestions, to see her afresh. In tandem at a typewriter set on the kitchen table, we pounded out draft after draft in those endless days before word processing.

Months later, we were piled together in the car, halfway to the limit of our land and on the way to Hanover for a visit to the midwife in anticipation of our first-born child, when John McCauley, delivering the mail from the opposite direction, honked his horn to make us stop. Through the rolled-down windows he handed over the fat brown envelope that held the galley set in real type, with a peach cover, soon to be out on its own in the world. We left the motor idling, remained there turning the pages, incredulous and terrified and proud all at the same time.

After *The Beet Queen,* after *A Yellow Raft in Blue Water,* after *Tracks,* after the birth of another daughter and amidst the expectation of a third, Louise moved her office across the street to a small house we had previously leased in exchange for child care. Actually, "house" doesn't do the story justice. The Smiths immediately previous to us had a firecracker of a scheme—a hot dog stand for snowmobilers. Before they ran out of capital and sold us the property, they had poured a concrete foundation, run in wiring, and secured a variance for the installation of the largest septic tank in Cornish—old-timers, twenty years later, still pause their trucks and point out the site to visitors as part of the standard tour of the town.

We finished the building, dividing the structure into three rooms, and over the years an unforgettable array of tenants occupied the premises: a woman who drove a L'Eggs pantyhose van had her driver's license suspended for D.W.I. She was succeeded by a man who operated a Pepsi truck, and then he by a couple seized by a series of, as they put it, "$100,000 ideas": a car repair operation in our falling-down barn, dog-breeding kennels for their mongrel pack, and finally a book about how a small rental home could be "beautified" with ingenuity but practically no cash outlay on the part of the owner.

The single common trait shared by all these people was unapparent during our initial interviews with them, but ultimately, in all cases, surfaced within weeks of occupancy: a passion for motorcycles. Perhaps it was the frustrated spirit of snowmobiles, still haunting the environs, but sooner or later, a morning always came when we were startled out of sleep by the proud rev of an unthrottled engine, the hacking cough of a chrome tailpipe, the haughty snap of a kickstand preparatory to lift-off. Would this obsession infect Louise, we worried, when at last we were financially able to survive without supplementary income and converted the house into her studio? Would the drive to write be replaced by the drive to drive, the call of the tarmac? Would her wardrobe suddenly run to black leather? Would she henceforth insist that our children address her as "Pretty Mama" instead of "Mom"?

Not yet, anyway, and with peace and quiet restored, animals ventured forth from the surrounding woods—wild turkeys, woodchucks, ravens, deer, foxes, and porcupines. A placid skunk established residence beneath the entrance and a blue heron began to fish the shallow pond. Tiny birds built nests in every eave. Within the garland of their song, Louise's second book of poetry, *Baptism of Desire,* was completed and a series of nature essays—to be eventually published as *The Blue-Jay's Dance*—begun.

It was in Cornish we learned, reluctantly and painfully, that our three older adopted children, two sons and a daughter, were each crippled to one degree or another by the lifelong effects of prenatal exposure to alcohol. I recorded our dawning sorrow and frustration in *The Broken Cord,* a book that somehow refused to be written during daylight. I would rise each morning at 3 or 4, release my mind to recollection until the sun rose, and then reread the pages before bed at night.

As with most victims of fetal alcohol syndrome or fetal alcohol effect, the successes of our older children's lives seemed to peak early, around age ten. The family reveries guarded before that invisible marker are happy: beautiful, trusting, loving boys and girl, full of enthusiasm and energy, their futures brimming with promise. And then we watched helpless as, one after the other, they were overtaken, as the balance of their respective lives narrowed toward limitation, veered toward trouble. Their development either plateaued or regressed, their anger and resentment grew at a world that became increasingly incomprehensible to them in its expectations and demands. Now, the resonation of their youthful exuberance—free, hearty, brief as the hour of a May fly—reverberates through the apple trees around our house like the echo of music.

It was to Cornish where our beloved aunt came to stay, two years past, while receiving daily radiation treatments at a nearby hospital. During those months of uncertainty, of necessary hope and repressed anxiety, Louise and I completed the final drafts of *The Crown of Columbus,* a book we tried to infuse with laughter and optimism as well as meaning. At the end of each day we would retreat to Louise's little house, become Vivian Twostar and Roger Williams for an hour or two, to lose ourselves in words and fictions, in the foibles of intellectual geometry and romance, to, as Roger himself put it, "meet in the present, in this house that holds the treasure."

Three Penny Review
June 1993

CUTTING GRASS

In the ambiguous borderland in which it's spring at night and in early morning but summer in midafternoon, the yard awakens, stretches after a long sleep, and starts to grow. At our house the runoff from the hills to the east is still in full procession in late May and early June, making the ground soft, a mud cushion, a natural petri dish that nurtures nascent seeds into bloom. It's a race to the sun, a vertical graph in which the hardiest weeds outdistance all rivals in their naive exuberance. They are the signal to haul the power mower from the barn, to take it to Fleury's for cleaning and sharpening. Almost every year the rope-pull of the starter must be replaced, as if during the atrophy of winter storage it has unraveled in grief.

I perform the annual search for my old shoes, their tread worn smooth from many passages back and forth across the property. They have adjusted so precisely to my feet that laces are no longer necessary, and when I extract them from their paper bag in the basement they exude like sharp memory that sour-sweet scent of sun and dirt which is their medium.

I always wait too long for the first mowing. I measure the

growth with my bare feet, my toes the ruler, and by the time I surrender to commence a new routine, certain patches have become too tough to cut. Oases of wilderness, islands marooned by a green sea, they progress toward fall untended: raggedy fists spreading seeds of revolt.

Poet & Critic
Fall 1990